The French Romantics

2

The French Romantics

VOLUME 2

edited by

D.G. CHARLTON

Professor of French in the University of Warwick

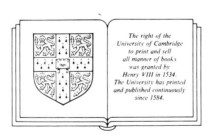

The right of the
University of Cambridge
to print and sell
all manner of books
was granted by
Henry VIII in 1534.
The University has printed
and published continuously
since 1584.

CAMBRIDGE UNIVERSITY PRESS

Cambridge

London   New York   New Rochelle

Melbourne   Sydney

Published by the Press Syndicate of the University of Cambridge
The Pitt Building, Trumpington Street, Cambridge CB2 1RP
32 East 57th Street, New York, NY 10022, USA
296 Beaconsfield Parade, Middle Park, Melbourne 3206, Australia

First published 1984

Printed in Great Britain at
the University Press, Cambridge

Library of Congress catalogue card number: 83–21010

British Library Cataloguing in Publication Data

The French romantics.
Vol. 2
1. Romanticism – France 2. France –
Civilization – History
I. Charlton, D.G.
944.04   DC33.5
ISBN 0 521 25971 1 hard covers
ISBN 0 521 27779 5 paperback

SE

Contents

Illustrations

Preface

This work aims to describe and evaluate the collective achievements of the French Romantics and to reassess, some 150 years after their heyday and in the light of recently increasing scholarly attention, their significance and persisting value. To that end certain delimitations have been adopted, in part for reasons advanced in chapter 1 in Volume One. First, this is not a study of Romanticism and tries to eschew definitions of that much-defined abstraction; secondly, it seeks to examine the 'French Romantic movement' in itself, to the extent to which that is possible – in isolation from European Romanticism as a multi-national phenomenon and in isolation also from the numerous other developments within French culture during what has sometimes been rather over-inclusively termed 'the age of Romanticism'. The purpose, by contrast, is to focus upon the works of the French Romantics themselves and the movement they cumulatively created, and here a presupposition must be stated that explains the very design of the work (a view for which the editor alone is responsible, even though his collaborators may share it to a greater or lesser extent). This is that they and their movement have to be interpreted not only in the perspectives of literary history and criticism, as has quite often been the case in even the best and most helpful of previous studies, but, equally and much more broadly, of intellectual and cultural history in general. The Romantics' salons and *cénacles* included historians, painters and illustrators, men of politics, composers, critics and philosophers alongside poets, novelists and dramatists, and, furthermore, even the literary men themselves had far wider preoccupations than we today tend to connect with 'literature'. They lived at a time when works from Mme de Staël's *De la littérature* (1800) to surveys like Alfred Nettement's histories of French literature under the Restoration and under the July monarchy (1852 and 1854) commonly included under that term works of history, philosophy, even religious thought, as much as poems, novels and plays, and the Romantics themselves fully shared that range of interests, as the sheer diversity of their works readily illustrates.

As a consequence, this study of them contains chapters on the visual arts, music and opera, historians, religious and political thought, and criticism and theory, as well as on the main literary genres, and that in turn has entailed a practical conclusion. The present editor, at any rate, could not single-handedly write such a book (as kindly suggested by the Cambridge University Press initially); only a collaborative study, enriched by a variety of specialists, could hope to be adequate. I am most grateful to the distinguished scholars who accepted my invitations and pleased that, whilst most of them are by design British or American, the very considerable renewal of scholarly work on the Romantics in France is represented here by the chapters from Professors Fayolle and Milner. Another advantage may result: instead of a single, inevitably limited, interpretation the reader is offered several. The resulting differences of emphasis and judgment, the 'variations on a theme' played by my colleagues, will, I hope, make the total examination the more comprehensive and stimulating, not least where conflicting assessments are evident. We have not even sought complete agreement, indeed, as to *who* 'the French Romantics' *are* (a multi-sided problem discussed in chapter 1), and each contributor is finally responsible for the dramatis personae of his own chapter, whatever pragmatic guide-lines the editor may have suggested. It may be tempting to appeal to Henri Bremond's well-known half-truth, salutary though it is for those seeking portable generalisations: 'Il y a autant de romantismes que de Romantiques.' Against that, my colleagues and I are agreed that there did exist, in the first half of the nineteenth century, a 'French Romantic movement' – slow though most of its rather loosely linked members were to become conscious of it and diverse as was their commitment in both duration and conviction. Our attempt is to reconsider it, but without ever attributing as much interest to the movement itself – finally an abstraction – as to individuals; the title, *The French Romantics* (*sic*), says what is intended.

The ordering of the following chapters is in good measure arbitrary, reflecting the claim that no aspect or genre has significant priority over any other, and so also is the division between the two volumes required by present publishing economics. Only the first chapter, surveying the movement as a whole and its rise, development and aims, fell naturally into place, and as well, to conclude, on chronological grounds, Professor Milner's chapter, which presents a final group of writers whom he describes as essentially 'les romantiques *marginaux*', translated here, with allusion to 'fringe theatre' and the like, as 'Romantics on the Fringe'. The chapters between have been re-ordered to the last, until choice became unavoidable. Chapter 1 is followed by two complementary chapters (II and III) on different aspects of what, in my view, was a fundamental intellectual commitment on the part of the French Romantics (whatever be true of their English, German and other counterparts), an intended *engagement* of which a recognition is basic for a full understanding of their concerns and works. Thereafter the literary genres are studied in turn: poetry (IV), prose fiction (V), drama (VI), literary criticism and theory (VII), and – seen as 'literature' by Nettement but perhaps not by Professor Johnson and other modern scholars – the work of the Romantic historians (VIII). (As to the specific ordering here a minor consideration should be mentioned; since the three chapters written by myself rest on a particular interpretation – which my colleagues may or may not share, though I naturally hope they do in good part – it seemed easier for the reader to judge it if they were placed in the same volume.) Chapters IX and X consider the other cultural forms prized by the Romantics as part of their belief in 'la fraternité des arts': the visual arts, and music and opera. Chapter XI, on the 'fringe' Romantics, completes the work, to which by intention there is no formal Conclusion. The current profusion of scholarly work on the Romantics, in France and abroad, would make conclusions more than normally premature at this time; secondly, any editor would be presumptuous, not to add hard-pressed, to attempt an agreed communiqué from his diverse colleagues. The worth-while conclusion, moreover, is really that the reader should eventually put aside this work and repair to the bookshelves, the concert halls and the art galleries. To help him to do so the more rewardingly, however, each chapter ends with a bibliographical essay, albeit firmly selective and biased in part to studies in English. Notes have been kept to the minimum needed, in the view of each separate contributor, in order, where thought desirable, to identify the sources referred to.

I feel greatly indebted to my fellow authors, and, for his frequent encouragement and advice, to Professor Garnet Rees, and equally so to the Syndics and to the Publisher and his colleagues at the Cambridge University Press; they have been especially generous, particularly in the present financial climate, in the length they themselves suggested, in agreeing to translation of chapters VII and XI from the original French and to the inclusion of illustrations, contained in the second volume, for chapters VI, IX and X, and in their constant helpfulness during the process of preparation and publication.

University of Warwick   D.G.C.
January 1983

Acknowledgments

Permission to reproduce illustrations is gratefully acknowledged: for number 1 from the Neue Pinakothek, Munich; for number 2 from the Mansell Collection, London; for number 3 from the Photo Agence de Presse Bernand; for number 4 from Agnès Varda; for numbers 6, 7, 8, 10, 11, 13, 15, 16, and 19 from the Musée du Louvre, Paris; for number 9 from the Musée de l'Armée, Palais des Invalides, Paris; for number 12 from the Musée des Beaux-Arts, Ghent; for number 14 from the Wallace Collection; for number 17 from the Musée des Beaux-Arts, Nîmes; for number 18 from the National Gallery, London; and for number 21 from the Bibliothèque Nationale, Paris.

Note

The place of publication of works cited is Paris unless otherwise stated.

VI · *Drama*

W.D. HOWARTH

'THE MOUSE THAT STIRRED . . .': SHAKESPEARE AND THE
FRENCH

Of the 8000 plays known to have been performed in Paris between 1830 and 1850,[1] only a handful are ever considered to be examples of 'Romantic drama': whatever that term does signify, it is certainly not a purely chronological label. The period around 1830 was one of unprecedented activity in the French theatre: new establishments proliferated in Paris – Balzac's novels provide a vivid record of the vital role played by the theatres in the social life of the capital – and there was a vigorous theatrical activity in the major provincial cities. The vast majority of the plays performed, however, were as unambitious as they were undistinguished: they are the theatre's equivalent of the ephemeral journalism of the day. Standing out from these are the plays which represent the successful commercial drama of the period. Eugène Scribe was the most successful, the most popular, and in many ways the most representative playwright of his age; but he is rightly not considered a Romantic dramatist. Scribe gauged to perfection the taste of the public for whom he wrote, and if he is remembered somewhat condescendingly today for his manipulation of the mechanics of plot-construction according to the formula of the 'well-made play', this was a formula calculated to produce the blend of suspense and surprise that his patrons required.

The body of works we call Romantic drama was in contrast the product of an avant-garde minority. If there is a common denominator linking plays as different as *Hernani* and *Antony*, *Chatterton* and *On ne badine pas avec l'amour*, it is surely this: that they were all created to express the ideology, or the sensibility, of a cultural elite, and to express this in a consciously literary or artistic manner. Hugo, Dumas, Vigny and Musset were above all innovators, determined to impose on the Parisian theatregoing public new forms, new ideas, and a challenging theatrical experience, the product of an aggressively iconoclastic aesthetic. The most forceful expression of that aesthetic is to be found in the Preface with which Victor Hugo accompanied his historical drama *Cromwell* in 1827; however, in order to understand the originality and the impact of Hugo's ideas, it is necessary not only to look at the cultural context of the 1820s in France, but also to trace the development of what may be called 'pre-Romantic' attitudes to drama in the previous half-century or so.

If the term 'pre-romanticism' has any validity, it surely denotes – and this is more abundantly true in the field of drama than elsewhere – that intermediate stage in French cultural evolution, when the ideology and the sensibility that we call 'Romantic' were already widely in evidence, but when the literary and linguistic medium did not yet exist that could have given them effective expression. If we look sideways at the German example, there is no such gap between 'fond' and 'forme' in the masterpieces of *Sturm und Drang* drama, Goethe's *Götz von Berlichingen* (1773) and Schiller's *Die Räuber* (1782), both of which express a vigorous challenge to established values in the name of a revolutionary individualism. But whereas Lessing had already prepared the way in his *Hamburgische Dramaturgie* (1767–8), by persuading his fellow Germans to reject the restricting influence of French neo-classicism and to look favourably on the example of Shakespeare, in France the determined resistance to Shakespeare by the theatrical establishment provides an excellent indicator of the narrow-minded conservatism which governed the writing of serious drama throughout the eighteenth century. Voltaire, who in the eighteenth letter ('Sur la tragédie') of his *Lettres philosophiques* (1734) had put himself forward as the champion, albeit a somewhat patronising one, of English drama, hitherto unknown to the French, had moved by the end of his life to an attitude of uncompromising hostility: Shakespeare, hailed in 1734 as a poet of genius, had become, by the time of the Preface to *Irène* (1778), 'un sauvage avec des étincelles de génie qui brillent dans une nuit horrible'. It is true that by this time the English dramatist had acquired more sympathetic interpreters in France; but not only was the prestige of Voltaire such as to outweigh the favourable attitudes of Letourneur, Ducis or Mercier, whose 'translations' or adaptations of Shakespeare in any case stopped well short of a faithful, unadulterated rendering of the English text: his rooted distrust of any genuine innovation in the field of the arts was also in line with the conservatism of the Théâtre-Français whose position as a monopoly theatre, enabling it to resist all change, was a major factor in ensuring the survival of the derivative neo-classical forms of tragedy and 'haute comédie', with hardly any modification at all, from the late seventeenth until well into the nineteenth century.

Voltaire's denigration of Shakespeare had focused on three principal heads: uncouth construction, typical of a poet who wrote 'sans la moindre connaissance des règles'; 'le mélange des genres', which offended against that implicit fourth unity, unity of tone, which was even more important than the notorious three unities of time, place and action; and failure to preserve the dignity required of tragic diction. Repeatedly, Voltaire returned to the attack; and one of his prime targets was the passage from the beginning of *Hamlet* where the guard Francisco, asked if he has had a quiet night, replies: 'Not a mouse stirring'. This banal colloquialism is scornfully contrasted (in the *Lettre à l'Académie Française*, 1776) with the line from Racine's *Iphigénie* in which the stillness of the night is also evoked: 'Mais tout dort, et l'armée, et les vents, et Neptune', a line Voltaire commends for its 'beauté admirable' and its 'harmonie'. He continues:

Je vous dirai qu'il n'y a ni harmonie ni vérité intéressante dans ce quolibet d'un soldat: *Je n'ai pas entendu une souris trotter*. Que ce soldat ait vu ou n'ait pas vu passer de souris, cet événement est très-inutile à la tragédie d'Hamlet; ce n'est qu'un discours de gilles, un proverbe bas qui ne peut faire aucun effet. Il y a toujours une raison pour laquelle toute beauté est beauté, et toute sottise est sottise.

Such total inability to accept a freer and more suggestive poetic expression, as a valid alternative to 'le style noble' from which all concrete, technical or everyday vocabulary was excluded, was the principal obstacle to the creation of a drama capable of expressing the new ideas of the Age of Sensibility. Voltaire's translation of the 'To be or not to be . . .' soliloquy from *Hamlet* in the *Lettres philosophiques* (no. 18) is a clear demonstration of the incompatibility of two imaginative processes: Shakespeare's rich, colourful imagery is throughout replaced by the colourless abstractions and the cliché-like epithets that characterised the neo-classical tragedies themselves. And the tragedies of 1820 showed little change from those of 1720 in this respect. The same hierarchical attitude to language still prevailed, and although the setting might now, as an alternative to Greek mythology or Roman history, be medieval France, Palestine at the time of the Crusades, or South America at the time of the Spanish conquest, dramatists were still deprived of the linguistic resources with which to represent local colour, or to express ideas and feelings specific to a given time or place. If the hero of Voltaire's *Mahomet* (1742) wants to refer to the Moslem practice of total abstinence, he must say:

> J'ai banni loin de moi cette liqueur traîtresse,
> Qui nourrit des humains la brutale mollesse;

if De Belloy, in *Le Siège de Calais* (1765), wants to express the idea that the beleaguered citizens were reduced to eating their dogs, he can get no nearer than this laboured periphrasis:

> Le plus vil aliment, rebut de la misère,
> Mais, aux derniers abois, ressource horrible et chère,
> De la fidélité respectable soutien,
> Manque à l'or prodigué du riche citoyen;

and that matters were not changed in this respect by the French Revolution is shown by the following example, cited by Stendhal, from Legouvé's *La Mort de Henri IV* (1806), in which the King's famous saying, 'Je voudrais que le plus pauvre paysan de mon royaume pût du moins avoir la poule au pot le dimanche', is rendered by an equally absurd circumlocution:

> Je veux enfin qu'au jour marqué pour le repos
> L'hôte laborieux des modestes hameaux
> Sur sa table moins humble ait, par ma bienfaisance,
> Quelques-uns de ces mets réservés à l'aisance[2].

Some progress was made, however, especially in the period following the Revolution, in the gradual familiarisation of the French public with the example of Shakespeare. Mme de Staël, arguing in *De la littérature* (1800) that a nation's cultural taste depends on specific geographical, political and social factors affecting that nation, justified Elizabethan drama by reference to the historical background against which it had been produced – though her cultural relativism did not disguise her preference for the greater refinement of taste that had produced Racinian tragedy. Similarly Benjamin Constant, though a sympathetic translator and interpreter of Schiller's *Wallenstein*, lacked the courage to go beyond an unadventurous compromise with 'la dignité de la tragédie'; and it was Guizot, a historian with a specialist interest in Tudor England, who in his *Shakespeare et son temps* (1820) showed the most enlightened understanding of a valid alternative to neo-classical tragedy, an alternative actually to be preferred because of its vigour and its truth to life.

Even the Théâtre-Français itself now possessed, in the person of Talma, the greatest actor of his generation, a devotee of Shakespeare – at any rate, of Shakespeare as acclimatised in France by the timid pen of Ducis. After Talma's death in 1826, an outstandingly successful visit by a company of English actors in 1827–8 brought a much wider public into contact not only with Shakespeare's language, but also with the less formal, more 'natural' style of acting associated with Kemble, Kean, Macready and Harriet Smithson. Finally, the performance of Alfred de Vigny's adaptation of *Othello*, *Le More de Venise*, at the Théâtre-Français in 1829 played an important role in breaking down the residual opposition. However, to accept *Othello*, the most regular of Shakespeare's tragedies, accommodated as it was into Vigny's more or less blameless alexandrines, was one thing: the real challenge was still to come, in the shape of a native French drama which much more provocatively rejected the rules and the conventions on which serious French theatre had been based for two hundred years. It was the arrival of such a play, the publicity which attended its first performances, and the head-on collision between its enthusiastic young supporters and the conservative upholders of tradition, that produced the 'bataille d'*Hernani*' in 1830.

The story is a familiar one; and the opening line of Hugo's play, with its outrageous enjambement:

> Serait-ce déjà lui? C'est bien à l'escalier
> Dérobé

is deservedly memorised by every student of Romantic drama. But provocative as this was, it was not metrical innovation that constituted Hugo's most fundamental challenge to the established order of things. A more significant portent of the subversive nature of his dramatic verse was to be found in the opening line of his *Cromwell*:

> Demain, vingt-cinq juin mil six cent cinquante-sept . . .

In this line which, in George Steiner's phrase, 'drew tragic verse down to the gross world of clocks and calendars',[3] the young Hugo was already proclaiming the full measure of his linguistic revolution. And it was as a revolutionary in matters of vocabulary especially that he saw himself, as is shown by his proud boast in the poem 'Réponse à un acte d'accusation':

> Je fis souffler un vent révolutionnaire.
> Je mis un bonnet rouge au vieux dictionnaire.
> Plus de mot sénateur! plus de mot roturier!
> Je fis une tempête au fond de l'encrier . . .
> Je massacrai l'albâtre, et la neige, et l'ivoire;
> Je retirai le jais de la prunelle noire,
> Et j'osai dire au bras: Sois blanc tout simplement.[4]

'LA "PRÉFACE DE CROMWELL" N'EST PAS LA PRÉFACE DE "CROMWELL"'

In 1825, Stendhal had formulated this forthright definition: 'Le Romantisme appliqué au genre tragique, c'est une tragédie en prose qui dure plusieurs mois et se passe en divers lieux.'[5] As an ambitious young dramatist, at the spearhead of the assault on the Théâtre-Français, Victor Hugo knew better: neo-classical verse tragedy could be successfully challenged only by Romantic drama in verse. And to take the strictest possible view of the history of Romantic drama, this can be almost exclusively identified with the fortunes of Hugo's verse dramas. The Théâtre-Français may have opened its doors to historical melodrama in prose, with Dumas's *Henri III et sa cour*, in 1829; Hugo may himself have made his début in the theatre with a prose play, *Amy Robsart*, in 1828; he was also to return to prose for the sequence *Lucrèce Borgia – Marie Tudor – Angelo* in the middle 1830s; and it would be impossible to ignore the distinctive contribution made by such plays as *Antony*, *Chatterton* or *Lorenzaccio* in arriving at an assessment of the achievements of the major Romantic writers in the field of drama. But *Lorenzaccio* was a 'spectacle dans un fauteuil', not written for stage performance; *Antony* was played at a boulevard theatre, the Porte-Saint-Martin; and even *Chatterton*, though played at the Théâtre-Français, was a prose drama in a modern setting. So that if one takes the view, as contemporary playgoers and critics evidently did, that the vital issue was the Romantics' challenge to verse tragedy at the Théâtre-Français, then the series of plays *Cromwell* (1827), *Hernani* (1830), *Marion de Lorme* (1831), *Le Roi s'amuse* (1832), *Ruy Blas* (1838), *Les Burgraves* (1843), has a quite unique importance[6]. And it is as a manifesto for this whole sequence of plays Hugo was to launch as an attack on the theatrical establishment that the *Préface de 'Cromwell'* should be regarded.

In many ways, the *Préface* is Hugo's most accomplished achievement as a dramatist: a 'profession de foi' that deliberately turns its back on two hundred years of French drama, and proposes entirely new aesthetic principles for the theatre of the future. Its devastating criticism of the sterile neo-classical tragedy goes hand in hand with positive recommendations for a distinctive new form; and the whole is presented within the framework of a historical survey which, though highly subjective, still impresses us with its imaginative sweep and its suggestive power. World literature is divided by Hugo into three ages: the first, primitive, era is characterised by the simple lyrical expression of the ode, while the second, theocratic era has the epic as its characteristic form – though the basic affinity between epic and ancient tragedy is stressed: 'mêmes fables, mêmes catastrophes, mêmes héros . . .'; and it is only with the advent of Christianity that the necessary conditions were produced for the development of the third, modern, epoch: Christianity, with its peculiar insistence on the double nature of man: 'Pour premières vérités, elle enseigne à l'homme qu'il a deux vies à vivre, l'une passagère, l'autre immortelle; l'une de la terre, l'autre du ciel.' And to this philosophical dualism corresponds an artistic duality: 'Tout dans la création n'est pas humainement *beau* . . . le laid y existe à côté du beau, le difforme près du gracieux, le grotesque au revers du sublime, le mal avec le bien, l'ombre avec la lumière.'

The vital aesthetic intuition of a need for the synthesis of 'sublime' and 'grotesque' had been grasped by such writers as Dante, Rabelais or Cervantes, and by Callot and Goya among the visual artists; but in the field of dramatic writing, says Hugo, Shakespeare offered a unique example that had been ignored by the neo-classical tradition, with its much more limited aspiration towards an exclusive notion of the sublime. The new drama, 'le drame', must reject any such constraints:

La poésie née du christianisme, la poésie de notre temps est donc le drame; le caractère du drame est donc le réel; le réel résulte de la combinaison toute naturelle de deux types, le sublime et le grotesque, qui se croisent dans le drame, comme ils se croisent dans la vie et dans la création. Car la poésie vraie, la poésie complète, est dans l'harmonie des contraires. Puis . . . tout ce qui est dans la nature est dans l'art.

Rather than the moral challenge of Christian dualism – the exhortation to man to subordinate his earthy nature to his finer, spiritual potential – which Chateaubriand, for instance, had stressed in *Le Génie du christianisme*, it is the aesthetic possibilities of *contrast* that attract Hugo; and this essential basis of his approach to character in a dramatic context has an obvious affinity with the way in which other Romantic artists approached the human personality: most clearly, perhaps, Baudelaire with his compelling pair of opposites 'le spleen' and 'l'idéal'.

When Hugo writes 'tout ce qui est dans la nature est dans l'art', he is far from adopting the 'naturalism' of Diderot and other eighteenth-century exponents of domestic drama. In a vital paragraph, he takes up the familiar notion of art 'holding a mirror up to nature' – but only to stress the particular qualities essential to such a mirror, as he sees it: 'Si ce miroir est un miroir ordinaire, une surface plane et unie, il ne renverra des objets qu'une image terne et sans relief, fidèle, mais décolorée . . . Il faut donc que le drame soit un miroir de concentration qui, loin de les affaiblir, ramasse et condense les rayons colorants.' As this striking image demonstrates, the *Préface* presents a blueprint for a poetic drama, offering an idealised, heightened picture of life. The nature of this 'heightening' may be very different from that adopted by the classical dramatist, in that it consists in the selection of 'grotesque' elements to provide the necessary contrast with the 'sublime'; but Hugo's *drame* has this in common with neo-classical tragedy (as well as with Shakespeare), that the representational portrayal of everyday life is rejected out of hand as lacking aesthetic interest.

The philosophical conviction that the human personality is composed of two contrasting elements, 'ange' and 'bête', and that these must both be reflected in any art form that claims truth to life, not only provides the key to the characterisation that typifies Hugo's theatre; it has other important corollaries affecting both the structure and the style of his plays. If we accept the thesis of the *Préface de 'Cromwell'*, then 'le mélange des genres' is no structural idiosyncrasy, but an essential part of any attempt to portray life in its entirety; as Hugo says of 'le grotesque':

Grâce à lui, point d'impressions monotones. Tantôt il jette du rire, tantôt de l'horreur dans la tragédie. Il fera rencontrer l'apothicaire à Roméo, les trois sorcières à Macbeth, les fossoyeurs à Hamlet. Parfois enfin il peut sans discordance, comme dans la scène du roi Lear et de son fou, mêler sa voix criarde aux plus sublimes, aux plus lugubres, aux plus rêveuses musiques de l'âme.

Similarly, the linguistic richness and metrical virtuosity of the new drama are no mere superficial embellishment; they are an essential consequence of an aesthetic programme which called for a comprehensive poetic representation of reality. And this is how Hugo defines the stylistic medium of the new drama:

un vers libre, franc, loyal, osant tout dire sans pruderie, tout exprimer sans recherche; passant d'une naturelle allure de la comédie à la tragédie, du sublime au grotesque; tour à tour positif et poétique, tout ensemble artiste et inspiré, profond et soudain, large et vrai; sachant briser à propos et déplacer la césure pour déguiser sa monotonie d'alexandrin; plus ami de l'enjambement qui l'allonge que de l'inversion qui l'embrouille; fidèle à la rime, cette esclave reine, cette suprême grâce de notre poésie, ce générateur de notre mètre . . . lyrique, épique, dramatique, selon le besoin; pouvant parcourir toute la gamme poétique, aller de haut en bas, des idées les plus élevées aux plus vulgaires, des plus bouffonnes aux plus graves, des plus extérieures aux plus abstraites, sans jamais sortir des limites d'une scène parlée; en un mot, tel que le ferait l'homme qu'une fée aurait doué de l'âme de Corneille et de la tête de Molière. Il nous semble que ce vers-là serait bien *aussi beau que de la prose.*

Although the *Préface de 'Cromwell'* can be said to have predicted with some measure of success the form that the most notable Romantic drama of the next fifteen years was to take, this does not mean, of course, that all prose theatre was incompatible with the essence of Hugo's theoretical programme. The banalities of everyday life, the ordinariness of everyday language, were excluded, certainly; but prose dialogue of a more ambitious literary character, capable of expressing the feelings and ideas proper to the young avant-garde of the day, was a different matter, and in any assessment of the achievements of the Romantic dramatists, Musset's sensitive handling of imagery and prose rhythms in *Lorenzaccio* deserves especial consideration. This is poetic drama in the only sense that counts, and in the final analysis, *Lorenzaccio* is surely the most successful embodiment of Hugo's aesthetic doctrine.

HEROES AND ANTI-HEROES

What Lilian Furst implies in her chapter title 'The Romantic hero, or is he an anti-hero?'[7] is particularly valid in the context of French Romantic drama: one of the essential features of the Romantic hero is that he calls in question heroic attributes that had been taken for granted for centuries. Corneille's Rodrigue or Nicomède, self-reliant, self-confident, and acting in the name of principles endorsed by those around them, represent the supreme avatar of conventional heroism; but the Romantic dramatists reject moral distinction as well as elevation of rank. Instead, they look for the psychological singularity which is the distinguishing feature of post-Cartesian man. 'Si je ne vaux pas mieux, au moins je suis autre', Rousseau had said in the preamble to his *Confessions* (1781); and to suit the tastes of a generation brought up on *Adolphe* and *René*, playwrights now set out first and foremost to portray clearly delineated individuals. The Romantic hero is forever conscious of what distinguishes him – indeed, sets him apart – from his fellows. He is no leader of men, for he lacks both the commitment to the common good, and the common denominator of shared human qualities, that marked his predecessor in the classical age. Whether he is cast in the dynamic, Byronic mould, or reproduces the reflective indecision of a Werther, he is an 'être d'exception'. If on the one hand he is inordinately susceptible about his real or fancied disadvantages, physical or social, he can be equally arrogant about his intellectual superiority. But the concept of the divided self to which Hugo gave explicit expression in the *Préface de 'Cromwell'* was adopted more or less consciously by other playwrights, too; as a result, the new-style hero is beset by doubts, and has constantly to justify himself both against the misunderstandings of others and against the tortures of self-criticism. Far from being an exemplary figure like the Cornelian *généreux*, the Romantic hero is an outlaw (Hernani), a bastard (Antony), or physically deformed (Triboulet); he is a flawed genius (Kean), or a social parasite (Chatterton). Where altruistic idealism exists, it is corrupted, as in Musset's Lorenzo, by cynicism and disillusionment; and if a gift for political leadership is to be found, it is in the unlikely person of Ruy Blas, a lackey.

Hugo had argued for the juxtaposition of 'grotesque' and 'sublime' on the grounds that the synthesis of these contrasting elements would produce a greater truth to life; but more often than not in his own practice a convincing synthesis is lacking, and characterisation stops short at antithetical contrast. Perhaps the crudest example of such an antithesis is Triboulet, the central character of *Le Roi s'amuse*. As we see him in Act I, Triboulet, the court jester to François I, is the epitome of physical and moral deformity, his misanthropy symbolised by his hunched back as he gloats over the misfortunes of the noblemen whose wives and daughters have been seduced by the King. The act closes with Saint-Vallier, one of these courtiers, pronouncing a curse on Triboulet; and a phrase from Hugo's Preface provides an unconscious clue to the reason for the lack of coherence in the central character: 'Cette malédiction, sur qui est-elle tombée? Sur Triboulet fou du roi? Non. Sur Triboulet qui est homme, qui est père, qui a un cœur, qui a une fille.' The character we see in Act II – indeed, throughout the rest of the play – is no less idealised, as the devoted father of Blanche, than the perverted pander of Act I had been a caricature. This is not a viable synthesis, and it is almost as if retribution were falling on an innocent person: as if the sins of the court jester were being visited on a complete stranger in Blanche's father.

'La paternité sanctifiant la difformité physique, voilà *Le Roi s'amuse*; la maternité purifiant la difformité morale, voilà *Lucrèce Borgia*', writes Hugo in the Preface to the latter play. Here we have another case of schematic characterisation on the a priori basis of the contrast between 'sublime' and 'grotesque': Lucrèce's 'difformité' – the monstrous evil of the legendary poisoner – is contrasted with the self-abnegation of her love for her son Gennaro, brought up, like Triboulet's daughter Blanche, away from the corruption of the court. However implausible such a juxtaposition may seem in the light of normal human psychology, there is no doubt that the contrast produces a powerful dramatic effect – sustained, in this case, throughout the play. For while Triboulet's physical deformity remains constant, his moral depravity gives way completely after Act I to what we are intended to see as the 'sublime' side of his character, and the dramatic interest centres on his attempts to avenge himself on the King for the seduction of Blanche; in the case of Lucrèce, however, it is the opposition within the character herself between lust for evil and remorse that provides the dramatic focus of the later play.

A similar formula underlies the attitude to character in *Marion de Lorme*, but it is much less arbitrary in its application. Indeed, one of the attractive features of this curiously undervalued play is that the character of Marion herself is based on a psychological contrast whose inherent truth we can all recognise. A celebrated courtesan, Marion has renounced the meretricious glamour of her notorious past to indulge in an idyllic love for the young Didier; but the past has inescapable consequences, and it leads inexorably to her humiliation and to Didier's death. We do not constantly feel – as we do on reading *Le Roi s'amuse* or *Lucrèce Borgia* – that the character's only *raison d'être* is the illustration of an abstract formula: the fallen woman rehabilitated by a pure love may later have become one of the clichés of Romantic literature, but Hugo makes Marion a thoroughly convincing portrait of the strength as well as of the weakness of human nature.

The most compelling embodiment of the *sublime/grotesque* antithesis, however, is not a creation of Victor Hugo's. There appears to be no evidence of how the young Musset of the early 1830s responded to the theoretical ideas of the *Préface de 'Cromwell'*; but there is no doubt that soon after this, he became thoroughly disillusioned with the grandiose extravagances of Hugo's type of Romantic drama. However, in 1834 the conjunction of 'milieu' and 'moment' was exactly right to produce in the central figure of his *Lorenzaccio* a character who not only offers a synthesis of contrasting elements much subtler than anything Hugo himself was ever to achieve, but also combines in his person a convincing representation of the historical Lorenzo with the introspective poet–hero of the 1830s.

One clue to Musset's success is surely his sympathetic understanding of Shakespeare. *Lorenzaccio* is the most Shakespearean of Romantic dramas; and Lorenzo is by far the most Shakespearean of characters. Not only because of the superficial resemblance to Hamlet, of which so much has been made; but much more fundamentally, because of the piecemeal, cumulative approach to characterisation that is common to both dramatists. The antithetical formula on which Hugo's heroes are constructed never leaves us in any doubt: Hernani is from the start a bandit with a noble character, Ruy Blas a lackey with a statesmanlike vision. But Lorenzo does not fit into any such pattern: he is, quite simply, an enigma for the first two acts of the play, and we share the bewilderment, the frustration and the contempt expressed by other characters as partial glimpses of his personality are revealed. Indeed, not until the middle of Act III is attention focused on Lorenzo as the central character: only in the long confessional dialogue with Philippe Strozzi in Act III, scene iii does he really emerge as Musset's hero. In this crucial scene, and in a series of soliloquies in Act IV, Lorenzo reveals the key to the enigma of the first two acts, and makes an eloquent appeal to our sympathy. He is the idealist in a corrupt world, prepared to sacrifice himself for his fellow men; but the mask of debauch he has assumed in order to win the confidence of the tyrant Alexandre has become a second nature to him: 'Le vice a été pour moi un vêtement, maintenant il est collé à ma peau' (III, iii). A modern commentator writes of Lorenzo 'playing at being Lorenzaccio',[8] but this misses the point; he *is* Lorenzaccio the idealist, and he *is* Lorenzaccio the contemptible pander. No arbitrary, a priori antithesis, but a completely plausible synthesis, the character is built up inductively, by the suggestive touches of a playwright who knew his Shakespeare thoroughly.

Hugo's a priori approach to character, based on a simpler antithesis, is expressively epitomised in a line from *Ruy Blas*: 'Je suis un ver de terre amoureux d'une étoile.' The portrait of a character who escapes from his humble role as lackey not only to enjoy a brief but successful career as prime minister, but also to persuade the Queen to reciprocate his idealised, platonic love for her, may not pose the same problems in terms of psychological plausibility as do the cases of Triboulet and Lucrèce Borgia; but from the point of view of external plausibility – the relationship between character and context – it requires a massive suspension of disbelief. Ruy Blas possesses certain attributes that must be accounted 'heroic': he is capable of ruling his country; and he loves, and is loved by, his Queen. But his lowly social condition, the *grotesque*, 'ver de terre' aspect of his character, makes him an anti-hero. Dr Anne Ubersfeld, in her edition of *Ruy Blas*, emphasises the 'dream-like' quality of the play which, she suggests, links it to the 'conte de fée'. Here, perhaps, is a pointer to a means of reconciling the contradictory attributes of the central character: in this play in which 'le héros délivre la reine prisonnière du méchant enchanteur, extermine les forces du mal et meurt',[9] we can all live out at second hand the fantasies of our own dream world, fantasies that we are prevented from realising by our unheroic natures.

However, there is another tradition to which the characters in a play like *Ruy Blas* must also be related. When Charles Nodier, one of the founding fathers of Romanticism in the first *Cénacle* in the 1820s, wrote in 1841 that 'la tragédie et le drame de la nouvelle école ne sont guère autre chose que des mélodrames relevés de la pompe artificielle du lyrisme',[10] he may have been expressing a deliberately disparaging view of Hugo's verse drama; but the affinity he alleges with the popular theatre of the early years of the century is none the less real. As established by Pixerécourt and others around 1800, 'le mélodrame' was a simple, unsophisticated art form for the entertainment, and the moral instruction, of a simple, unsophisticated audience – Pixérécourt claimed that he wrote 'pour ceux qui ne savent pas lire'[11] – and the formula was one that was to remain recognisably the same throughout the popular theatre of the nineteenth century and into the early days of the cinema. A strong, uncomplicated story-line, with moral issues polarised into a crude opposition between black and white, strong and weak; stock characters, of whom the essential nucleus is provided by the 'traître', or villain, and the heroine – the latter usually accompanied by the conventional hero-figure, who is often backed in turn by the 'naïf', his well-meaning servant or friend; a denouement which brings about the punishment of the villain, whether or not the heroine is rescued in time: these features can be identified over and over again throughout the repertoire of the *boulevard* theatres in the period between 1800 and 1830. And of all Hugo's plays, none fits the formula as closely as *Ruy Blas*. For the eponymous hero, content to nurture his hopeless love in silence, is caught up in a vendetta carried out by the evil Don Salluste against the Queen of Spain, who has rejected his advances; and it is this melodramatic confrontation of black and white that provides the motive force of the plot. The hero is half helped, half hindered by the well-intentioned Don César, an obvious development of the *naïf*; and though the hero dies in the end, this does not happen until he has saved the innocent heroine and sent the *traître* to his death.

Beyond all doubt, then, the structural model for such a play would be recognised by contemporaries as that of the popular melodrama; and it is surely no coincidence that for its production at the Théâtre de la Renaissance in 1838 Hugo entrusted the roles of Ruy Blas and the Queen to Frédérick Lemaître and the latter's current mistress, Atala Beauchêne, both trained in the *boulevard* theatres and Frédérick himself, though never a member of the Comédie-Française, generally held to have been among the very greatest of French actors. And it should be remembered that *Ruy Blas* was by a long way the most successful of Hugo's plays.

'It would only be a slight exaggeration', writes Peter Brooks, 'to argue that in France melodrama quite literally lies at the source of Romantic aesthetics of dramatization, in the theatre and the novel.'[12] Professor Brooks's attempt to rescue melodrama from the opprobrium with which it has traditionally been regarded, and to rehabilitate it as a critical term central to the understanding of the Romantic imagination, is most successful in the case of Balzac's fictional world: there, the dynamic opposition of good and evil – or at any rate of strong and weak

– does seem to reflect a Manichaean conflict on a cosmic scale, and this helps to give *La Comédie humaine* its distinctive metaphysical dimension. In Hugo's dramas, it must be admitted, the cosmic dimension is lacking: the polarisation into black and white, in the examples of *Lucrèce Borgia* or of *Ruy Blas*, is a more gratuitous contrivance, and it is difficult not to conclude that whereas Balzac's creative imagination allowed him to transcend the limitations of the melodramatic mode, Hugo stays nearer to its origins, and reflects the relatively unambitious aspirations of a popular art form.

1 and 2. 'La tragédie et le drame de la nouvelle école ne sont guère autre chose que des mélodrames relevés de la pompe artificielle du lyrisme' (p. 216). *Below:* Daumier, *Le Mélodrame; opposite:* Grandville, La Bataille d'*Hernani*.

On the other hand, the affinity with melodrama, however marked, is only part of the story: if they were melodramas, Hugo's verse plays were, in Nodier's phrase, 'des mélodrames *relevés de la pompe artificielle du lyrisme*'. We must now examine the nature of this 'pompe', and attempt to assess the contribution made by the 'lyrical' quality of the writing to the total effect of Hugo's verse drama.

PASSION AND PERSUASION

It may be useful, in considering the role of the lyrical element in Hugo's dramatic writing, to bear in mind an illustration of the practice of a classical playwright for the purposes of comparison. The well-known soliloquy spoken by Corneille's Don Rodrigue in Act I of *Le Cid* is often

referred to as consisting of 'stances lyriques'; but the adjective is misleading, except in the limited technical sense that it denotes a temporary departure from the dominant alexandrine. There is nothing 'lyrical' about Rodrigue's soliloquy, if by that we mean the expansive expression of the character's (or the poet's) sensibility: on the contrary, this is a strictly *dramatic* scene, as Corneille's hero debates possible courses of action, the reiterated terms 'père' and 'maîtresse' and the repeated rhyme 'peine/Chimène' giving forceful articulation to the dialectical process that is taking place within his mind. It is a crucial scene of decision, highlighted according to the practice of the 1630s by being written in a distinctive verse-form; and the dialectical reasoning of Corneille's hero sets an example that will be followed by his successors in serious French drama for nearly two hundred years.

Hugo, on the other hand, can be shown in his verse plays genuinely to be writing in the manner of the lyric poet, the manner that is characteristic of his own *recueils* such as *Les Feuilles d'automne* or *Les Contemplations*; this can be seen in passage after passage, where the logical requirements of a traditional dramatic structure give way to the development, extension and embellishment of standard lyric themes of a personal or confessional nature. To quote Sarcey's excellent appraisal: 'Tout l'art de Victor Hugo consiste à mettre violemment ses person-nages dans une position où il puisse aisément, lui poète, s'épancher en odes, en élégies, en imprécations, et d'un seul mot, en pièces de vers. Il se prépare, comme un habile librettiste à un compositeur, des airs de bravoure, des duos, des trios, des finales.'[13] It is often suggested, somewhat dismissively, that these passages alone redeem the triviality, or the absurdity, of the rest of the play (this suggestion may indeed have been implicit in Nodier's comment quoted above); but it is possible, I think, to see them as an integral part of a new dramaturgy, not merely as an accidental embellishment of an essentially second-rate formula. For Hugo's originality as a dramatist – and as Sarcey recognises, in this he combines the functions of librettist and composer in operatic terms – is to have rejected the linear plot-development of traditional neo-classical drama, in favour of a structure in which 'plot' becomes a framework for a succession of solos and duets, arias and recitatives, of a much more static nature. The action is halted, as it were, while Hugo's characters who, like Shakespeare's, are able to look outwards from their particular predicament, take the dramatic context as a *pretext* for imaginative developments of universal lyric themes. And Hugo's imagery in such passages fills the same role as the music in nineteenth-century opera: it expresses the poet's creative imagination in striking, memorable form, moving, rousing or uplifting the spectator as the case may be.

To see how this works in practice, let us look in the first place at *Hernani*. The clearest example of Hugo writing as a lyric poet is perhaps Don Ruy Gomez's speech at the beginning of Act III, in the course of which he departs from the immediate context of his conversation with Doña Sol to deliver a moving elegy on old age that transcends the particular circumstances of his half-pathetic, half-ridiculous old man's jealous love for his ward:

> Quand passe un jeune pâtre – oui, c'en est là! – souvent,
> Tandis que nous allons, lui chantant, moi rêvant,
> Lui dans son pré vert, moi dans mes noires allées,
> Souvent je dis tout bas: O mes tours crénelées,
> Mon vieux donjon ducal, que je vous donnerais,
> Oh! que je donnerais mes blés et mes forêts,
> Et les vastes troupeaux qui tondent mes collines,
> Mon vieux nom, mon vieux titre, et toutes mes ruines,
> Et tous mes vieux aïeux qui bientôt m'attendront,
> Pour sa chaumière neuve et pour son jeune front!
> Car ses cheveux sont noirs, car son œil reluit comme
> Le tien, tu peux le voir, et dire: Ce jeune homme!
> Et puis, penser à moi qui suis vieux. Je le sais!
> Pourtant j'ai nom Silva, mais ce n'est plus assez!
> Oui, je me dis cela. Vois à quel point je t'aime!
> Le tout, pour être jeune et beau, comme toi-même!
> Mais à quoi vais-je ici rêver? Moi, jeune et beau!
> Qui te dois de si loin devancer au tombeau!

(lines 735–52)[14]

Other instances of virtuoso solo performances include Hernani's evocative description of the bandit's life (125–46); his soliloquy beginning 'Oui, de ta suite, ô roi, de ta suite! J'en suis' which closes Act I (lines 381–414); and Don Carlos's long monologue in Charlemagne's tomb (1433–599). (Of the last example, the critic of *Le Moniteur* was warm in his praises, finding it 'souvent riche de la plus belle poésie . . . le fond appartient à Bossuet en très grande partie et même à Béranger'; what the features were which suggested an affinity with the court preacher and the popular *chansonnier* is not revealed to us, but it is interesting to note that neither reference is to a *dramatic* poet.) And finally, there is the remarkable lyrical inspiration of the love-duet which brings the play to a close. In any prosaic summary, the mechanics of Hugo's plot, with Don Ruy Gomez adopting the role of melodramatic *traître*, and Hernani's 'honneur castillan' making him obey the call of the latter's horn and surrender his life just as he is about to consummate his marriage to Doña Sol, must appear as the height of absurd contrivance; but it is surely impossible to see, or even to read, the closing scenes of *Hernani* without being persuaded by the lyrical transports of the lovers that their death constitutes the only acceptable ending to the play, and that the irrational equation of love with death has an aesthetic rightness which overcomes all common-sense objections.

The passages cited from *Hernani* can be matched with similar examples from other plays, covering the whole range of Hugo's lyrical expression. At one extreme we have the intimate, anecdotal style, reminiscent of the *Feuilles d'automne*, in Didier's self-portrait in *Marion de Lorme*:

> J'ai pour tout nom Didier. Je n'ai jamais connu
> Mon père ni ma mère. On me déposa nu,
> Tout enfant, sur le seuil d'une église. Une femme,
> Vieille et du peuple, ayant quelque pitié dans l'âme,
> Me prit, fut ma nourrice et ma mère, en chrétien
> M'éleva, puis mourut, me laissant tout son bien,
> Neuf cents livres de rente, à peu près, dont j'existe.
> Seul, à vingt ans, la vie était amère et triste.
> Je voyageai. Je vis les hommes, et j'en pris
> En haine quelques-uns, et le reste en mépris;
> Car je ne vis qu'orgueil, que misère et que peine
> Sur ce miroir terni qu'on nomme face humaine.
> Si bien que me voici, jeune encore et pourtant
> Vieux, et du monde las comme on l'est en sortant;
> Ne me heurtant à rien où je ne me déchire;
> Trouvant le monde mal, mais trouvant l'homme pire.
> Or, je vivais ainsi, pauvre, sombre, isolé,
> Quand vous êtes venue, et m'avez consolé.

(lines 107–24)

In the same play, the courtiers' word-play in Act II, scene i recalls the comic invention of certain poems in *Les Orientales*. Similarly, the spirited invective of *Les Châtiments* is prefigured in Saint-Vallier's curse on the King and his jester in *Le Roi s'amuse*, in Triboulet's soliloquy at the beginning of Act V of the same play as he glories in his forthcoming vengeance on the King, and in Ruy Blas's 100-line tirade addressed to the corrupt ministers:

> Bon appétit, messieurs! O ministres intègres!
> Conseillers vertueux! voilà votre façon
> De servir, serviteurs qui pillez la maison!
> Donc vous n'avez pas honte et vous choisissez l'heure,
> L'heure sombre où l'Espagne agonisante pleure! . . .
> Donc vous n'avez ici pas d'autres intérêts
> Que remplir votre poche et vous enfuir après!
> Soyez flétris, devant votre pays qui tombe,
> Fossoyeurs qui venez le voler dans sa tombe!

(*Ruy Blas*, lines 1058–66)

And *Les Burgraves*, evoking as it does titanic struggles between mythical figures of superhuman stature, foreshadows the grandiose abstractions of *La Légende des siècles*:

> Eh bien! je suis le meurtre et je suis la vengeance.
> Je vais, fantôme aveugle, au but marqué d'avance;
> Je suis la soif du sang . . .

(lines 533–5)

Romantic verse drama in Hugo's hands is in the fullest sense of the expression a 'drame lyrique', in which the poet borrows the persona, or mask, of his characters in order to address himself to the audience. This kind of play no longer aims, as the neo-classical theatre had done, to represent the realistic interplay of more or less credible characters, with the spectator in the position of privileged eavesdropper: it consists rather – and in this respect it harks back to the pre-classical theatre of the late sixteenth and early seventeenth centuries, as well as looking forward to the masterpieces of nineteenth-century opera – of a series of 'exercices de style' whose aim is to move or persuade us, the spectators, much more directly: lyrical displays of mood or feeling which are co-ordinated, in the final analysis, less by a coherent conception of character than by the possibilities of variety and contrast offered to the author by the theatrical medium.

It goes without saying that in Hugo's prose plays, the same formula works a good deal less successfully. In Hugo's dramatic prose, passions are cruder, persuasion is more blatantly rhetorical. Triboulet had been crude enough, in all conscience, as an embodiment of the *grotesque/sublime* antithesis; but the power of Hugo's verse enables us to forget this as we listen to the magnificent expression of his *folie de grandeur* which occurs as a virtuoso soliloquy in Act v of *Le Roi s'amuse*:

> Songer que si demain Dieu disait à la terre:
> – O terre, quel volcan vient d'ouvrir son cratère?
> Qui donc émeut ainsi le chrétien, l'ottoman,
> Clément-Sept, Doria, Charles-Quint, Soliman?
> Quel César, quel Jésus, quel guerrier, quel apôtre,
> Jette les nations ainsi l'une sur l'autre?
> Quel bras te fait trembler, terre, comme il lui plaît?
> La terre avec terreur répondrait: Triboulet!
> Oh! jouis, vil bouffon, dans ta fierté profonde.
> La vengeance d'un fou fait osciller le monde!

(lines 1457–66)

But in *Lucrèce Borgia*, for example, this aesthetic justification is lacking, and in place of the vivid imagery, the melodious rhythms and the original rhyming of the verse plays, we have to rely on the same features of repetition, balance and antithesis that give such forceful articulation to the argument of the *Préface de 'Cromwell'*:

Gubetta! Gubetta! S'il y avait aujourd'hui en Italie, dans cette fatale et criminelle Italie, un cœur noble et pur, un cœur plein de hautes et de mâles vertus, un cœur d'ange sous une cuirasse de soldat; s'il ne me restait, à moi, pauvre femme, haïe, méprisée, abhorrée, maudite des hommes, damnée du ciel, misérable toute-puissante que je suis; s'il ne me restait, dans l'état de détresse où mon âme agonise douloureusement, qu'une idée, qu'une espérance, qu'une ressource, celle de mériter et d'obtenir avant ma mort une petite place, Gubetta, un peu de tendresse, un peu d'estime dans ce cœur si fier et si pur; si je n'avais d'autre pensée que l'ambition de le sentir battre un jour joyeusement et librement sur le mien; comprendrais-tu alors, Gubetta, pourquoi j'ai hâte de racheter mon passé, de laver ma renommée, d'effacer les taches de toutes sortes que j'ai partout sur moi, et de changer en une idée de gloire, de pénitence et de vertu, l'idée infâme et sanglante que l'Italie attache à mon nom?

(I, iii)

Professor Brooks writes of this play: 'It is no accident that Hugo's most purely melodramatic play, *Lucrèce Borgia*, is also dramatically the most successful. When Romantic authors tried to invent something wholly other than melodramatic expressionism, they fell into bookishness and non-theatre.'[15] Such a judgment seems to me seriously to undervalue the poetic qualities of Hugo's verse drama: qualities that, as I have tried to show, are no mere superficial decoration, but an integral part of the play's dramatic effect. By the same token, Brooks's dismissive comment on *Lorenzaccio* – '*Lorenzaccio*, despite its poetic moments, is at least as hollow intellectually as Hugo's plays, and it does not offer Hugo's compensating sense of dramatic enactment'[16] – betrays a blind spot with regard to Musset's masterpiece. For the same remarks about the contribution of a playwright's poetic imagination to the overall character of a Romantic drama apply here too. The prose medium does not imply a prosaic tone; far from it, and Musset's play is more truly poetic than any of Hugo's verse plays. If Hugo's lyrical inspiration can persuade us to accept the exaltation of a Hernani, a Didier or a Triboulet as a convincing expression of the intensity of a character's experience, how much easier this is in the case of Lorenzo. As has been said, this character makes a thoroughly enigmatic impression during the first two acts; but once he assumes the centre of the stage, so to speak, he is soon established as the quintessential Romantic hero: an idealist of superior sensibility, conscious of having reached the limit of his endurance, and appealing to us by qualities at once representative of our own natures and exceeding anything we are capable of feeling. The three confessional soliloquies in Act IV are less self-sufficient, more closely integrated into the dramatic structure of the play, than is the case with Hugo's more 'operatic' monologues; on the other hand, Musset's imagery is more suggestive, less susceptible to rational explication, than Hugo's:

Par le ciel! quel homme de cire suis-je donc! Le Vice, comme la robe de Déjanire, s'est-il si profondément incorporé à mes fibres, que je ne puisse plus répondre de ma langue, et que l'air qui sort de mes lèvres me fasse ruffian malgré moi? J'allais corrompre Catherine. – Je crois que je corromprais ma mère, si mon cerveau le prenait à tâche; car Dieu sait quelle corde et quel arc les dieux ont tendus dans ma tête, et quelle force ont les flèches qui en partent. Si tous les hommes sont des parcelles d'un foyer immense, assurément l'être inconnu qui m'a pétri a laissé tomber un tison au lieu d'une étincelle dans ce corps faible et chancelant . . .

(IV, v)

If we accept Musset's Lorenzo not only as a convincing representation of the Lorenzo de Medici of sixteenth-century Florence, but also as a compelling expression of the Romantic sensibility of the 1830s, this is an example of indirect persuasion. At the same time, however, there were Romantic dramatists who used their plays for the direct persuasion, or indoctrination, of contemporary audiences; and although their theses have no more than a historical interest for the modern reader, it should be remembered that the theatre was a powerful medium for the dissemination of the Romantic ideology.

THE IDIOM OF AN IDEOLOGY

Two of the four major Romantic dramatists, Alfred de Vigny and Alexandre Dumas *père*, seem totally opposed to each other in background, upbringing, temperament and taste. The former was a fastidious aristocrat, a serving officer, ill at ease in the competitive, thrusting theatrical milieu; while the latter, a poor civil-service clerk, was immensely energetic and prolific, and was constantly seeking the formula for sure box-office success. The common charge against Vigny is that he was too much the intellectual to be a successful man of the theatre; while Dumas is only grudgingly accepted into the group of Romantic dramatists by virtue of that handful of plays out of his vast output, which succeed in rising above the banalities of popular melodrama. Nevertheless, it was these two authors, not Hugo nor Musset, who saw, and grasped, the opportunity to use the theatre as a means of expressing in challenging form ideas prevalent among the artists and thinkers of the Romantic generation.

François Ponsard, who with Émile Augier was to spearhead the reaction against Romanticism in the theatre in the 1840s, proposes the following yardstick for distinguishing between 'le drame' and 'le mélodrame':

J'appellerai *drame* toute pièce qui se préoccupera surtout de représenter des caractères, de développer des passions, ou de résumer l'esprit et les mœurs d'un siècle, en les personnifiant dans les grands hommes de l'époque, et qui subordonnera l'intrigue à cette idée dominante. Toute pièce, au contraire, qui ne cherchera qu'à étonner et émouvoir le spectateur, par la succession rapide des aventures et l'imprévu des péripéties, sera un *mélodrame*.[17]

Judged by Ponsard's criterion, Hugo's three prose plays of the period 1833–5 come perilously near to melodrama, even if they do not qualify outright for that label. In spite of Hugo's somewhat pompous declaration in the Preface to *Angelo* –

On ne saurait trop le redire, pour quiconque a médité sur les besoins de la société, auxquels doivent toujours correspondre les tentatives de l'art, aujourd'hui, plus que jamais, le théâtre est un lieu d'enseignement. Le drame, comme l'auteur de cet ouvrage voudrait le faire, et comme le pourrait faire un homme de génie, doit donner à la foule une philosophie, aux idées une formule, à la poésie des muscles, du sang et de la vie, à ceux qui pensent une explication désintéressée, aux âmes altérées un breuvage, aux plaies secrètes un baume, à chacun un conseil, à tous une loi –

there is little sign of an animating ideology in *Lucrèce Borgia*, *Marie Tudor* or *Angelo*; or rather, if such a philosophical impulse does exist, it has been badly served by the prose medium. There can be no such doubt in the case of Dumas's *Antony*. In place of Hugo's vague, unconvincing philosophy of history, Dumas's play embodies a simple, unambiguous message of considerable contemporary relevance. For *Antony* is a 'pièce à thèse': first and foremost, it is a *plaidoyer* on behalf of the illegitimate who are denied a place in society – a social handicap which, allied to the material endowments and the psychological make-up of Dumas's hero, justifies his defiant anti-social attitude. The portrait of Antony himself may not strike us all as attractive – even among contemporaries there were those who were sceptical about the social stigma of illegitimacy, and who saw in him an awful warning against Romantic individualism[18] – but the prejudices of society are most tellingly represented. And above all, Adèle d'Hervey is a most sympathetic heroine: victim of a loveless marriage, she tries to remain faithful to her husband, but is defeated by a combination of circumstances and the ruthless opportunism of Antony himself. However, she emerges as an 'authentic' character, admirable in her sincerity when compared with the shallow, hypocritical attitudes of her friends. Moreover, even to the modern reader – and we can guess how much more this would have been the case with Dumas's contemporaries – the focus of interest is not so much on Antony, or on

Adèle, as individuals, as on the couple and on their idealised love, which is denied its full fruition by the conventions and the prejudices of the social order.

One of the most striking innovations of Romantic literature is the myth of a shared love, incompatible with the exigencies of real life, and condemned to find consummation only in death. There are earlier instances of this myth to be found in Western literature, of course, the most celebrated being no doubt the stories of Pyramus and Thisbe and of Romeo and Juliet. But in neo-classical tragedy the obstacle faced by a couple of true lovers had normally been the jealousy of a third party; and the accepted idiom of tragedy had always invested unhappy love with the fatalism that was one of the hallmarks of the genre: even Shakespeare, it will be remembered, presents Romeo and Juliet as a pair of 'star-crossed' lovers. But for the Romantic generation this fatalistic dimension is lacking: the individual is no longer the plaything of the gods, but the victim of the society into which he is born; and the obstacle to the happy union of two lovers is now to be found in the community to which they belong, its political and social institutions, its economic pressures or its prejudices about birth and rank. *Antony*, then, is ostensibly a thesis-play attacking the prejudice against illegitimacy that had decreed that a man without a name, however rich and talented, could not be accepted as a suitor for the hand of Adèle; but has it not also another, much more insidious, thesis? For the events of the play take place three years after the day when Antony, her mysterious, passionate lover, had disappeared from Adèle's life; in the meantime she has become wife and mother, and is integrated into fashionable Parisian society. Antony's return threatens the values of this society, and the emotive force of Dumas's writing is such that we are persuaded to accept the adulterous liaison as the *real* relationship, and the institutions of marriage and the family as a hypocritical sham. A crucial scene in this respect is the discussion of contemporary drama that develops in Act IV in the salon of the Vicomtesse de Lacy. The poet Eugène d'Hervilly has been maintaining that 'le drame moderne' is impossible in a contemporary setting, since passions are masked by the universal conformism of the day. The perfidious Mme de Camps disagrees:

Il y a encore des amours profondes qu'une absence de trois ans ne peut éteindre, des chevaliers mystérieux qui sauvent la vie à la dame de leurs pensées, des femmes vertueuses qui fuient leur amant, et, comme le mélange du naturel et du sublime est à la mode, des scènes qui n'en sont que plus dramatiques pour s'être passées dans une chambre d'auberge . . .[19] Je peindrais une de ces femmes . . .

The calculated insult to Adèle is accepted by Antony, who throws it back in the speaker's face, as a challenge to the shallow, insincere society she represents:

Oui, madame a raison, monsieur! et, puisqu'elle s'est chargée de vous tracer le fond du sujet, je me chargerai, moi, de vous indiquer les détails . . . Oui, je prendrais cette femme innocente et pure entre toutes les femmes, je montrerais son cœur aimant et candide, méconnu par cette société fausse, au cœur usé et corrompu; je mettrais en opposition avec elle une de ces femmes dont toute la moralité serait l'adresse; qui ne fuirait pas le danger, parce qu'elle s'est depuis longtemps familiarisée avec lui; qui abuserait de sa faiblesse de femme pour tuer lâchement une réputation de femme, comme un spadassin abuse de sa force pour tuer une existence d'homme; je prouverais que la première des deux qui sera compromise est la femme honnête, et cela, non point à défaut de vertu, mais par manque d'habitude . . . Puis, à la face de la société, je demanderais justice entre elles ici-bas, en attendant que Dieu la leur rendît là-haut.

(IV, vi)

This is an almost programmatic exposition of Romantic individualism. The emotively charged epithets 'innocente', 'pure', 'aimant', 'candide' are opposed to the equally loaded 'fausse', 'usé', 'corrompu'; and the playwright explicitly adopts the role of agent of human justice, as a preliminary to the divine judgment that can be confidently predicted. The institution of marriage, the accepted notion of the wife's duty to her husband, all the values of society, are under attack; and this play proclaimed more eloquently than any other the threat posed by amoral individualism to the established social order. While the vogue for this ideology lasted, it was above all with Dumas's name that it was connected; and though similar themes recur in later plays, in none are they expressed with the persuasive force of *Antony*. Add to this the tremendous theatrical sense that is demonstrated particularly in the 'coups de théâtre' which bring to an end Acts I, III and V, and the acting of Bocage and Marie Dorval, both ideally suited to their parts,[20] and it is small wonder that the production of *Antony* in 1831 should have been one of the high moments of Romantic drama. In his *Gabrielle* of 1849, Augier was to take issue with the Romantic challenge to marriage in the name of a great passion that knows no laws, as an ideology that had subverted a whole generation:

– Les bonheurs négatifs sont faits pour les poltrons:
Nous serons malheureux, mais du moins nous vivrons.
– Voilà certe une belle et vive poésie.
J'en sais une pourtant plus saine et mieux choisie,
Dont plus solidement un cœur d'homme est rempli:
C'est le contentement du devoir accompli,
C'est le travail aride et la nuit studieuse,

Tandis que la maison s'endort silencieuse,
Et que pour rafraîchir son labeur échauffant
On a tout près de soi le sommeil d'un enfant.
Laissons aux cerveaux creux ou bien aux égoïstes
Ces désordres au fond si vides et si tristes,
Ces amours sans lien et dont l'impiété
A l'égal d'un malheur craint la fécondité.

(v, v)

It is as though, across the years, this was a specific rejoinder to Antony and his individualist ethic.

Chatterton, the poet–hero of Vigny's play of 1835, belongs to the tradition of Werther and René, passive rather than dynamic or 'Byronic' examples of the Romantic hero. Here the focus is firmly on the single figure, not the couple; for although Chatterton has nourished an unspoken love for Kitty, the wife of his landlord John Bell, and she in response has conceived an attachment for him that she has hardly formulated even to herself, this relationship achieves dramatic prominence only at the end of the play, so that if *Chatterton* does in its way illustrate the Romantic notion of an ideal love opposed to the harsh realities of marriage, it does so by offering an example of a platonic union of souls, which achieves consummation in death as Chatterton takes his own life and Kitty dies of a broken heart. The central thesis reflects Vigny's conversion to Saint-Simonian doctrines, and the conviction that the poet has a duty to use his gifts to enlighten and guide his fellow men. *Chatterton* is an example of what would be called in our own day 'littérature engagée': as Vigny writes in 'Dernière Nuit de travail', the preface to the play, it is 'un plaidoyer en faveur de quelques infortunés inconnus'. The play's first spectators were invited to accept the thesis that just as the genius has a duty to follow the call of his inspiration, and cut himself off from the distractions of the busy world around him, so society in its turn has a duty to support the young artist of genius, and to enable him to dedicate himself in this way. The immediate occasion of the play was a series of suicides of starving poets deprived of this resource. 'La cause', says Vigny, 'c'est le martyre perpétuel et la perpétuelle immolation du Poète. – La cause, c'est le droit qu'il aurait de vivre. – La cause, c'est le pain qu'on ne lui donne pas. – La cause, c'est la mort qu'il est forcé de se donner.' Théophile Gautier, looking back in his *Histoire du romantisme*, provides eloquent testimony to the impact on the play's first audiences:

Lorsqu'on n'a pas traversé cette époque folle, ardente, surexcitée, mais généreuse, on ne peut se figurer à quel oubli de l'existence matérielle l'enivrement, ou si l'on veut l'infatuation de l'art poussa d'obscures et frêles victimes qui aimèrent mieux mourir que de renoncer à leur rêve. L'on entendait vraiment dans la nuit craquer la détonation des pistolets solitaires.[21]

But for us 150 years later, Vigny's thesis has lost its relevance, the play's *raison d'être* has disappeared, and the modern reader may well feel that *Chatterton* retains at best a purely technical interest, as a notable example of *drame bourgeois* in Diderot's manner, and the most important link between eighteenth-century didactic theatre and the social drama of the Second Empire.

Vigny marks his conversion to social romanticism by turning his back on the historical subject-matter of *La Maréchale d'Ancre* (1831) as well as on the poetic idiom of his *More de Venise* (1829); and in a stirring 'profession de foi' at the end of his Preface, he parts company implicitly with all that Victor Hugo stands for as a dramatist:

Puisse [la forme d'art que j'ai créée] ne pas être renversée par l'assemblée qui la jugera dans six mois! avec elle périrait un plaidoyer en faveur de quelques infortunés inconnus; mais je crois trop pour craindre beaucoup. Je crois surtout à l'avenir et au besoin universel de choses sérieuses; maintenant que l'amusement des yeux par des surprises enfantines fait sourire tout le monde au milieu même de ses grandes aventures, c'est, ce me semble, le temps du DRAME DE LA PENSÉE.

It was perhaps inevitable that in this demonstration of 'l'homme spirituel étouffé par une société matérialiste' the latter term should be portrayed more effectively than the former. John Bell is an impressive piece of characterisation, larger than life but no caricature; the embodiment of the profit motive, he ruthlessly exploits his workmen, tyrannises his wife, and has nothing but scorn for his unworldly lodger. In the case of Chatterton himself, we have to take his genius on trust; but more than this, he is too much the symbol to be a convincingly human portrait; and Vigny himself virtually confesses as much: 'Le Poète était tout pour moi; Chatterton n'était qu'un nom d'homme; et je viens d'écarter à dessein des faits exacts de sa vie pour ne prendre de sa destinée que ce qui la rend un exemple à jamais déplorable d'une noble misère.' But the ardent young spectators of 1835 were not worried by such critical scruples: they were more than willing to identify themselves with the martyr, feeling the same scorn as Chatterton himself for the Lord Mayor's offer (surely not unreasonable by any objective standards) of a job as a footman:

(*Il décachète la lettre, lit . . . et s'écrie avec indignation.*) Une place de premier valet de chambre dans sa maison! . . . Ah! pays damné! terre du dédain! sois maudite à jamais! (*Prenant la fiole d'opium.*) O mon âme, je t'avais vendue! je te rachète avec ceci. (*Il boit l'opium.*) . . . Libre de tous! égal à tous, à présent! Salut, première heure de repos que j'aie goûtée! Dernière heure de ma vie, aurore du jour éternel, salut! Adieu, humiliation, haines, sarcasmes, travaux dégradants, incertitudes, angoisses, misères, tortures du cœur, adieu! Oh, quel bonheur, je vous dis adieu! Si l'on savait! si l'on savait ce bonheur que j'ai . . . on n'hésiterait pas si longtemps! (*Ici, après un instant de recueillement durant lequel son visage prend une expression de béatitude, il joint les mains et poursuit:*) O Mort, ange de délivrance, que ta paix est douce! j'avais bien raison de t'adorer, mais je n'avais pas la force de te conquérir. Je sais que tes pas seront lents et sûrs. Regarde-moi, ange sévère, leur ôter à tous la trace de mes pas sur la terre. (*Il jette au feu tous ses papiers.*) Allez, nobles pensées écrites pour tous ces ingrats dédaigneux, purifiez-vous dans la flamme et remontez au ciel avec moi. (*Il lève les yeux au ciel et déchire lentement ses poèmes, dans l'attitude grave et exaltée d'un homme qui fait un sacrifice solennel.*)

(III, vii)

There is one other vigorous play of ideas in a modern idiom which deserves mention. If less obviously a 'pièce à thèse', Dumas's *Kean, ou Désordre et génie* (1836) is an equally remarkable expression of the Romantic ethos. The great Edmund Kean, who had died in 1833, had visited Paris in 1827, and was already a legendary figure. Dumas's play was written as a vehicle for his nearest French counterpart, Frédérick Lemaître, in whose case too the flamboyant life-style, as well as his professional achievements, already contributed to the creation of a similar legend. We may well feel that in Dumas's text 'désordre' is more in evidence than 'génie'; but no doubt Frédérick's acting was a powerful aid to belief in the other side of the equation. In Sartre's adaptation of 1954, the play became an existentialist enquiry into 'authenticité', a study in growing self-awareness; for Dumas, however, Kean represented a simpler, more recognisably Romantic type: the man of genius whose 'désordre' is explained and justified by his invidious position, at odds with the society that both patronises and persecutes him.

'LE THÉÂTRE N'EST PAS UN COURS D'HISTOIRE'

In a postscript to his 'drame militaire' about Napoleon, *La Barrière de Clichy* (1851), Dumas was to justify putting into the Emperor's mouth 'des pensées de liberté qu'il n'avait pas dans le cœur' with the argument that 'le théâtre n'est pas un cours d'histoire, mais une tribune par laquelle le poète répand et propage ses propres idées'. The truth is, of course, that the theatre never had been a 'cours d'histoire', in France at any rate: the historical tragedy of Corneille or Voltaire had similarly served as a vehicle for the display of ideas and attitudes of a personal nature. One eighteenth-century Frenchman at least, however, C.-J.-F. Hénault, had shown himself capable of recognising the virtues of a different tradition when he wrote this appreciation of Shakespeare's *Henry VI*:

J'ai trouvé les faits à peu près à leurs dates; j'ai vu les principaux personnages de ce temps-là mis en action, ils ont joué devant moi; j'ai reconnu leurs mœurs, leurs intérêts, leurs passions qu'ils m'ont apprises eux-mêmes; et tout à coup oubliant que je lisais une tragédie, et Shakespeare lui-même aidant à mon erreur par l'extrême différence qu'il y a de sa pièce à une tragédie, je me suis cru avec un historien, et je me suis dit: Pourquoi notre histoire n'est-elle pas écrite ainsi?[22]

Only in very rare instances before the nineteenth century – Sébastien Mercier's plays, for instance, on the wars of religion – can we find the attitude to history that Hénault acknowledges in Shakespeare's practice: the historical event interpreted not as the predetermined working-out of an individual's tragic fate, but as the product of a complex relationship of cause and effect in particular circumstances of time and place.[23] However, for a brief period in the 1820s a number of writers, for the most part members of a group associated with Stendhal, Mérimée and *Le Globe*, experimented with a kind of historical drama that was equally distinct from neo-classical tragedy on historical subjects and from the historical play that was to make such a prominent contribution to the Romantic drama of the following decade. The 'scène historique', as this minor genre was called, aimed to present a sober, well-researched account of the historical event, with a minimum of selection and arrangement, and without reducing the complexities of the historical process to the simplified personal dilemma of an individual protagonist. Over-academic in inspiration, and wholly lacking in theatrical qualities (though they had some affinity with the historical *novel* of the period), the *scènes historiques* of the 1820s made only one notable contribution to the story of Romantic drama; for as a result of Musset's liaison with George Sand, the latter's *Une Conspiration en 1537* passed into his hands, and was to provide the essential source for *Lorenzaccio*.

Thanks to modern editors, like Dimoff and Masson, it is possible to see in detail how the historical material has evolved in this case, from the Renaissance chronicle, Varchi's *Storia fiorentina*, though Sand's *scène historique*, to Musset's play. While *Une Conspiration en 1537* is a major source for *Lorenzaccio*, it is no more than that; and Musset's creative imagination was necessary to give genuinely dramatic shape to the material: not only to develop the compelling figure of the enigmatic hero, but also to bring to life the city of Florence, and to persuade us that the events portrayed are the product of a specific historical contingency. The ability to create convincing atmosphere – not the superficial 'local colour' applied so crudely in Dumas's historical melodramas, nor yet Hugo's more suggestive, but essentially subjective, 'couleur des temps', but something more like Shakespeare's sense of the relationship between main characters, minor characters, and historical background: this is Musset's unique achievement. The only other historical drama of the period to show anything like the same responsible attitude towards historical sources is *La Maréchale d'Ancre*; but like the *scènes historiques*, Vigny's play suggests the novelist's approach to history rather than that of the true dramatist. The text is provided with scholarly footnotes; the dialogue seems designed for literary, rather than theatrical, effect; and, although *La Maréchale d'Ancre* enjoyed a reasonable run at the Odéon in 1831, it cannot be said to have succeeded in establishing a new form of historical drama.

As for Hugo and Dumas, a study of their plays on historical subjects can lead to only one conclusion: that with very few exceptions, the historical setting was no more than a subsidiary consideration, a vehicle for Romantic tragedy on the one hand, for spectacular melodrama on the other; and that this was not 'historical drama' in the strictest sense. Dumas has at least the merit of candour when he confesses:

Je commence par combiner une fable; je tâche de la faire romanesque, tendre, dramatique . . ., je cherche dans l'histoire un cadre où la mettre, et jamais il ne m'est arrivé que l'histoire ne m'ait fourni ce cadre, si exact et si bien approprié au sujet, qu'il semble que ce soit, non le cadre qui ait été fait pour le tableau, mais le tableau pour le cadre[24]

– a confession which could surely have been made, *mutatis mutandis*, by nearly every author of historical plays in the French tradition, from Corneille through to Anouilh. Characteristically, the French playwright looks to history for a setting in which to display preconceived attitudes; and Hugo's claim that plays like *Hernani* and *Ruy Blas* have a lesson to offer about the philosophy of history (see the closing paragraphs of the Preface to the latter play) rings rather hollow when one realises that in both cases the historical setting was chosen after the main lines of the plot had been conceived. '*Ruy Blas*, pas plus qu'*Hernani* qui lui ressemble tant, n'est un drame véritablement historique', writes Anne Ubersfeld[25]; and an early reviewer had already delivered the same judgment: 'M. Hugo se contente d'emprunter le nom de ses principaux personnages et ne consulte en les dessinant que sa fantaisie. M. Hugo ignore, oublie, ou méprise l'histoire . . . Il est évident que l'histoire ne joue aucun rôle dans les drames de M. Hugo.'[26] If this applies to *Hernani*, *Le Roi s'amuse* and *Ruy Blas*, it applies even more forcefully to Hugo's three prose dramas of the 1830s, just as it had to the early *Amy Robsart* (1828) which, adapted from Scott's *Kenilworth*, had helped to set the pattern for the fictional exploitation of history in Scott's own manner – for, shorn of their laborious, erudite expository passages, Scott's novels provide the perfect formula for historical melodrama; and his example contrasts markedly with that of the *scène historique*, Vigny's novel *Cinq-Mars*, or *La Maréchale d'Ancre*. A similar adverse judgment could be passed (and no doubt was passed by contemporaries) on Dumas's sensational melo-dramas *Henri III et sa cour* (1829) and *La Tour de Nesle* (1832). But there were interesting exceptions; and in practice neither Hugo nor Dumas was so completely wedded to a single formula as such a sweeping judgment might suggest.

Cromwell itself was never played, so that in some respects it was written, like *Lorenzaccio*, with an experimental freedom that would have been impossible in a work written for stage production; and if the central figure himself corresponds to the theoretical formula of the *Préface*, and therefore to some extent anticipates characters like Triboulet, Lucrèce Borgia or Ruy Blas, *Cromwell* stands out from the rest of Hugo's theatre by the enormous breadth and variety of the historical scene in which it is set. This broadening of context is of course a feature of all Romantic history plays: historical events are no longer reduced to the interaction of a handful of significant characters, each attended by his functional *confident*. But nowhere else has a Romantic dramatist gone so far in the other direction: *Cromwell* contains over seventy named characters, and a veritable army of supernumeraries: Cavaliers, Roundheads, soldiers, bourgeois and common people; and the only way to stage such a colourful parade would be to use the resources of twentieth-century cinema. Within this vast framework, the treatment of Cromwell's personal dilemma has a strangely old-fashioned look; presented as it is in the tight time-scale of little more than twenty-four hours, it could easily have satisfied the requirements of neo-classical tragedy. Consequently, there is a certain lack of cohesion between the dramatic subject and the theatrical framework: the profuse and vigorous local colour, which constitutes the most memorable feature of the play, remains external to the study of Cromwell and his dilemma. *Marion de Lorme*, in 1831, achieved a much more satisfactory balance. Not only is this the most moving of all Hugo's plays in terms of intimate personal tragedy, it also presents an authentic picture of seventeenth-century France, not by overwhelming the reader or spectator with indiscriminate local colour in the manner of *Cromwell*, but by a more selective display of attitudes and preoccupations, so that the trio Marion – Didier – Saverny appears at the apex of a pyramid, as it were, of representative supporting roles, and the heroine's individual tragedy is convincingly related to its specific historical context.

Dumas's evolution as a dramatist follows a similar pattern in his historical plays as in those set in contemporary life: although he initially aspired to make his mark by contributing to the literary drama of his day, gradually his literary ambitions gave way to the desire for commercial success, as play followed play written to the same mechanical formula. Indeed, this is even more clearly the case in his historical plays, where from the mid 1840s onwards his collaboration with Auguste Maquet was to produce for the audiences at the Ambigu-Comique and the Théâtre-Historique dramatised versions of those novels – *Monte-Cristo, Les Trois Mousquetaires, La Reine Margot* and *Le Chevalier de Maison-Rouge* among others – which had already brought history perilously near to the simplified stereotypes of the strip-cartoon. In contrast to these adventure stories, even *Henri III et sa cour* can be seen to be a serious attempt at a genuine history play; and Dumas deserves credit for being the first of the Romantic playwrights, before Hugo with *Hernani*, to achieve performance at the Théâtre-Français. In *Christine*, a verse play performed at the Odéon in 1830, he attempted to create a triptych of seventeenth-century history, as the subtitle (*Stockholm, Fontainebleau et Rome*) indicates; and if the effects are cruder than those of *Marion de Lorme*, at least *Christine* is not unworthy of comparison with Hugo's masterpiece. *Caligula* (also in verse, 1837) is a by no means unsuccessful attempt to apply the new methods of the history play to the ancient world; and the conflict between Christianity and the pagan civilisation is convincingly related to the unique historical context. But it is an early prose play, *Napoléon Bonaparte*, presented at the Odéon in 1831, which best illustrates Dumas's eclecticism and (at any rate at the outset of his career) freedom from the limitations of a set formula; for in this play he assimilates the techniques of the *scène historique*, but does so by building up a series of episodic tableaux in the documentary manner. These are linked by the person of Napoléon himself, but also by a fictional character, L'Espion, who is pardoned by Napoléon in Act I, and reappears in various guises throughout the play to show his devotion to the Emperor. This highly imaginative device, an attempt to solve the problems of the documentary play in the naturalistic manner by non-naturalistic means, was far in advance of its times. It may well be that the play's success was largely due to the playing of Frédérick Lemaître in the title role; but *Napoléon Bonaparte* possesses qualities that have never been fully appreciated, and it is certainly the only historical play of its period that looks forward to the epic drama of Brecht.

MUSSET, OR THE ARMCHAIR IRONIST

Discouraged by the failure of *La Nuit vénitienne* at the Odéon in 1830, the young Musset (he was only twenty at the time) resolved never to write for the theatre again. Not only his historical dramas *André del Sarto* and *Lorenzaccio*, but also the 'comédies' and 'proverbes' which made such a distinctive contribution to the dramatic literature of the period, were therefore written for publication as 'spectacles dans un fauteuil'. As an author of 'armchair drama' Musset can be seen, with the benefit of hindsight, to have enjoyed several advantages. Most notably in *Lorenzaccio*, he was able to write with total freedom from the constraints of the staging practice current in the 1830s; but more generally, he was freed from the problems of a personal and material nature that beset the other playwrights. The choice of theatre for each particular play; the casting of the play, under pressure from managers and mistresses; the susceptibilities of actors and the caprices of critics; the unpredictable role of the censor: these were the constant preoccupations of Hugo, Dumas and Vigny, and played no small part in determining the stage fortunes of Romantic drama. Aloof from the battle, Musset was able to write in order to please himself and to appeal to posterity.

Alongside the strongly marked sense of period which, as we have seen, characterised *Lorenzaccio* in particular, Musset's two historical dramas also both display a full-blooded Romantic individualism. *André del Sarto* (1833) is a demonstration of the unprincipled rights of passion, just as much of its time as Dumas's *Antony*. The lover, Cordiani, who with Lucrèce betrays the latter's husband André, cries: 'De quel droit ne serait-elle pas à moi?'

– De quel droit?
– Silence! j'aime et je suis aimé. Je ne veux rien analyser, rien savoir; il n'y a d'heureux que les enfants qui cueillent un fruit et le portent à leurs lèvres sans penser à autre chose, sinon qu'ils l'aiment et qu'il est à la portée de leurs mains.

(I, i)

But André himself is also a Romantic individualist, prepared to sacrifice honour and integrity to passion, and finally driven to suicide by a *mal du siècle* that belongs to the nineteenth century rather than to the Renaissance. A similar attitude is illustrated in *Lorenzaccio*, where the hero embodies what must have been a familiar Romantic cliché: the character young in years, but who has already accumulated a lifetime of experience. The whole of the crucial central scene in Act III with Philippe Strozzi is an elaboration of this topos; but the cumulative build-up of Lorenzo's character is so effective, and the imagery he develops in this scene is so compelling, that what might elsewhere seem like a cliché here becomes totally credible as the authentic expression of a real personality:

Ah! vous avez vécu tout seul, Philippe. Pareil à un fanal éclatant, vous êtes resté immobile au bord de l'océan des hommes, et vous avez regardé dans les eaux la réflexion de votre propre lumière. Du fond de votre solitude, vous trouviez l'océan magnifique sous le dais splendide des cieux. Vous ne comptiez pas chaque flot, vous ne jetiez pas la sonde; vous étiez plein de confiance dans l'ouvrage de Dieu. Mais moi, pendant ce temps-là, j'ai plongé – je me suis enfoncé dans cette mer houleuse de la vie; – j'en ai parcouru toutes les profondeurs, couvert de ma cloche de verre; – tandis que vous admiriez la surface, j'ai vu les débris des naufrages, les ossements et les Léviathans.

(III, iii)

Elsewhere, however, these same themes and attitudes are treated in a spirit of irony, almost in some cases of parody. And where they are treated seriously, it is often with a lightness of touch that sets Musset apart from his fellow Romantics.

Musset wrote no further historical drama. Several of his plays, it is true, are set in a geographically remote location; but place and time are so vaguely indicated that the predominant affinity is with Shakespeare's courts of Illyria and Navarre. The playwright's aim was clearly to distance his readers from the here and now of France in the 1830s, without creating a precise reality elsewhere. The labelling of his plays is not entirely consistent, but for convenience it is most useful to treat as 'comédies' those set in this unreal imaginary world, and displaying a considerable degree of fantasy; and to class as 'proverbes' those plays, whether originally called 'proverbes' or 'comédies', which observe a greater fidelity to the portrayal of recognisable reality.

Although *comédies* and *proverbes* are characterised respectively by fantasy and realism in terms of their setting, they are linked by the affinity of both groups of plays with the psychological comedy of Marivaux. More than any other dramatist, until we reach Giraudoux and Anouilh in our own day, Musset shows an intuitive awareness of the crucial role dialogue can play in furthering the progress of a love relationship: an intuition which, in the case of the eighteenth-century playwright, had led to the coining of the term 'marivaudage'. In *On ne badine pas avec l'amour* (1834), for instance, the young lovers Perdican and Camille are kept apart, like Marivaux's pairs of lovers, not by any external factor but by the powerful psychological obstacles of pride, vanity and mistrust; and at each of their meetings, their courtship takes the form of a defensive skirmishing. But this is *marivaudage* with a difference: the emotions of an innocent third party are involved, and Musset's bitter-sweet comedy ends with the death of the *ingénue* Rosette, a victim of the couple's self-absorbed trifling with love. Perdican's 'profession de foi' may be justly celebrated as a *locus classicus* of Romantic idealism:

Tous les hommes sont menteurs, inconstants, faux, bavards, hypocrites, orgueilleux et lâches, méprisables et sensuels; toutes les femmes sont perfides, artificieuses, vaniteuses, curieuses et dépravées; le monde n'est qu'un égout sans fond ou les phoques les plus informes rampent et se tordent sur des montagnes de fange; mais il y a au monde une chose sainte et sublime, c'est l'union de deux de ces êtres si imparfaits et si affreux. On est souvent trompé en amour, souvent blessé et souvent malheureux; mais on aime, et quand on est sur le bord de sa tombe, on se retourne pour regarder en arrière, et on se dit: – J'ai souffert souvent, je me suis trompé quelquefois, mais j'ai aimé. C'est moi qui ai vécu, et non pas un être factice créé par mon orgueil et mon ennui

(II, v)

– but the note on which the play ends reflects a pessimism peculiar to this period of Musset's life. The same pessimism had already found expression in *Les Caprices de Marianne*, published in the previous year, 1833. The cynicism and the idealism that are united in the same character in the case of Perdican, are here represented by two separate characters; and in the denouement of this play, as the trusting idealist Coelio goes to his death thinking (quite wrongly) that he has been betrayed by his friend Octave, Musset's irony achieves a bitter intensity that seems to belie the label 'comédie'.

From this point onwards, however, the mood of the *comédies* shows a marked change, as passionate intensity gives way to a more detached form of irony – reverting, in fact, to the tone of *Fantasio*, an idiosyncratic little piece published between *Les Caprices de Marianne* and *On ne badine pas*. In *Le Chandelier* (1835) the naïve young hero, Fortunio, is being used as a decoy, to divert the attention of a jealous husband from Jacqueline and her established lover Clavaroche; but his devotion is rewarded when Jacqueline deserts the worldly Clavaroche and transfers her attention to the youthful idealist – a clear reversal of the theme and message of *Les Caprices de Marianne*. *Barberine* (also published in 1835) demonstrates an even greater change of mood; and this play, a serene celebration of the strength of conjugal love, is the clearest possible illustration of the extent of Musset's independence of current ideologies.

The *proverbes* show a similar independence, not only in their subject-matter but especially in their manner. The *proverbe* – essentially a conversation-piece, or documentary sketch, portraying the domestic life of the leisured classes of the playwright's own day – was developed by Musset from a society entertainment, popular in the late eighteenth century, in which a short dramatic sketch illustrated a proverb which the spectators were invited to identify. The charade element has now disappeared, though several of Musset's *proverbes* do offer an illustration of the proverbial saying which serves as their title. *Il ne faut jurer de rien* (1836) represents a halfway stage between *comédie* and *proverbe*: its setting is recognisably that of Musset's own world, and the fantasy of the earlier comedies has gone – though the dialogue retains a lyrical exaltation which suggests the Romantic poet rather than the realist social observer in Musset. The pure *proverbe*, on the other hand, convinces us of its authenticity as a record not only of the manners, but also of the speech, of Musset's day. The genre is illustrated by *Un Caprice* (1837) – important because this was the play which led to Musset being revived at the Théâtre-Français, in 1847; *Il faut qu'une porte soit ouverte ou fermée* (1845); and *On ne saurait penser à tout* (written for the Théâtre-Français, and performed there in 1849). The second of these plays is comedy of manners reduced to the proportions of an exquisite miniature: sophisticated, witty, urbane. Plot is minimal; though it is interesting to note how, as with Marivaux's comedy, it is the act of conversing that provides such plot as there is. As Le Comte confesses, when he has been led to propose marriage to La Marquise (they are the only two characters of this charming little play):

Je conviendrai, tant que vous voudrez, que j'étais entré ici sans dessein; je ne comptais que vous voir en passant, témoin cette porte que j'ai ouverte trois fois pour m'en aller. La conversation que nous venons d'avoir, vos railleries, votre froideur même, m'ont entraîné plus loin qu'il ne fallait peut-être.

Wit, urbanity and poise are not attributes one necessarily associates with the writing of the Romantic generation in France. Inasmuch as they are undoubtedly characteristic of Musset's *proverbes*, it may well be felt that these pieces, although the work of one who in so many ways was the most Romantic of the Romantics, escape classification as genuine examples of Romantic drama.

ROMANTIC DRAMA IN RETROSPECT: ACHIEVEMENT AND INFLUENCE

'On ne doit pas oublier que nous sommes dans la transition d'un goût ancien à un goût nouveau': so wrote Victor Hugo in a 'Note' appended as a postscript to *Marion de Lorme* in 1831. In so far as the 'goût ancien' refers to the writing of derivative tragedies in the neo-classical manner, it is true enough that one positive achievement of the 1830s was to have killed this off once and for all. 'Le passé ne se recommence pas', wrote Gautier, reviewing Ponsard's *Lucrèce* in 1843;[27] and this play, often hailed as marking a 'return to classicism', in fact reveals a distinct tendency to compromise on the author's part, both in construction and in poetic manner. As regards the performance, and appreciation, of the masterpieces of Corneille and Racine, although they were regarded with disfavour by the young Romantic iconoclasts – 'Nous en avons fini avec le classique; Melpomène est enfoncée; nous sommes délivrés des harangues de Corneille, des fadeurs de Racine, du clinquant et des jongleries de Voltaire. Bravo! bravo!'[28] – performances had suffered only a partial setback even at the height of the Romantic vogue; and the advent of Rachel, bringing a freer, less conventional acting style to the Théâtre-Français in the early 1840s, soon re-established these authors in popular esteem. Here too, indeed, one can see a similar compromise in taste between the old and the new, for Rachel, relying on natural grace rather than on stylised technique, had more in common with Marie Dorval or Harriet Smithson than with Mlle Mars.

If the 'goût ancien' has been tempered in this way, and accommodated to the changing fashion, what of the 'goût nouveau'? It must be said that the eclipse of Romantic drama was by the end of the 1840s remarkably complete. After *Les Burgraves* in 1843, Hugo was to write nothing more for the stage; Vigny had written nothing since *Chatterton*; and Musset's 'armchair drama' began to be staged only towards 1850. Dumas alone remained active as a force within the theatre; but as has been seen, what Romantic inspiration he had earlier shown had faded by the end of the 1830s. However, there were still isolated cases of plays in the Romantic idiom, or plays strongly marked by Romantic influences, by other authors. Nerval, for instance, made repeated attempts to succeed in the theatre throughout his career: he collaborated with Dumas more than once, and on his own account wrote a historical drama *Leo Burckart* (1839) and a play on the Faust theme *L'Imagier de Harlem* (1851). Gautier, too, offered a historical drama, *La Juive de Constantine*, in 1846; and the 60-year-old Lamartine produced an ambitious 'tragédie moderne' in verse, *Toussaint Louverture*, in 1850, with Frédérick Lemaître in the role of the black Haitian leader. And what is to be made of Balzac's work as a dramatist? It would be wrong to try to locate him squarely in the Romantic tradition; but in two bourgeois tragedies, *L'École des ménages* (not staged until 1910) and *La Marâtre* (1848), as well as in the social comedy *Mercadet* (performed posthumously in 1851), he showed how his idiosyncratic blend of Romantic imagination and sober realism could be transferred from the novel to the theatre. Better than any other playwright of the Romantic period, Balzac suggests the possibility of a new kind of drama, capable of analysing the forces motivating the behaviour of representative individuals in contemporary society.

This new social drama was the goal of the dramatists of the new generation, Dumas *fils* and Augier. The latter, following Ponsard, took a moralist's stance resolutely opposed to the excesses of Romantic individualism; but although Dumas too was later to pose as the champion of marriage and the family as the essential bases of a healthy society, he is really remembered for one play only, *La Dame aux camélias* (1852), which is a powerful expression of the individualist ethos. Its theme updates that of *Marion de Lorme*, transposing it from the story of the seventeenth-century courtesan to that of a contemporary *demi-mondaine* who had died in 1847. Although the intellectual argument presented by the play may emphasise the triumph of social morality and the defeat of the individual, the emotional appeal is wholly on the side of the lovers; and the curtain-line: 'Dors en paix, Marguerite! il te sera beaucoup pardonné, parce que tu as beaucoup aimé!' is an eloquent restatement of the familiar Romantic ideology of the 1830s. Like *Hernani*, *Marion de Lorme*, *Antony* and *Ruy Blas*, *La Dame aux camélias* is one of the most memorable embodiments of a tenacious Romantic myth.

After what is conventionally regarded as the 'failure' of Romantic drama, its liberating influence remained. Even when the Romantic playwrights were no longer there to present an active challenge to the notion of a hierarchy of values based on the supremacy of classical tragedy, those hierarchical values remained much diluted. If, to quote the Preface to *Hernani*, 'le romantisme . . . n'est, à tout prendre . . . que le libéralisme en littérature', then the real achievement of 1827 and 1830 was to have secured for the Romantics' successors a greater freedom of choice.

Only occasionally have those successors opted for a style that Hugo and his colleagues might have acknowledged as their own. The poetic revival of the end of the century produced, in the plays of Banville, Villiers de l'Isle-Adam and Maeterlinck, something much more esoteric than the characteristic manner of the 1830s, showing more affinity with German than with French Romanticism. Edmond Rostand, however, in *Cyrano de Bergerac* (1897), produced not only the greatest theatrical success of the century, but also the most faithful illustration of the Romantic dramatists' theories. Larger-than-life characterisation based on the *sublime/grotesque* antithesis; a convincing evocation of the atmosphere of a historical period; a verse-form that provides an admirable vehicle for comedy, satire, invective, imaginative flights of fancy and intimate lyricism; the poignant expression of the Romantic myth of a shared love frustrated by the realities of life: all is there, as a triumphant vindication of the *Préface de 'Cromwell'* – and one can but trust that Hugo's ghost was generous enough to applaud his successor's triumph.

3 and 4. 'The true "première" [of *Lorenzaccio*] was the production at Avignon in 1952 . . .' (p. 244). *Above*: Marguerite Jamois as Lorenzo (Théâtre Montparnasse, Paris, 1945) represents the end of the old tradition; *opposite*: Gérard Philipe (Théâtre National Populaire, Avignon, 1952) inaugurates a new interpretation.

If Claudel and Cocteau, Montherlant and Anouilh, each in his different way, all produced a kind of drama that would have been inconceivable without the breakthrough of the 1830s, the Romantic dramatists themselves have enjoyed a steadily declining popularity in the twentieth century. Both as subjects of serious academic study and in terms of performance in the theatre, plays that were once universally known are now badly neglected; and where revivals do take place, they are often, perversely, of the less distinguished plays, chosen as a pretext for gratuitous travesty.[29]

Musset stands out as the exception here. Not only have a number of his *comédies* and *proverbes* – *Le Chandelier*, *Un Caprice*, *Il faut qu'une porte soit ouverte ou fermée* – remained firm favourites as curtain-raisers at the Comédie-Française, but *Lorenzaccio* is now belatedly established as the one major play of its generation with permanent appeal both on stage and in the study. First performed in 1896 with Sarah Bernhardt in the title role, in an adaptation by Armand d'Artois (which transposed the 'Shakespearean' construction of Musset's play into a tidy affair with five different sets, one for each act – showing no advance on the staging pattern of Hugo's plays, for instance, in the 1830s), *Lorenzaccio* continued for another fifty years or so to be played, if at all, with a woman in the part of Lorenzo, and in a form which completely betrayed the author's intentions. The true 'première' of Musset's play was the production by Jean Vilar for the TNP (Théâtre National Populaire) at Avignon in 1952, with Gérard Philipe as Lorenzo. Having waited nearly 120 years to be accepted as the masterpiece it undoubtedly is, *Lorenzaccio* has now become, by a strange irony, the only play of its period to enjoy a regular place in the national repertory, and the Romantic drama which best represents, for audiences of the 1980s, the aspirations and achievements of the playwrights of the 1830s.[30]

NOTES

1. See C.B. Wicks and J.W. Schweitzer (eds.), *The Parisian Stage, Part III (1831–50)* (University of Alabama Press, 1960).
2. *Racine et Shakespeare*, ed. H. Martineau (Divan, 1928), p. 47.
3. *The Death of Tragedy* (London, Faber, 1963), p. 243.
4. *Les Contemplations* (1856): poem written in 1834.
5. *Racine et Shakespeare*, p. 113.
6. See W.D. Howarth, 'Victor Hugo and the "failure" of French Romantic drama', *L'Esprit Créateur*, 16 (1976), 247–56.
7. *The Contours of European Romanticism* (London, Macmillan, 1979), pp. 40–55.
8. H.S. Gochberg, *Stage of Dreams: the Dramatic Art of A. de Musset* (Geneva, Droz, 1967), pp. 173, 174.

9. *Ruy Blas*, ed. A. Ubersfeld (Besançon and Paris, Les Belles Lettres, 1971), I, 80.
10. Pixérécourt, *Théâtre choisi*, ed. C. Nodier (Nancy, by the author, 1841–3), I, p. vii.
11. Quoted by W.S. Hartog, *Guilbert de Pixérécourt, sa vie, son mélodrame, sa technique et son influence* (Champion, 1913), p. 191.
12. P. Brooks, *The Melodramatic Imagination: Balzac, Henry James, Melodrama, and the Mode of Excess* (New Haven and London, Yale UP, 1976), p. 90.
13. *Quarante Ans de théâtre* (Bibliothèque des Annales, 1901), IV, 2.
14. For an analysis of this passage, see W.D. Howarth, *Sublime and Grotesque: a Study of French Romantic Drama* (London, Harrap, 1975), pp. 165–6.
15. P. Brooks, *The Melodramatic Imagination*, p. 92.
16. *Ibid.*, p. 218.
17. Quoted by P. and V. Glachant, *Le Théâtre de V. Hugo: les drames en prose* (Hachette, 1903), p. 9.
18. In an interesting passage from an article which appeared in *La Revue des deux mondes* in 1831, Vigny interprets Antony as a 'type effrayant, et il est utile par cela même'. See also D.O. Evans, *Le Drame moderne à l'époque romantique* (1923; Geneva, Slatkine reprint, 1974), pp. 160ff.
19. Needless to say, these references summarise the action of the first three acts of the play.
20. Cf. the eloquent testimony of Gautier's account of the first night in *Histoire du romantisme* (Charpentier, 1911), pp. 167ff.
21. *Ibid.*, p. 154.
22. Quoted by L. Breitholtz, *Le Théâtre historique en France jusqu'à la Révolution* (Uppsala, A.B. Lundequistska Bokhandeln, 1952), p. 136.
23. See W.D. Howarth, 'History in the theatre: the French and English traditions', *Trivium*, I (1966), 151–68.
24. Quoted by H. Parigot, *Le Drame d'Alexandre Dumas: étude dramatique, sociale et littéraire* (C. Lévy, 1899), p. 243.
25. *Ruy Blas*, ed. A. Ubersfeld, I, p. 78.
26. Quoted by D.O. Evans, *Le Drame moderne à l'époque romantique*, p. 17.
27. *Histoire de l'art dramatique en France depuis vingt-cinq ans* (Brussels, Hetzel, 1859), III, 48.
28. *Le Constitutionnel*, 2. iii (1829), quoted by O.E. Fellows, *French Opinion of Molière (1800–1850)* (Providence, R.I., Brown UP, 1937), p. 15.
29. A recent production of Hugo's *Marie Tudor* by Jean-Luc Boutté at the Comédie-Française (Easter 1982) provided an outstanding example of this. Simon Renard's curtain-line ('Qui a osé. . .? – Moi. J'ai sauvé la reine et l'Angleterre') served as the cue for the playing of 'God Save the Queen', and this was sadly in keeping with the whole spirit of the production, whose inspiration seemed to more than one critic to reflect the influence of the circus.
30. See B. Masson, *Musset et le théâtre intérieur: nouvelles recherches sur Lorenzaccio* (A. Colin, 1974), pp. 225–400, for a detailed analysis of stage productions of the play.

BIBLIOGRAPHY

Among first-hand accounts by participants or observers, the following stand out: Adèle Hugo, *Victor Hugo raconté par un témoin de sa vie* (Lacroix, Verboeckhoven, 1863); A. Dumas *père*, *Mes Mémoires*, ed. M. Josserand (5 vols., Gallimard, 1954–68); and T. Gautier, *Histoire du romantisme* (Charpentier, 1874). Modern works which present the story of Romantic drama from the point of view of the personalities involved, in a highly readable anecdotal manner, include R.A.E. Baldick, *The Life and Times of Frédérick Lemaître* (London, Hamish Hamilton, 1959) and Linda Kelly, *The Young Romantics*

(London, The Bodley Head, 1976). M. Descotes, *Le Drame romantique et ses grands créateurs* (PUF, n. d. (1955)) is outstanding as a factual historical account, based on contemporary documents.

General interpretative studies, which combine historical narrative with critical evaluation, include P. Nebout, *Le Drame romantique* (Lecène, Oudin, 1895); P. Ginisty, *Le Théâtre romantique* (Morancé, 1922); F.W.M. Draper, *The Rise and Fall of the French Romantic Drama, with special reference to the influence of Shakespeare, Scott, and Byron* (London, Constable, 1923); D.O. Evans, *Le Théâtre pendant la période romantique (1827–48)* (1925; Geneva, Slatkine reprint, 1974). M. Carlson, *The French Stage in the Nineteenth Century* (Metuchen, NJ, The Scarecrow Press, 1972) focuses in chapter 2, 'The Age of Romanticism (1827–1850)', on the history of the Paris theatres during this period. W.D. Howarth, *Sublime and Grotesque: A Study of French Romantic Drama* (London, Harrap, 1975) sets the central study of the major Romantic dramatists in a wide literary and social context, and evaluates the theatrical as well as the literary qualities of the plays concerned; it is to date the most comprehensive treatment of the subject as a whole.

The relationship between melodrama and Romantic drama is well treated in P. Brooks, *The Melodramatic Imagination: Balzac, Henry James, Melodrama and the Mode of Excess* (New Haven and London, Yale UP, 1976; see especially chapters 1–4); and Michèle H. Jones, *Le Théâtre national en France de 1800 à 1830* (Klincksieck, 1975) studies the relationship with the 'scène historique'. D.O. Evans, *Le Drame moderne à l'époque romantique (1827–1850)* (1923; Geneva, Slatkine reprint, 1974) provides a good background for those Romantic dramas with a modern social setting. For the staging of Romantic plays, see Marie-Antoinette Allevy, *La Mise en scène en France dans la première moitié du dix-neuvième siècle* (Droz, 1938).

General works on drama which offer valuable critical interpretations of French Romantic drama include G. Steiner, *The Death of Tragedy* (London, Faber, 1963), M. Lioure, *Le Drame de Diderot à Ionesco* (A. Colin, 1973; see chapter 2, 'Le Drame romantique'), and H. Lindenberger, *Historical Drama: The Relation of Literature and Reality* (Chicago and London, U. of Chicago Press, 1975).

Turning to the coverage of individual authors, studies of Vigny's theatre have been notably lacking in recent years. The best remains that by E. Sakellaridès, *Alfred de Vigny auteur dramatique* (Éditions de la Plume, 1902); see also E. Estève, *Alfred de Vigny, sa pensée et son art* (Garnier, 1923), especially Book 2, chapter 2, 'Le Théâtre'. More recent articles include R.C. Dale, '*Chatterton* is the essential Romantic drama', and E. Kushner, 'Histoire et théâtre chez Vigny', in *L'Esprit Créateur*, 5 (1965), 131–7 and 147–61 respectively.

On Dumas, H. Parigot, *Le Drame d'Alexandre Dumas: étude dramatique, sociale et littéraire* (C. Lévy, 1899) remains the fullest study. See also F. Bassan, 'Dumas père et le drame romantique', *L'Esprit Créateur*, 5 (1965), 174–8; S. Chevalley and F. Bassan, *Alexandre Dumas père et la Comédie-Française* (Lettres Modernes, 1972); G.M.S.C. Simon, *Histoire d'une collaboration: A. Dumas et A. Maquet* (G. Crès, 1919); and A. Ubersfeld, 'Désordre et génie', *Europe*, 490–1 (1970), 107–18.

Recent studies of Hugo's theatre include C. Affron, *A Stage for Poets: Studies in the Theatre of Hugo and Musset* (Princeton, NJ, Princeton UP, 1971); M. Butor, 'Le Théâtre de V. Hugo', *Nouvelle Revue Française*, 24 (1964), 862–78, 1073–81; 25 (1965), 105–13; S. Chahine, *La Dramaturgie de Victor Hugo (1816–1843)* (Nizet, 1971); J. Gaudon, *Victor Hugo dramaturge* (L'Arche, 1955); and A. Ubersfeld, *Le Roi et le bouffon, étude sur le théâtre de Hugo de 1830 à 1839* (Corti, 1974). Earlier works of value include the two volumes by P. and V. Glachant, *Le Théâtre de V. Hugo: les drames en vers* (Hachette, 1902) and *Le Théâtre de V. Hugo: les drames en prose* (Hachette, 1903); G. Lote, *En préface à Hernani* (Librairie Universitaire, 1930), and A. Sleumer, *Die Dramen Victor Hugos* (Berlin, E. Felber, 1901).

It is Musset's work for the theatre that has attracted the most attention in recent years. Useful studies include: C. Affron, *A Stage for Poets* (see above); E.L. Gans, *Musset et le 'drame tragique'* (Corti, 1974); H.S. Gochberg, *Stage of Dreams: the dramatic art of A. de Musset* (Geneva, Droz, 1967); B. Masson, *Musset et le théâtre intérieur: nouvelles recherches sur Lorenzaccio* (A. Colin, 1974); and D. Sices, *Theater of Solitude: The Drama of A. de Musset* (Hanover, NH, U. Press of New England, 1974). Joyce Bromfield, *De Lorenzino de Medicis à Lorenzaccio: étude d'un thème historique* (Didier, 1972) assesses the source material of *Lorenzaccio*; H. Lefebvre, *Musset* (L'Arche, 1955) offers a Marxist interpretation of this same play; and valuable studies of Musset's language in his plays are provided by A. Brun, *Deux Proses de théâtre* (Gap, Ophrys, 1954); B. Masson, *Théâtre et langage: essai sur le dialogue dans les comédies de Musset* (Minard, 1977); and F. Tonge, *L'Art du dialogue dans les comédies en prose d'Alfred de Musset* (Nizet, 1967). Among earlier studies, L. Lafoscade, *Le Théâtre d'A. de Musset* (Hachette, 1901) is still of use. P. Dimoff's invaluable *La Genèse de Lorenzaccio* (Droz, 1936), which presents a critical edition of the text of Musset's play, has recently been supplemented by the edition by B. Masson (Imprimerie Nationale, 1978): in both cases, the text of *Lorenzaccio* is accompanied by the essential source texts of Varchi and George Sand.

Among other playwrights of the period, Balzac is represented by a recent complete edition of his plays, *Théâtre*, ed. R. Guise (3 vols., Les Bibliophiles de l'Originale, 1969–71) and by the two volumes by D.Z. Milatchitch, *Le Théâtre de Honoré de Balzac* and *Le Théâtre inédit de Honoré de Balzac* (both Hachette, 1930).

VII · *Criticism and theory*

ROGER FAYOLLE
(translated by Janet Lloyd)

FROM THE AGE OF ENLIGHTENMENT TO THE ROMANTIC PERIOD

It is impossible to understand the renewal that the Romantics brought to traditional aesthetic ideas in France without taking into consideration the crisis in which French society found itself during the last decades of the eighteenth century. Rigidified institutions had become unequal to the task of coping with the new forces that were making themselves felt. The practice of Art (at least, of what was recognised as true Art) was limited to providing an occupation or distraction for a few privileged people and to lending lustre to the pomp and importance of a handful of patrons. It was obliged to accommodate itself to outworn aesthetic theories and barren critical dogmas. The guiding principle of classical art, namely, to imitate the beauties of nature, had become no more than a rule the effects of which were totally retrograde. What was expected was the imitation of the great classicists whom no one could ever hope to surpass or even match. Arrested in its admiration of the past, post-classicism was concerned simply with producing increasingly subtle refinements on the minute precepts of an increasingly formal dogmatism whose fundamental ideas were losing all significance. The anonymous author of *Un Voyage au Parnasse*, published in 1762, was full of scorn for critics capable of doing no more than everlastingly repeat 'les mots: Diction, Goût, Harmonie . . . Je leur demandai ce que ces mots signifiaient: je les vis embarrassés; ils me lancèrent un regard affreux qui me fit prendre la fuite.' In 1843, in an article on Barante, Sainte-Beuve, amazed at this dearth of ideas among the critics of the Age of Enlightenment, exclaimed: 'Chose singulière! La critique littéraire, à la fin du xviiième siècle, de cette époque éminemment philosophique, était devenue chez la plupart des disciples, purement méticuleuse et littérale: elle ne s'attachait guère qu'aux mots.' In truth, the precepts of men such as Marmontel or Daurat (whom Stendhal, in *La vie de Henri Brulard*, reflecting on his childhood reading, refers to as 'canailles') were chiefly concerned to ensure that rhetoric was correctly used and to impose equilibrium and regularity upon the arrangement of subject-matter: critics appeared to be reading simply for the purpose of counting the pages and lines and going to the theatre armed with a watch in one hand and a schoolteacher's ruler in the other, with the sole aim of suppressing any attempts to strike at the nobility of the work's form.

The formal trivialisation resulting from the tyranny of the rules was compounded by the increasing dullness of the taste of a society obsessed by respect for the proprieties. The only enjoyment admissible was that derived from works that conformed to the conventions of French good manners. Homer, Cervantes, Dante or Shakespeare were tolerable only once their excessive lapses of taste had been expunged. Under conditions such as these, any kind of poetry was practically inconceivable, apart from periphrases and conceits in the style of Delille.

This straitjacket was nevertheless unable totally to prevent the effects that a growth of information and historical knowledge was having, on the level of aesthetic sensibilities. In the course of the eighteenth century, more and more newspapers appeared, informing French readers about what was being published in England, Germany and Italy. Admittedly, not much space was devoted to (what was not yet known as) 'la littérature'. Nevertheless, this precarious accessibility to outside influences favoured the development of 'l'anglomanie', sufficiently strong to alarm even Voltaire when Le Tourneur set about translating Shakespeare and the English critics' prefaces to his works. Alongside this discovery of English authors to rival the French classics and considered just as dangerous, was the rediscovery – thanks to the appearance of the first great studies of literary history – of the works of the past. These drew attention to the origins of French literature and promoted the budding taste for a literary mode not at all in keeping with the canons of classicism: namely, the 'troubadour' genre. However, 'anglomania' and the 'troubadour' genre were both ephemeral phenomena and did not give rise to any work striking enough to attract the attention of the legislators of Parnassus.

The critics and theorists paid more attention to other demands which stemmed from the transformations taking place in economic and social life, the development of commerce and industry and an improvement in the material conditions of life, of which the effect was to encourage a sense of the importance of the family. The new society confusedly desired a new kind of art, one more relevant to its needs and way of life, an art which would be of some use by helping to promote and celebrate the new values: notably, work and the family. For example, it called for and encouraged a non-classical genre of drama: the *drame*, in which the new public of the second half of the eighteenth century tried to identify with representations of virtuous bourgeois and philosophical business-men, just as the public of 1630 had sought to identify with characters representing heroes or valorous princes. Nevertheless, so long as literature continued to bring readers or audiences an ideal image of what they believed themselves to be, it remained steeped in dignity. It was quite possible, in the field of painting as well as that of literature, to tackle new subjects and glorify modern heroes simply by appropriating, with a few formal adjustments, the techniques, conventions and rules of classical art over which the traditional aristocratic public had ceased to hold a monopoly. The fact is that aesthetic conflicts were fought essentially over the formal aspects of art (for example, over the role of verse in drama), even when new themes or sources of inspiration were generally recognised to be necessary. The attitude was: 'Let us be *philosophes* and *sensibles* as bourgeois businessmen would like to be, but let us be so with all the *bienséance* and *distinction* dear to the hearts of the courtiers of the *Grand Siècle*.'

Sainte-Beuve underlined this kind of contradiction between desire for renewal and techniques of appropriation when, in the article 'Barante' cited above, he wrote: 'Quand je dis que la critique issue en droite ligne de la philosophie du XVIIIème siècle se prenait surtout aux mots, je sais bien que, parmi les mots, on faisait sonner très haut ceux de *philosophe* et de *raison* mais sous ce couvert imposant et creux, on était trop souvent puriste et servile.' The truth is that the liberating ideology of the *encyclopédistes* was not free from uncertainties and obscurities of its own. The advance towards liberty never proceeds equally rapidly in all domains. Those who are preoccupied by the urgent need for economic and social change find it difficult at the same time to realise that there is also a need for radical change in the domain – always considered a privileged one – of the Fine Arts. In this respect, the hesitancies of the eighteenth-century bourgeois and those who purveyed their ideology may be compared to those felt by proletariats of the nineteenth and twentieth centuries. One of the by no means negligible feats of many of those determined to restore the earlier social order has been to present and glorify liberty of expression and artistic creation as an essential aspect of individual liberation. Perhaps this might even explain why modern histories of literature often present the image of the Romantic movement in France as one of a movement of overall liberation, but without ever posing the question: liberation from whom? and at the cost of what new or recreated servitude?

True, many *encyclopédistes* or *philosophes* who were opposed to the practices of classical art expressed their intention to promote an art which would be more than simply a distraction for the aristocracy and would fulfil the function of 'une espèce d'instruction publique' (Mercier, in the Preface to his *Molière*, 1776). True, Diderot, among others, voiced the claims of *l'homme sensible* and, in opposition to the insipidity of an art designed for a leisured and frivolous society, championed the authenticity of an art rich in powerful emotions. Both expressed a protest against the decadence of a society more concerned with its pleasures than with its duties, more prone to preciosity than to real passion. But before hailing such tendencies as the first manifestations of the new art that Romanticism was to be and before speaking of a 'pre-Romantic' tendency, it is important to take account of the ambiguity of the word 'sensibilité' bandied about so freely in the eighteenth century. It may either refer to the free expression of individual feelings or else to the expression of strong public sentiments; and Romanticism, in the most usually accepted sense of the term, appears to have related only to the first of these two possibilities. Here, the work of Jean-Jacques Rousseau is an exception, combining as it does the expression of civic 'sensibilité' with appealing confessions from a passionate heart. It contains the seeds of two types of art which the future was to distinguish between and oppose: the Revolutionary art that made a fleeting appearance in 1792 and the Romantic art of 1830. In order to understand the latter, it is important not to consider the period inaugurated by the 1789 Revolution as one hostile to the Muses and alien to all forms of artistic and literary expression. Romanticism was born in a revolutionised France. Before the Revolution, criticism had been steeped in 'philosophie' and involved in the fight of philosophes against traditionalists. After the Revolution, it was steeped in politics and involved in the ceaseless struggles of the Résistance and the Movement.

But there is one important difference which may explain how it is that historians of literature have so often been mistaken in this context: in the eighteenth century, philosophy was openly appealed to in the course of literary conflicts and it often happened that, despite all the grand new words, 'la littérature' itself remained altogether traditional and more than somewhat repetitive. In the nineteenth century, in contrast, however real and important the political implications of literary discussions may have been, they were not openly recognised: 'pure' literature took pride of place once more and conflicts of an essentially social or political nature were used as an opportunity for a genuine renewal of literary forms and themes. During the Age of Enlightenment, most artists and writers played a part in the movement which led to the 1789 Revolution even while they clung, essentially, to modes of expression inherited from the classical period. During the century that followed, artists and writers, now placed in a new situation by bourgeois society, found themselves masters of nothing but their own material and words, and these they used in new ways, as Romantics, as Realists, as Symbolists, and so on: it was a century of social revolutions that were failures and aesthetic revolutions that were successful. The first of the latter was the 'Romantic revolution'.

REVOLUTIONARIES AND ÉMIGRÉS– THE FIRST SKIRMISHES IN THE ROMANTIC QUARREL

Let us attempt to define how the great Revolutionary upheaval of French society also altered the function of artists and the concept of art, in particular the function of writers and concept of literature.

Under the *ancien régime*, whilst Latin, the language of clerks, was the language of knowledge – a knowledge inseparable from faith and theology – French was first and foremost the language of the king, the language of power. The mission of writers strictly dependent upon aristocratic patronage, itself subject to royal surveillance, consisted to a large extent in demonstrating that the language of the king and the nobility was capable of producing masterpieces worthy of the prestigious models of antiquity. (It was indeed to this that the great classical writers of the age of Louis XIV owed their renown.) For the great writers of that period it was clearly a matter of rivalling antiquity in a contest for greatness: the glorious renown of the King had to equal that of Alexander or of Augustus. Theirs was an art that was totally aristocratic and it was quite different and radically separated from popular traditions, and from a national past that was both ignored and despised.

With the Revolution, French became (or was soon to become) the language of the entire nation and the depository of power. Writers and artists had a role to play in this transformation. It was to promote a necessary consciousness of the changes that had taken place and to prolong the effects of those changes by striving through their works to forge a national unity. The appalling conditions of war against a coalition of kings made it almost impossible for the young Republic to develop a new collective kind of art linked to great national demonstrations and great public festivals or even to gain recognition for such an art from the 'experts in aesthetics'. The new literature had no time to invent for itself either language or forms and so, in its patriotic odes, anthems and dramas addressed itself to the 'people' in the emphatic and pompous language of neo-classicism. Meanwhile, there were hesitant attempts to establish a new art neither classical nor romantic but 'national'; that is to say, to use the term which Mme de Staël invented expressly for it, an art of 'vulgarity'.

In the meantime the nation had banished the 'erstwhile' aristocrats, who were in a way the proprietors of classical art, and many of them had chosen exile. Emigration provided them with the opportunity to discover that, in other countries such as Germany or England, the function of art and literature in society was not the same as in France; that other artists, despite being just as close to aristocratic circles, did not show the same concern to emulate antiquity, the model that had been thought to be impossible to transcend. Here was a truth to be recognised and some (such as Charles de Villers, in 1806, in his *Érotique comparée*) proclaimed it: there is no universal form of beauty and no untouchable aesthetic model. There was surely a positive connection between the aesthetic theories which had been imposed upon France over nearly two centuries and the power of the absolute monarchy. Was not literature 'l'expression de la société', as Bonald in 1802 recognised it to be? The truth was that other societies, with different histories, fully accepted arts and literatures oblivious of the radical separation between religious feeling and aesthetic expression that had been imposed upon France by the cult of pagan antiquity. Nor did they despise their feudal and gothic pasts: in these societies great works of art had also been produced by chivalry and faith. Why not try to renew French art in a similar fashion once it became possible to bring about the Restoration in France?

However, the moment for such a Restoration was delayed by the appearance, in France itself, of new aristocrats who appropriated the young power of the nation. The nobles of the Empire, many of them risen from the popular strata of this victorious nation and in alliance with industrialists and bankers, helped to restore to honour the pompous formalism of classical art, for the purpose of glorifying their own, French, Augustus. But the new classicism betrayed more arrogant ambitions than that of the age of Louis XIV: now it was a matter of proclaiming to all and sundry the superiority of France in every domain, including religion. Chateaubriand's rapid rise to literary fame may be understood within this framework. Can one really speak of Romanticism in connection with his *Génie du christianisme* (1802) and the texts used to illustrate it? Above all they demonstrated in striking fashion that the language inherited from the classical age could perfectly well be used to express Christian, hence modern sentiments and that the great representations of the supernatural in the Christian religion had even more to offer the artistic imagination than the myths of pagan antiquity.

It is at this point, during the 1810s, that the word 'romantisme' made its appearance, and it soon became the focus of a conflict, namely the opposition of 'good Frenchmen', faithful to their national traditions on the one hand, and dangerous apologists for foreign cultures on the other. Initially the attack was aimed against only the restricted circle of admirers of German culture such as Villers, mentioned above. The least obscure member of this circle, Benjamin Constant, in his *Réflexions sur la tragédie de Wallstein et sur le théâtre allemand* (1809), deplored the obstinacy of Frenchmen 'qui se refusent à comprendre l'esprit des nations étrangères'. Upon discovering the German theatre, Constant realised to what extent the rule of the three unities ran contrary to 'nature'. French tragic authors, obliged to respect that rule, could not rival the Germans who, enjoying greater freedom, had been able to create characters endowed with 'cette mobilité ondoyante qui appartient à la nature humaine et qui forme des êtres réels'. Constant was in effect doing no more than echo the opinion of Wilhelm Schlegel, one of the founders of the German school. As early as 1798 Schlegel had declared at Jena that 'les pièces françaises ne sont d'un bout à l'autre qu'une seule et même faute contre le goût, car que peut-il y avoir de plus contraire au goût que ce qui est hors de la nature?' In 1807, in his *Comparaison entre la 'Phèdre' de Racine et celle d'Euripide*, he had even dared to denigrate the idol of the French critics: the immortal Racine.

To gauge the extent to which the criteria of the most influential critics were revised within a period of twenty years, it is perhaps useful to recall the vehement terms in which one of the most respected pundits of the day. Dussault, critic for the *Journal des débats*, refuted the theses of Schlegel in his articles of February–March 1808. For him, Schlegel 'n'est qu'un sophiste et un rhéteur' who had the audacity to speak of innovation when 'les bases de la littérature sont depuis longtemps fixées', and there exist 'des principes communs dictés par le bon sens et par la raison qui sont applicables à tous'. If there were theatres (such as the German theatre) which ignored 'ces règles constantes et invariables' while others (such as the French theatre) conformed to them, 'il est évident qu'il ne peut pas y avoir plus de comparaison à faire entre ces deux espèces qu'entre la science et l'ignorance, entre la folie et la raison, entre la politesse et la barbarie'.

Up until 1813 the conflict remained extremely limited. To be a Romantic was to be lacking in good taste and to appeal to some new kind of nature or liberty haughtily disdained by the upholders of tradition – tradition which was identified with the truth and with all that was reasonable and refined. In March 1808, Dussault demonstrated alarm at the impending publication of a work by Mme de Staël which 'se propose de porter les dernières atteintes à notre gloire littéraire'. The book was *De l'Allemagne*. In 1810, the Emperor prohibited its publication and it did not appear until 1813 in London and the following year in Paris.

With the collapse of the Empire the classicists lost their official government support. Between the spring of 1813 and that of 1814 three publications of Swiss or German origin made their appearance in France and this collective blast gave the impression of a concerted attack against the European hegemony of French classical literature. The works were Sismondi's *De la littérature du midi de l'Europe* in four volumes in the spring of 1813; Mme Necker de Saussure's translation of Schlegel's *Cours de littérature dramatique* in December 1813; and the first French edition of Mme de Staël's *De L'Allemagne* in May 1814. Of the three, Sismondi's is particularly important for it lent a new dimension to the debate on Romanticism. By linking the word 'romantisme' to the adjective 'roman, romane', Sismondi gave the concept of 'romantique' a wider historical and geographical significance. The description 'romantique' was applied to the whole civilisation that stemmed from the interaction of the Ancient and the Germanic worlds, a civilisation characterised essentially by Christianity and chivalry. This civilisation is reflected in romantic literatures in which can be found 'ce mélange d'amour, de chevalerie et de religion qui a formé les mœurs romantiques et qui a donné à la poésie un caractère particulier'. Taken all in all, the literatures of Europe had retained that character, with the one exception of French literature which was romantic only during the Middle Ages and which since the Renaissance 's'est complètement séparée de la littérature romantique'. To be sure, Chateaubriand, in his *Génie du christianisme* had celebrated the poetic splendours of Christianity and the world of chivalry, but his concept of art nevertheless remained profoundly classical, as can be seen plainly from his *Martyrs*.

The new Romantic poetics, as defined by Sismondi, were therefore certainly in tune with the French public's desire – already manifested on a number of occasions – to give poetry a new life through the inspiration of Christianity, but now this desire was linked with an attempt to justify new artistic techniques based on German examples and hitherto generally condemned in the name of *vraisemblance* and nature. Sismondi, too, praised the drama of foreign cultures. He was particularly enthusiastic about the Spanish theatre of the sixteenth and seventeenth centuries and he suggested to his French readers that to adopt chivalric and Christian subjects, as Chateaubriand recommended, would mean abandoning the Graeco-Latin aesthetics of the age of Louis XIV. In opposition to him, as in 1808, Dussault vehemently defended classicism as the only concept of art acceptable and he was vigorously supported by Charles Nodier (the future organiser of the Romantic salon of the Arsenal) who denounced Romanticism as a false, grotesque and monstrous genre: 'le genre rêveur'. But his words were no more than vain repetitions of postulates already outworn. Such convictions were swept aside by the collapse of the Empire. The future now belonged to Mme de Staël.

In chapter XI of Part II of *De l'Allemagne* entitled 'De la poésie classique et de la poésie romantique', Mme de Staël develops a spirited defence for romantic literature as defined by Sismondi: 'celle qui est née de la chevalerie et du christianisme'. The Schlegelian antithesis of North/South is openly replaced by the antithesis of Romantic/classical. Considerations of race, religion and moral disposition come to the fore, pushing into second place the geographical considerations beyond which, in 1800, the author of the treatise *De la littérature* had not ventured. Now the clash between two forms of poetry, the classical and the Romantic, corresponded to the opposition between Latins and Germans, paganism and Christianity, antiquity and the Middle Ages, Graeco-Latin institutions and chivalry. Which path should be followed? Mme de Staël's choice is clear:

La question pour nous n'est pas entre la poésie classique et la poésie romantique, mais entre l'imitation de l'une et l'inspiration de l'autre. La littérature des anciens est chez les modernes une littérature transplantée; la littérature romantique ou chevaleresque est chez nous indigène et c'est notre religion et nos institutions qui l'ont fait éclore . . .

To choose Romanticism is thus to bring literature up to date and also to restore its national roots to it. But it is also to align oneself with the idealistic, subjective, individualistic concept of beauty accepted by the Germans. Mme de Staël, in effect, opposes the classical ideal of a rational imitation of nature with a Romantic ideal of free creativity and personal art: 'Les Allemands ne considèrent point, ainsi qu'on le fait d'ordinaire, l'imitation de la nature comme le principal objet de l'art; c'est la beauté idéale qui leur paraît le principe de tous les chefs-d'œuvre.' How should this beauty be defined? Power is the criterion for it, and liberty the essential condition for its realisation. Mme de Staël emphasises that taste, skill and the merit inherent in overcoming difficulties are values vastly overrated by classical criticism. All that helps to inhibit genius:

'La première condition pour écrire, c'est une manière de sentir vive et forte. Les personnes qui étudient dans les autres ce qu'elles doivent éprouver et ce qui leur est permis de dire, littérairement parlant, n'existent pas.' French poetry must be liberated from the 'lois prohibitives' by which it is oppressed: 'En France, il y a maintenant trop de freins pour des coursiers si peu fougueux.'

These few quotations will suffice to pinpoint what was at stake in the quarrel surrounding the blossoming of the Romantic movement in France. Two major claims were being expressed with increasing force: first, a change of subject was needed – it was time to have done with the myths of pagan antiquity and speak instead of France's own religion and history; and second, genius must be allowed to express itself with all its force and with all the greater chance of being understood given that it would now be speaking to a public that shared its feelings. Insistence was laid upon the affirmation of the self as a source of creative energy and above all upon the desire to further recognition of a national consciousness based upon common religious feelings and historical traditions. It was an insistence that was extremely revealing in respect of the situation of France in 1815. Thanks to the staggering changes and astonishing social ascents that had been achieved during the Revolutionary and post-Revolutionary periods, a new feeling had emerged: namely, that the individual exists and his existence is not absolutely determined by his initial membership of a particular social class.

There were many who had learned to hope that they might become other than that which their birth 'predestined' them to be. However, a vanquished France, now confined within frontiers that had suddenly become too restricting, was no longer able to satisfy such aspirations. For a whole new generation this was a time of frustrated ambitions, of the *mal du siècle*: since action was impossible, all it could do was dream of an ideal. The self, apparently destined to win many victories, became a theatre for imaginary conflicts and a refuge for unsatisfied passions. At the same time, men's minds could not but be disturbed by the astonishing course of recent history: an age-old monarchy had fallen to be replaced by an empire soon toppled. All the evidence appeared to lend support to a new idea: that of historical evolution. History could no longer be considered as an affirmation of an immutable social model. Now it meant instability and those whom the Restoration had re-established amid their former privileges sought to protect themselves against it: France had to rediscover its roots and origins and borrow from its own past myths that could take the place of the glorious myths of antiquity.

However, it was not possible to erase all traces of upheavals so recent and so profound. Anxiety, pessimism and guilt presided over the re-establishment of the old power and the old social hierarchy. The class that now won back its privileges was still stunned at having ever lost them and was, above all, fearful that it might once again be dispossessed. In order to consolidate those privileges it was prepared to go to any lengths, even to affirm in every way possible the art of the new 'models' of virtue. It co-operated in the radical condemnation of the classical credo, the most recent manifestations of which were connected with the Napoleonic adventure. It wanted to *be* France and also to promote an art in conformity with its own idea of what that France was – a France united around the throne and the altar. However, the truth was that it was *not* France and the reason why the problem of the French nation loomed so large in the polemics of the critics was perhaps that the nation was itself deeply divided.

'ULTRA' ROMANTICS AND LIBERAL ROMANTICS: FROM
CONFRONTATION TO CONCILIATION AND VICTORY

Most royalist aristocrats (of more or less noble extraction and more or less proven loyalty) favoured the new so-called 'romantic' literature, that is to say a chivalric and Christian literature, because it seemed that it might cure society of the philosophic rationalism denounced as being responsible for the Revolution. They gave their encouragement to 'right-thinking' authors such as one former councillor of State for the Empire, now converted to the art of literature, Alexandre Soumet. To him must go the credit of discovering and banding together the young religious and monarchist poets of *La Muse française*: Lamartine, Hugo, Vigny and the Deschamps brothers. First, however, this group had to be detached from a royalist clique who had quite different ideas about the national literature and continued to defend Racine against the Germano-philes.' This was the highly legitimist Société des Bonnes Lettres, founded in 1821 and concerned to gather together 'les défenseurs de toutes les légitimités et de toutes les vraies gloires, du sceptre de Boileau comme de la couronne de Louis-le-Grand'. In other words, in the 'ultra' camp, the need to renounce the conventions of the classical poetics for reasons of national urgency certainly did not seem so unquestionable to all and sundry.

The other France, that is to say the France of the liberals, was still more inclined to declare itself for classicism, out of its loyalty to rationalism, and in order to oppose an invasion of feudal romanticism of foreign inspiration which cast discredit upon the French literature of the seventeenth and eighteenth centuries. The convictions of this group are summed up in the *Cours analytique de littérature* given in lecture form in 1817 at the Athénée, the refuge of liberal professors, by Népomucène Lemercier who, among other peremptory pronouncements, produced the following declaration: 'Les erreurs des nations dont le goût n'est pas encore formé ne font pas autorité contre les principes du vrai beau, dont les anciens nous ont donné des exemples admirables.' However, there were also a number of liberal circles who had paid attention to the lessons of Manzoni's Italian romanticism rather than to those of Schlegel and who were thus in a position to associate literary freedom with political freedom. A contrast to the 'ultra' salon of the Deschamps brothers was provided by the Delécluze salon where Rémusat, Stapfer and Stendhal were deploring the chauvinism of young liberals among whom *Le Constitutionnel* had whipped up feeling against English actors and against Shakespeare.

During the early 1820s, the major difficulty for French Romantics (whether liberal or 'ultra') arose from the fact that in the eyes of a large section of public opinion (including their own party) they appeared as defenders of foreign theories and works. However, positions were soon to change. The former *émigré* ultras were anxious to efface the memory of their foreign connections and to identify themselves with the nation now reconciled with the King. They therefore became increasingly mistrustful of certain aspects of the new art that they considered to be too inclined to idealism. The royalism and mystical appeal of the 'young poets' suited them so long as the latter did not plunge into a vague religiosity and confused mysticism which provided easy targets for adverse critics bent on denouncing Germanic influences. If they were willing to encourage a renewal of literature, it was only in order to promote new themes of a definitely political and religious character. Their attitude was: help us to restore a good society by giving us good literature. Among the liberals a radical hostility was initially felt towards 'une école de germanisme et d'anglicisme'. They totally rejected the mystic, medieval themes of royalist romanticism. However, loyalty to classicism out of loyalty to 'l'esprit voltairien' soon began to appear to many of them as a retrograde attitude and *Le Globe*, the mouthpiece of the doctrinaire liberals, went so far as to denounce, in the name of liberty and truth, all that was petrified and dead in the literature directed towards imitation of the great models of the past.

Stendhal, who in his turn became an *émigré*, but in his case in order to escape from the return of the Bourbons, was one of the first to express such opinions. In 1814 he elected to settle in Milan. During his seven-year stay in that city, he became an enthusiastic witness of the birth of the Italian romantic movement which was closely linked with the currents of liberalism. On the strength of this initiation he became the spokesman for a 'romanticisme' that had nothing in common with the romanticism of the poets of *La Muse française*. In 1821, now returned to Paris, he tried to launch a periodical on the model of the English magazines. It was called *L'Aristarque, ou l'indicateur universel des livres à lire*. He only managed to publish the prospectus, introduced by the epigraph, 'la vérité toute nue', which gave some indication of his desire to unmask the false glories of the literature of the day. However, the opposition proved too strong for him. Denied the chance of playing the role of omnipresent judge, he now flung himself into the literary battle in the area where it was being most violently fought, namely the theatre, for here he found a meeting-ground for opposed public groups rather than solitary and isolated readers. On the pretext of the hostile demonstrations that in 1822 greeted the performances of a company of English actors, he launched a campaign against a theatre of boredom and in favour of a liberated theatre which took Shakespeare, not Racine, as its model. His pamphlet in two parts, *Racine et Shakespeare* (1823 and 1825) contains a famous definition of 'romanticisme': 'L'art de présenter aux peuples les œuvres littéraires qui, dans l'état actuel de leurs habitudes et de leurs croyances, sont susceptibles de leur donner le plus de plaisir possible'. For Stendhal, as for Mme de Staël – but in his case in the name of a bolder and more individualistic concept of aesthetic pleasure – to be a Romantic was to be resolutely modern. With his pitiless wit he lambasted all literature that was boring and outdated and all criticism that was pedantic and flat – in particular all that so-called romantic discourse inspired by the theories of Schlegel. He countered these ponderous dissertations with the alert, lively criticism devoid of theoretical pretensions that he himself was producing clandestinely between 1822 and 1828 in a number of English journals. 'Qui nous délivrera de Louis XIV?' he exclaimed, for example, 'voilà la grande question qui renferme le sort de la littérature française à venir. Les gens de lettres actuels se sont fait un point de doctrine de soutenir le genre à la Louis XIV et l'Académie française est devenue plus intolérante et presque aussi absurde que la Sorbonne!' But, although he declared war on the old bewigged champions of classicism, that did not mean that he would cry 'Long live the Romantics of the *Cénacle*!' On the contrary, he vilified Victor Hugo, 'le poète du parti ultra, toujours exagéré à froid'; he lampooned Vigny for his 'Éloa', 'incroyable mélange d'absurdité et de profanation qu'on ose célébrer à Paris comme une imitation réussie de

Byron'; and he lamented the fact that Lamartine, once the friend of liberty, had allowed himself to be taken over by the same party and was also indulging in '[des] idées vagues, communes et, de plus, fort obscures'. He even accused *Le Globe* of having encouraged the early successes of this base kind of Romanticism that was indistinguishable from confused mysticism.

During the last years of the Restoration, nevertheless, that liberal publication played a role of capital importance in clarifying the debate and was a powerful factor in the triumph of a Romanticism 'à la française'. The editors of *Le Globe* wanted to restore 'indépendance et vérité' to criticism, that is to say, 'la retirer du commerce et des ambitions politiques'. Their motto ('Liberté et respect du goût national') soon led them to a double rejection: of, first, the outworn traditions of neo-classicism and, secondly, the imported innovations of Anglo-German Romanticism. Thus, in March 1825, Duvergier de Hauranne, having denounced 'la critique étroite et arbitraire des classiques', went on to spell out how 'ce qu'on appelle le romantique doit triompher . . . pour que sa victoire soit pure et complète, qu'il évite l'obscur, le prétentieux, l'inintelligible; que surtout il se garde bien d'affecter la phrase anglaise ou allemande'.

Two years later these aspirations were fulfilled. There was a reconciliation between Romantics of different persuasions, between the liberals and the Germanophiles. It was helped by the evolution that the young Romantic poets, in particular Hugo, had undergone. In 1822, in the Preface to the first edition of his *Odes*, he had asserted that 'l'histoire des hommes ne présente de poésie que jugée du haut des idées monarchiques et des croyances religieuses'. In 1824 he declared that he would devote himself to promoting a literature that would be 'l'expression anticipée de la société religieuse et monarchique qui sortira sans doute du milieu de tant d'anciens débris, de tant de ruines récentes'. But in 1826, in the Preface to his *Odes et Ballades*, he was tackling the problem of liberty in art and in his famous *Préface de 'Cromwell'* (December 1827), he restated it in the boldest of terms. In the name of respect for nature and the truth (classical values, to be sure, but now invested with new meaning), he advanced a plea for absolute liberty for the artist, who should not be obliged to propose only an ideal and partial view of man and the world, 'car la poésie vraie, la poésie complète est dans l'harmonie des contraires', and the future works of poets would associate the beautiful and the ugly, the sublime and the grotesque: 'c'est de la féconde union du type grotesque au type sublime que naît le génie moderne, si complexe, si varié dans ses formes, si inépuisable dans ses créations, et bien opposé en cela à l'uniforme simplicité du génie antique'. In *Le Globe*, Rémusat shut his eyes to Hugo's fantastical historical reconstructions and pledged 'la bienveillante indulgence des critiques pour quelqu'un qui est de leur avis'. A less well-known text, published in 1828, namely the Preface to Émile Deschamps' *Études françaises et étrangères* marks the compromise with the liberal innovators even more clearly. Deschamps celebrates the new generation of French poets, associating in his praises the names of Hugo, Lamartine and Béranger. He declares that 'riche de tous ces nouveaux grands poètes, la France n'a plus besoin d'aller chercher des exemples hors de chez elle'. Finally, he borrows from *Le Globe* itself the following formula so characteristic of the romantic movement of liberation: 'Le temps des imitations est passé; il faut ou créer ou traduire.'

The evolution of these poets was matched by that of the young critic Sainte-Beuve. He had made his début on the literary scene at *Le Globe* where he expressed deep distrust of the 'royalism' and 'mysticism' of the 'Romantic school'. It was not long before he was won over by the anti-classical temerities of the new school. He became its propagandist and published a *Tableau historique et critique de la poésie et du théâtre français au XVIe siècle* (1828) in which he sought to 'chercher dans nos origines quelque chose de national à quoi se rattacher', in other words to absolve the poets of the *Cénacle* from the accusation of merely being imitators of foreign poets. For a brief period the young school of literary criticism thus adopted a different tone and, based on two new publications (*La Revue de Paris* and *La Revue des deux mondes*), took a militant line, encouraging a romantic renewal in poetry and in drama. Momentarily turning its back upon its classic role of fastidious custodian to Parnassus, literary criticism ceased to judge new works by reference to a sanctified past and instead, to use Sainte-Beuve's expression, became 'avant-courrière', announcing the arrival of new geniuses to the public, as they appeared. Sainte-Beuve himself was altogether typical of the change in orientation among the most influential group of critics (now no longer the old academicians but the younger generation of 1830). The inventor of the *Portraits littéraires* was thus concerned to 'faire le point' concerning whatever remained alive in the work of the French classical authors. His first series of portraits, published in *La Revue de Paris*, was introduced under the provocative rubric: 'Littérature ancienne'. Sainte-Beuve's purpose in dusting down the classical pantheon in this way was to put himself in a position to hail the new works – in particular those of Victor Hugo – as so many masterpieces. In December 1831, in an article in *La Revue des deux mondes*, devoted to Hugo's *Feuilles d'automne*, he drew a comparison between the militant criticism born from Romanticism and of a kind to assist 'le triomphe du poète contemporain' on the one hand, and 'la critique réfléchie et lente' produced by fastidious and virtually useless scholars on the other.

AGAINST 'INDUSTRIAL LITERATURE' AND TOWARDS A DIFFERENT KIND OF ROMANTICISM: HUGO, LAMARTINE, GAUTIER, BAUDELAIRE

The first great successes of Romantic literature, that is to say of a lyrical poetry liberated from the conventionalists and, above all, drama given a new lease of life by new subject-matter and new dramatic forms, were thus an occasion of fervent and happy collaboration between critics and creators. However, this experience, which allowed the critics to try out a new and unaccustomed role, was short-lived. It came to an end with the disturbances provoked by the failure of a great hope: the July revolution of 1830. The revolution had been made possible by the active rallying of all those who had regained confidence in progress and who refused to acquiesce in the re-establishment of the old order. The united front of the various trends in the Romantic movement, all of which abandoned the defence of a retrograde monarchy in order to ensure the liberty of art, appeared as one manifestation, among others, of the rejection of the past. But the Three Glorious Days were not successful in turning France into a nation united in support of its new great men: politicians, university teachers, generals, poets and artists. A new régime was installed under the protection of a mediocre bourgeois king, to the advantage of the manufacturers and bankers and in the midst of the bitter rivalry of factions. The Romantics had yearned to be the glorious representatives of a new art welcomed and recognised by history. In fact, that art was now regarded as no more than the art of a particular school or even chapel, and one much resented and opposed. As early as 1829, Henri de Latouche, one of the former *habitués* of the Deschamps salon, was envying the success of other poets younger and more inspired than himself and was warning that 'la camaraderie littéraire', born in the wake of the *Cénacle*, was degenerating into a self-adulatory plot within 'la petite église romantique'. And in truth, the artificial unity often fraught with ulterior motives soon changed to rivalry and jealousy as in the case of the row between Hugo and Sainte-Beuve. In 1840 Sainte-Beuve was stigmatising those whom he branded 'les gladiateurs en littérature', in other words, 'les admirateurs gloutons de M. Victor Hugo' who have sought 'à confondre, à troubler, à pervertir les saines notions de la critique, à réduire en industrie ou en fief le domaine des lettres'. This violent split between the critics and the creators was a new feature in the literary situation which was to deteriorate still further as the century passed. In 1836, Gustave Planche, speaking in his turn on the subject of 'literary friendships', remarked: 'Jamais plaideurs n'ont maudit leurs juges comme les poètes d'aujourd'hui maudissent leurs critiques.' It was a far cry from the Saint-Simonian aspirations that many Romantics had for one moment shared. In October 1830, in *Le Globe*, Sainte-Beuve had written: 'Peuple et poètes vont marcher ensemble . . . L'art est désormais sur le pied commun, dans l'arène avec tous, côte à côte avec l'infatigable humanité.'

The very conditions of literary activity and production had within a short time been transformed. Few literary men now enjoyed the leisure to devote themselves to dreaming of ideals or producing huge theoretical constructions. Up until 1830 books had still been considered the only mode of truly literary production and we have seen in what voluminous treatises the theoreticians of Romanticism had expressed their views, totally discounting the protests of the classical pamphleteers. But now books were becoming a luxury. Periodicals and newspapers were considered the best means of diffusing literary texts and these encouraged the success of literary genres hitherto regarded as minor – the novel and the short story, for instance, which had hardly ever been mentioned in the theoretical arguments between classicists and Romantics. The critic himself was increasingly likely to be a professional journalist attached to a particular newspaper or periodical, selecting his subjects at random as he endeavoured to get through the drudgery of the weekly reviews and striving to be as up to date as possible. Balzac disparagingly described the situation in his *Monographie de la presse parisienne*: 'La critique aujourd'hui ne sert plus qu'à une chose: faire vivre le critique.'

The fact was that new ideas and theoretical contributions towards a redefinition of Romanticism were no longer to be expected from the critics. In an article in *La Revue des deux mondes*, Gustave Planche presented a study of 'criticism in 1835' in which he drew attention to how diffuse its various and derisory activities had become and lamented the absence of this type of criticism which could be 'une invention dialectique aussi hardie, aussi laborieuse que l'invention poétique', capable both of 'explaining' the poet's creation and of anticipating and encouraging the appearance of new works.

So what *was* criticism concerned with? In 1844, Rémusat teasingly asked: how was it possible for criticism miraculously to be preserved from the 'industrialisation' that it condemned? And, paradoxically enough, just when critics, like others in the literary world, were benefiting from the commercial development of new forms of literary production, the speciality of most of them was denouncing 'le mercantilisme littéraire' and abusing 'la littérature industrielle'. Romanticism became confused with the latter and was enveloped in the same blanket of condemnation. Thus, Nisard in 1834, in his *Études de mœurs et de critique sur les poètes latins de la décadence*, categorically declared that 'ce temps-ci est mauvais' and waxed indignant at the idea that 'des entrepreneurs de littérature' could be considered as great writers. For him, the Romantics were to be compared to the poets of Lucan's time and were the representatives of a literature of decadence: they were to Racine what Lucan was to Virgil.

This resurgence of a dogmatism unshakeable in its resolution to preserve and laud the classical heritage was not confined to Nisard. The same intransigence is to be found in even the most important critics: Saint-Marc Girardin, Cuvillier-Fleury or even the renowned Jules Janin, known as 'le Prince des critiques'. For forty years he dominated the dramatic column of the *Journal des débats* and when hailing the renewal of classical tragedy that the appearance of Ponsard's *Lucrèce* in 1842 appeared to herald, he boasted of not having used the frightful word 'Romantic' more than ten times in his life.

After 1830, then, it is no good consulting the works of the critics to discover how the Romantic aesthetic was being defined or how it was evolving. It was summarily condemned even in the articles of the young *Revue des deux mondes* where Gustave Planche defended the classical tradition against Romantic poetry, which he dubbed 'la poésie réaliste de nos jours'. Meanwhile, Sainte-Beuve, following his failures as poet and novelist, had resigned himself to being a critic and no more. He was devoting himself to his literary portraits with all the detachment of an observer who abstains from all conviction. He did not, in fact, remain content for long in his role as adviser to the young Romantic poets, distilling his poetic precepts from the pages of *Les Pensées de Joseph Delorme* (1829) or as promoter for Victor Hugo, campaigning ardently for him in reviews that hailed the coming of a genius. He soon came to regard literary criticism no longer as education in a new art or as a propagandist activity, but rather as a physiological and moral enquiry through which it was possible to seize upon all the individual characteristics of a particular writer, feature by feature, and to 'trouver l'homme'. The first lines of the 'portrait littéraire' of Diderot, published on 26 June 1831, already contained a very precise definition of this meticulous and patient method of observation which made it possible to recreate the writer under consideration:

Au type vague, abstrait, général, qu'une première vue avait embrassé, se mêle et s'incorpore par degrés une réalité individuelle, précise, de plus en plus accentuée et vivement scintillante; on sent naître, on voit venir la ressemblance; et le jour, le moment où l'on a saisi le tic familier, le sourire révélateur, la gerçure indéfinissable, la ride intime et douloureuse . . . à ce moment l'analyse disparaît dans la création, le portrait parle et vit, on a trouvé l'homme.

However, this laborious preparation for 'critical creation' was not enough truly to bring criticism and poetry together. From 1830 onward it was the genuine creators, the poets, most of them products of the 'Romantic school' of 1830, who, confronted by the mistrust and cravenness of the critics, continued to reaffirm their own faith in art and their own conviction that it was beyond the reach of decadence and capable of renewing itself indefinitely.

Thus, Hugo remained faithful to his declaration in the Preface to his *Orientales* (1829): 'Le critique n'a pas de raison à demander, le poète pas de compte à rendre. L'art n'a que faire des lisières, des menottes et des bâillons. . .' Curiously enough, however, he was no longer interested in leading Romanticism's fight against the prohibitions of classicism. In 1864, in *William Shakespeare*, he declares, like Jules Janin, that he has never used the words 'Romanticism' or 'Romantic'. All the same, in this dazzling collection of aesthetic and critical reflections, he certainly places himself under the sign of Romanticism when he develops his scathing diatribes against what he calls 'la critique de l'école sobre' and its moralistic and dogmatic allies: 'la critique sacristaine' and 'la critique doctrinaire'. All three would like to restore the reign of 'good taste', 'cet autre droit divin qui a si longtemps pesé sur l'art et qui était parvenu à supprimer le beau au profit du joli . . .' Hugo himself avoids such triviality by extolling only 'the beautiful', a powerful and free creation of genius which has nothing to do with 'ni décadence, ni renaissance, ni plagiat, ni répétition, ni redite . . . chaque grand artiste refrappe l'art à son image' and 'nier que les génies survenants puissent être les pairs des génies antérieurs, ce serait nier la puissance continuante de Dieu'. The particular function of the new genius of the nineteenth century seems to him to be to free art from the preconceptions of 'une littérature de lettrés' who believed that French was spoken in France only in the seventeenth century – 'et cela pendant douze années'. No, 'la poésie n'est pas une coterie'; 1830 did not simply mark the temporary success of a new literary school but inaugurated a debate, literary on the surface but fundamentally social and human, which can only come to an end once a revolution both literary and social has taken place. In his conclusion to *William Shakespeare*, Hugo finally ventures to use the word Romanticism to underline an equivalence: 'Romantisme et socialisme, c'est le même fait' – for the principal virtue of the beautiful is that it is humanly and socially useful: 'Être grand et inutile, cela ne se peut . . . L'art, à la seule condition d'être fidèle à sa loi, le Beau, civilise les hommes par sa puissance propre, même sans intention, même contre son intention.'

It was a magnificent transformation for Romanticism half a century after its first incursions into French cultural life. There was no longer any question of placing a new art at the service of an aristocracy bent on regaining its privileges. It was now a matter of rising above all the squabbles between factions and schools and reaffirming the civilising power that living Art possessed, provided it could escape from the stranglehold of theoretical poetics and become the free expression of genius.

This desire to contribute to progress and strive for the coming of a more just and egalitarian society was shared by many of the first-wave Romantics. But they were not always successful in convincing themselves that art on its own can signify such progress. The path that Lamartine followed is significant in this respect. It was not long before he became dissatisfied at being no more than a poet, perhaps because, unlike Hugo, he did not know how to declare war on 'rhetoric' and remained 'étranglé par la forme vieille' (as Rimbaud was to remark). Perhaps it was also because, not being obliged to earn a living for himself and his family by pursuing the profession of a man of letters, he was in a better position to appreciate the full measure of verbal gesticulation inherent in the art of the poet, even when he does speak the language of commitment. Like Hugo, he defined himself in his *Ode sur les révolutions* (1832) as a resolute partisan of human progress and he pronounced upon the future *Destinées de la poésie* as follows: to be at the same time 'philosophique, religieuse, politique, sociale' and also 'intime, méditative et grave', but above all to be capable of touching the hearts of the people and communicating with simple souls. After that, however, he launched himself directly into the political arena, convinced that the revolution must be promoted and that the way to do so was not with odes: 'Y a-t-il eu ou n'y a-t-il pas eu de Révolution française? On est tenté de se le demander à chaque instant, lorsqu'on considère notre régime industriel' (speech of 25 March 1846). The only image of Lamartine that literary history for many years elected to retain was the emotive one of 'le poète mourant' of the *Méditations*. It was a convenient way to avoid admitting that the melancholic sensibility of the Romantics of 1820 might have expressed rather more than the agonising of wounded souls – such as, for instance, the rich ardour of generous hearts. After 1830 and following the revelation of the true nature of modern society, the aristocratic romanticism, devised to touch the hearts of elegant ladies disposed to tears, had grafted on to it a Revolutionary romanticism designed to call for the liberation of slaves everywhere.

Meanwhile, other poets from the Romantic school of 1830, while sharing Victor Hugo's aversion for the critics and, like him, proclaiming their religious devotion to *le Beau*, had a quite different concept of what *le Beau* was, a concept based upon their desire to see a radical break with 'ce siècle infâme'.

Thus, in 1835, Théophile Gautier, in the Preface to his *Mademoiselle de Maupin*, produced a blazing attack upon the critics – mediocre, impotent and jealous scribblers, as he saw them: 'Une chose certaine et facile à démontrer à ceux qui pourraient en douter, c'est l'antipathie naturelle du critique contre le poète, de celui qui ne fait rien contre celui qui fait, du frelon contre l'abeille, du cheval hongre contre l'étalon.' Again like Hugo, he attacked the abject timidity of good taste and in 1844 produced a series of studies collected under the title *Grotesques* in which he fearlessly rehabilitated Villon and a number of those victimised by Boileau: Scarron, Théophile de Viau, Saint-Amant. 'Le bon goût', he wrote, 'est une belle chose; cependant il n'en faudrait pas abuser: à force de bon goût, on arrive à se priver d'une multitude de sujets, de détails, d'images, d'expressions qui ont la saveur de la vie.'

At the same time, however, Gautier denounced the detestably commercial quality of utilitarian literature and did so just as vigorously as the critics of the *Journal des débats*. From this position he moved on to take refuge in the cult of *le beau*. Even as early as in the Preface to his *Albertus* (1832) he had proclaimed that *le beau* is incompatible with the useful whatever 'les utilitaires, utopistes, saint-simonistes et autres' might think. The propagandists of progress were in his eyes simply a particularly execrable category of critics anxious to make art serve the purpose of perfecting the human race. Such a concept of art seemed to him as harmful as it was fanciful. Art, for Gautier, was a luxury and by definition could have no useful purpose. In the Preface to *Mademoiselle de Maupin* he writes: 'Il n'y a de vraiment beau que ce qui ne peut servir à rien; tout ce qui est utile est laid, car c'est l'expression de quelque besoin et ceux de l'homme sont ignobles et dégoûtants, comme sa pauvre et infirme nature.'

Charles Baudelaire, apparently fascinated by this arrogant definition of *le beau*, hailed Gautier as 'l'écrivain par excellence, parce qu'il est l'esclave de son devoir, parce qu'il obéit sans cesse aux nécessités de sa fonction, parce que le goût du beau est pour lui un *fatum*, parce qu'il a fait de son devoir une idée fixe' (article on Gautier, 1859). But in what sense can such behaviour in an artist still be said to be Romantic?

When, in 1868, after Baudelaire's death, Gautier and Asselineau gave the title *L'Art romantique* to a collection of critical articles written by the author of *Les Fleurs du Mal*, they did not feel they were committing any anachronism or error of judgment. Nevertheless, those pages contain numerous attacks against Romanticism. Consider, for instance, the following passage taken from the 'notice pour les *Chants et chansons* de Pierre Dupont': 'Disparaissez, ombres fallacieuses de René, d'Obermann et de Werther; fuyez dans les brouillards du vide, monstrueuses créations de la paresse et de la solitude . . . Le génie de l'action ne vous laisse plus de place parmi nous.' But this paean of praise for commitment, as opposed to Romantic melancholy, reflects no more than an ephemeral inclination that assailed Baudelaire at the time of the 1848 revolution. His view was, on the contrary, that the best lesson that the 'French Romantic movement' had provided was in having seen fit, as did Edgar Allan Poe, to denounce what the latter called 'the great poetic heresy of modern times', 'the idea of direct utility'. But acceptance of this inheritance of ideas should not lead one to maintain, 'comme certains sectaires fanatiques insensés de Goethe et autre poètes marmoréens et antihumains, que toute chose belle est essentiellement inutile' ('notice sur Poe', 1852). In short, true Romanticism had yet to be invented, avoiding both an insistence upon morality and also the pretensions of insensibility. It was still possible, provided one did not accept the rulings of those 'sphynx sans énigme' who spoke of 'une littérature de décadence', and were incapable of welcoming or understanding anything new ('notes nouvelles sur Poe', 1857). Instead of remaining frozen in a regret for the past, criticism ought to be spurring on the artist to be 'naïvely' himself and above all to understand and express his own times. Baudelaire, who was inspired by preoccupations akin to those of Stendhal, wanted the *modern* artist to find ways of representing the *modern* hero. In order to do so, it was necessary to devote oneself passionately to one's task, even if this happened to be criticism: 'Pour être juste, c'est-à-dire pour avoir sa raison d'être, la critique doit être partiale, passionnée, politique, c'est-à-dire faite à un point de vue exclusif, mais au point de vue qui ouvre le plus d'horizons.' (*Salon de 1846*, chapter 1: 'A quoi bon la critique?') Criticism of this kind can really only be practised by poets: they alone can take the side of art passionately and show that it has nothing to do with the demands of a timeless morality but involves recognition of the original aspects of modern beauty and demands hard work and self-control.

The reason why the Romanticism of 1830 was not really successful was that writers such as Lamartine and Musset 'n'ont pas assez de volonté et ne sont pas assez maîtres d'eux-mêmes' ('notice sur Poe', 1852). Baudelaire in effect rejected one whole, mistaken side to the first Romantic theories: by refusing to accept rules and despising systems of rhetoric, 'ces théories fautrices de paresse . . . permettent au poète de se considérer comme un oiseau bavard, léger, irresponsable, insaisissable' (article on Hégésippe Moreau, published in L'Art romantique). The true originality of the modern 'Romantic' involves knowledge of and mastery over systems of rhetoric and prosody, for these 'ne sont pas des tyrannies inventées arbitrairement, mais une collection de règles réclamées par l'organisation même de l'être spirituel' and 'jamais les prosodies et les rhétoriques n'ont empêché l'originalité de se produire distinctement; le contraire, à savoir qu'elles ont aidé l'éclosion de l'originalité, serait infiniment plus vrai' (Salon de 1859, 4 – 'Le gouvernement de l'imagination'). If the modern 'Romantic' poet desires to be subject to nothing – neither morality nor the people nor any conventional idea of the beautiful – he must be first and foremost master of his art and know how to make a 'magician's' use of all the resources of his language.

It should be pointed out that for Baudelaire, as for Gautier, literary criticism was inseparable from art criticism: the writer was seen as simply one artist among others. Gautier was therefore quite right to call Baudelaire's collection of articles L'Art romantique. It was a way of underlining the point that Romanticism did not only affect poetry and the theatre but also made it possible to open up new avenues to Art as a whole, in all its different manifestations. This brief chapter has been devoted to describing the evolution solely of literary criticism: it is a partial view of the Romantic movement that other sections of this work will fortunately complement. But it is important not to forget that painters, sculptors, musicians, engravers, and others were also closely associated with the meetings and discussions of the literary salons. The theoretical debates that took place on the necessary transformation of the classical theatre and lyricism were inseparable from the passionate polemics in the course of which neo-classical academicism was obliged to fall back in the face of the fire and spirit of Delacroix in painting, Rude in sculpture and Berlioz in symphonic music. . . .

In its all too short triumphant phase (1828–31), the Romantic movement appears to have adhered totally to the idea of a positive social role for all artists. This belief in a useful 'fraternité des arts', and in their mission as guides of human progress is one of the most important aspects of the Saint-Simonian doctrine by which no Romantic remained completely unaffected. Remember, for example, how Sainte-Beuve, in an article in *Le Globe* (published on 11 October 1830 and entitled 'Espoir et vœu du mouvement littéraire et poétique après la révolution de 1830'), summed up the recent movement of liberation for the arts and for society and encouraged art and the people to continue to go forward together:

L'art est désormais sur le pied commun, dans l'arène avec tous, côte à côte avec l'infatigable humanité . . . Les destinées presque infinies de la société régénérée, le tourment religieux et obscur qui l'agite, l'émancipation absolue à laquelle elle aspire, tout invite l'art à s'unir étroitement à elle, à la charmer durant le voyage, à la soutenir contre l'ennui, en se faisant l'écho harmonieux, l'organe prophétique de ses sombres et douteuses pensées.

By considering the evolutions of Hugo, Lamartine, Gautier and Baudelaire, we have been able to indicate how the Romantics soon became divided amongst themselves and opposed to the idea of the social role of art. These few typical examples (others such as Vigny, Musset or even Balzac would also have made it possible to illustrate the various tendencies) may give an idea of the changes in the concept of literature and the social role of the writer that had taken place since the great Romantic debate of 1820. In conclusion, let us summarise the overall historical significance of the Romantic revolution in the context of the literary history of France. The earliest form of Romanticism was a response to the desires of the aristocracy following the trials and tribulations of the Revolution, at a moment when they were hoping for a Restoration. It was a matter of inventing a new literature of a kind to promote a social regeneration. Artists were invited to develop themes borrowed not, as hitherto, from classical mythology but from the Christian religion and the medieval and chivalric past of the French nation, and to give free rein to the expression of the original feelings of individuals whose lives had been upset by the chaotic course of history. Of these propositions, what the artists seized mainly upon was the encouragement to liberate themselves from the manifold fetters of classical aesthetics. The ultimate or implicit object of the exercise – namely to assist in the restoration of a society once more committed to God and to the King – was lost from view and its place was taken by a generous-hearted aspiration towards free expression for the self and of the peculiarities of present times: this seemed to be the very essence of

Romantic art. With the hopes born of the 1830 revolution, expressed again only to be smothered again in 1848, this Romantic literature experienced its first metamorphosis: concerned to serve no power, neither that of princes nor that of industrialists, it tried to promote the definitive affranchisement of the people itself. It thus developed in the various trends of committed literature and, having over the years absorbed a transition from grandiose illusions to lost ones, it is still to be found among those contemporary artists who claim an affiliation with revolutionary romanticism. But the Romanticism of 1830 has other heirs as well: those who, despairing of seeing the success of social revolution, have preferred to preserve artistic creation from any alien influences and have committed themselves to the pure cult of Art, radically protected from the commercial aspects of a degraded society. 'L'école de l'art pour l'art' is often presented as the manifestation of a rejection of the most complacently sentimental aspects of Romantic lyricism. It is, however, inseparable from another rejection: that of any subjection of art to utilitarian or moral prescriptions. Being oneself and striving to be oneself through a complete mastery over one's means of expression is a necessity that the Romantics helped to render indisputable in the eyes of today's artists and public alike.

BIBLIOGRAPHY

The principal general works on the areas covered by this chapter, in chronological order of publication, are:

A. Cassagne, *La Théorie de l'art pour l'art en France chez les derniers romantiques et les premiers réalistes* (Hachette, 1906; new edn 1960); J. Marsan, *La Bataille romantique* (2 vols., Plon, 1912; new edn 1924); F. Baldensperger, *Le Mouvement des idées dans l'émigration française, 1789–1815* (2 vols., Hachette, 1924); R. Bray, *Chronologie du romantisme: 1804–1830* (Boivin 1932; new edn 1963); P. Moreau, *Le Classicisme des romantiques* (Hachette, 1932); E. Eggli et P. Martino, *Le Débat romantique en France, 1813–1826, Pamphlets, manifestes, polémiques de presse* (Publications de la Faculté des Lettres d'Alger, Les Belles Lettres, 1933) – only vol. I was published: *1813–1816*; L. Emery, *L'Âge romantique* (2 vols., Lyons, 1957–1960); R. Wellek, *A History of modern criticism* (5 vols., London, Jonathan Cape, 1955–65), vol. II: *The Romantic Age*, 1958; P. Moreau, *La Critique littéraire en France* (Colin, 1960); P. Martino, *L'Époque romantique en France*, (4th edn, Hatier, 1962); R. Molho, *La critique littéraire en France au XIXème siècle* (Buchet-Chastel, 1963); H. Peyre, *Qu'est-ce que le romantisme?* (PUF, 1971); G. Delfau et A. Roche, *Histoire/Littérature. Histoire et interprétation du fait littéraire* (Éditions du Seuil, 1976); and R. Fayolle, *La Critique* (2nd revised and expanded edn, Colin, Collection U, 1978).

Modern editions of theoretical and critical texts by the Romantic writers include, in alphabetical order, the following:

É. Deschamps, *La Préface des Études françaises et étrangères*, ed. H. Girard (Les Presses françaises, 1923); T. Gautier, *Préface de 'Mademoiselle de Maupin'*, critical edn by G. Matoré (Droz, 1946); V. Hugo, *Préface de 'Cromwell'*, ed. G. Souriau (Boivin, 1897); V.

Hugo, *Littérature et philosophie mêlées*, critical edn by A.R.W. James (2 vols., Klincksieck, 1976); V. Hugo, *William Shakespeare*, ed. B. Leuilliot ('Nouvelle Bibliothèque romantique', Flammarion, 1973); C.-A. Sainte-Beuve, *Vie, poésies et pensées de Joseph Delorme*, critical edition by G. Antoine (Nouvelles éditions latines, 1957); Mme de Staël, *De la littérature considérée dans ses rapports avec les institutions sociales*, critical edn by Paul Van Tieghem ('Textes littéraires français', Droz, 1959); Stendhal, *Selected journalism from the English reviews with translations of other critical writings*, edited by G. Strickland (London, John Calder, 1959); Stendhal, *Racine et Shakespeare*, ed. R. Fayolle (Garnier–Flammarion, 1970); and Stendhal, *Du romantisme dans les arts*, ed. J. Starzynski (Hermann, 1966).

Works relating to particular aspects of the history of literary ideas during the period that are especially noteworthy are as follows:

C.M. Desgranges, *Le Romantisme et la critique: La Presse littéraire sous la Restauration* (Mercure de France, 1907); H. Maxwell King, *Les Doctrines littéraires de ' La Quotidienne', 1814–1830. Un chapitre de l'histoire du mouvement romantique en France* (Smith College Studies in Modern Languages, vol. I, Northampton, Smith College, and Paris, Champion, 1919–20); M.H. Peoples, *La Société des Bonnes-Lettres (1821–1830)* (Smith College Studies in Modern Languages, vol. V, Northampton, Smith College, and Paris, Champion, 1923); P. Trahard, *Le Romantisme défini par ' Le Globe'* (Les Presses françaises, 1934); and A.E. Jensen, *L'Évolution du romantisme: l'année 1826* (Droz–Minard, 1976). Amongst numerous important articles are: H.H. Remak, 'West European Romanticism: definition and scope' in *Comparative Literature, Method and Perspective* (Carbondale, Ill. 1961), and R. Wellek, 'The concept of Romanticism in literary history' and 'Romanticism re-examined', reprinted in *Concepts of Criticism* (Yale University Press, 1963).

The following works concern individual writers of the period and, in particular, their ideas on literature.

On Mme de Staël: I.A. Henning, *L'Allemagne de Madame de Staël et la polémique romantique* (Hachette, 1929); J. Gibelin, *L'Esthétique de Schelling et l'Allemagne de Madame de Staël* (Clermont, 1932); and S. Balayé, *Madame de Staël. Lumières et Liberté* (Klincksieck, 1979).

On Sismondi: J.R. de Salis, *Sismondi, la vie et l'œuvre d'un cosmopolite philosophe* (Plon, 1932); and *Sismondi européen* (Actes d'un colloque tenu à Genève en Septembre 1973, Geneva, Slatkine and Paris, Champion, 1976).

On Saint-Beuve: M. Regard, *Sainte-Beuve* ('Connaissance des lettres', Hatier, 1959); R. Fayolle, *Sainte-Beuve et le XVIIIe siècle ou Comment les révolutions arrivent* (Colin, 1972); and R. Molho, *L'Ordre et les ténèbres – Essai sur la formation d'une image du XVIIe siècle dans l'œuvre de Sainte-Beuve* (Colin, 1972).

On Baudelaire: A. Ferran, *L'Esthétique de Baudelaire* (Masson, 1933); and M. Gilman, *Baudelaire the critic* (New York, Octagon Press, 1971).

One may also consult the following works on certain personalities in the literary life of the time:

H. Girard, *Un Bourgeois dilettante à l'époque romantique: Émile Deschamps* (Champion, 1921); R. Baschet, *E.J. Delécluze, témoin de son temps, 1781–1863* (Boivin, 1942); M. Regard, *Gustave Planche, l'adversaire des romantiques* (2 vols., Nouvelles éditions latines, 1955); A.R. Oliver, *Nodier, pilot of Romanticism* (Syracuse UP, 1964); and C. Pichois, *Philarète Chasles et la vie littéraire au temps du romantisme* (2 vols., Corti, 1967).

VIII · *Historians*

DOUGLAS JOHNSON

INTRODUCTION

'L'histoire et la poésie lyrique, voilà les deux lacunes apparentes de notre littérature classique.' So wrote Gustave Lanson. He found in the centuries of classical French literature, only three authors of great historical works. They were Bossuet (with *Le Discours sur l'histoire universelle* and *L'Histoire des variations*), Montesquieu (with *L'Esprit des Lois*, although his *Considérations sur la grandeur et décadence des Romains* was very influential) and Voltaire (with *L'Essai sur les mœurs* and *Le Siècle de Louis XIV*). This attitude has been shared by many who have dated the French historical school from the writings of Augustin Thierry, the lectures of Guizot and the carefully nurtured projects of Michelet. But not only is this unfair to the many excellent and worthy scholars, such as the Benedictines of Saint-Maur or the learned Protestants of the sixteenth century, whose erudition was based upon their invaluable collections of documentary material; it is also to ignore the way in which the historians of the nineteenth century used them as a source of comparison and criticism. It was often in contrast to their predecessors that Thierry, Guizot and Michelet were able to distinguish themselves and to assert their importance.

The standard history of France by the end of the eighteenth century was that written by the abbé Velly. The first volumes of his *Histoire générale de France* had appeared in 1755, and after the author's death in 1759, further volumes were added thanks to the co-operation of certain authors, and rival editions were being printed after 1815. Napoleon had approved of Velly and had described him as 'le seul auteur un peu détaillé qui ait écrit sur l'histoire de France'. Velly's nearest rival was Louis-Pierre Anquetil who, although he was born in 1723 and had written various detailed studies about Rheims and about the League, had not published his voluminous *Histoire de France depuis des Gaulois jusqu'à la fin de la monarchie* until 1805, the year before his death. There were other, earlier historians who attracted attention (and sometimes admiration), such as Mézeray, whose *Histoire de France* was published in the mid seventeenth century, and Daniel, whose *Histoire de France* appeared in 1713, whilst Mably's *Observations sur l'Histoire de France* (1765) had for long been the bible of those who believed that there were historical origins for a constitutional and representative government in France.

These were amongst the historians whose works were available to those who sought to study and to teach history (and it might be noted that in 1814 those who taught the classical languages in *L'instruction secondaire* were required to teach a limited amount of history and geography during the summer term, and in 1818 it was laid down that the teaching of these subjects was to be entrusted to a specialised teacher). Louis Taillefer, a Paris teacher, set out in 1815 the expected tasks of a teacher of history, stating that he should confine himself to 'la simple exposition des faits historiques et la liaison naturelle qu'ils ont entre eux'. The same principle was stated again, in 1820, by the Commission de l'Instruction Publique, which claimed that the only objective of the teacher was to be useful to his pupils, and to 'graver dans leur mémoire les principaux faits de l'histoire'. Taillefer specifically recommended Velly and Anquetil, and a number of 'abrégés de l'histoire de France', all of which had been first published under the *ancien régime*.

It was against this method of teaching, and against this form of history itself, that some of the young historians first published criticisms and commentaries. Their criticisms were criticisms of the history in terms of inadequate scholarship and of an unsatisfactory perspective which often saw the history of France as the history of kings and courts, wars and gallantry. But it was also political. Since the recommended books dated from the *ancien régime* then by their nature they could not contain reflections on the Revolution, and with the Bourbon restoration after 1815 there was official unease at the prospect of accepting the existence of historical facts which for royalists were disastrous and humiliating.

It was these sentiments which caused Augustin Thierry to call upon his readers to beware of history, 'nous devons nous défier de l'histoire', since it could be made into a continual lie, and to reject a history which was 'froide et monotone', because it was arranged in advance. 'C'est la vérité qui doit y ramener le piquant et l'intérêt. Il faut que la perspective de ce but diminue l'ennui des sentiers arides qu'on doit traverser pour l'atteindre.' It was in July 1820 that Thierry began to publish his 'Lettres sur l'histoire de France' in *Le Courrier français*, a newspaper associated with a number of liberals who were also historians (including Guizot, Prosper de Barante and Villemain).

These articles called for the creation of a new history. 'La meilleure partie de nos annales, la plus instructive reste à écrire; il nous manque l'histoire des citoyens, l'histoire des sujets, l'histoire du public, l'histoire de la masse.' Historians should write, not about a small number of 'personnages' who claim the exclusive privilege of attention, but about 'ces hommes semblables en tout à nous-mêmes' and they should do so in a humanitarian spirit which allows for the celebration of liberty. He attacked Velly and Anquetil, as he savagely criticised those who had made the history of the conquering Franks into the history of France, and he surveyed the existing methods of writing history. There was the imaginative or poetic method, there was the narrative, 'forme sérieuse de l'histoire antique', and from the eighteenth century onward, there had developed a philosophical approach, in which the narrative was subordinated to the presentation of ideas and themes. Thierry, whilst hinting at his preference for the narrative, and whilst accepting the existence of more scientific means of verifying the accuracy of historical facts, suggested that the essence of historical studies was yet to be decided. All doors were open and writers of history were free to determine how they would proceed. As for himself he pursued the idea of conquest, and started on his *Histoire de la conquête de l'Angleterre par les Normands*, which was published in 1825, in which he continued to lament the disappearance of civilisations, but in which he sought to show how the defeated Britons (in contrast to the Gauls) had recovered their rights and preserved their identity.

Thierry, both in his observations on history in general, and in his first important historical work, had brought an emotional sympathy for the conquered and a sense of colour and variety to a determined erudition, since he had rigorously based his narrative upon primary documents. An even greater erudition was present in Guizot's revision of Mably's *Observations*, which he first published as a new edition of Mably but which subsequently appeared in 1825 as his *Essais sur l'histoire de la France*.

Whilst Thierry had had little experience as a historian, having taught for only a short time after he had left the École Normale Supérieure in 1813 before becoming secretary to Saint-Simon and a journalist, Guizot had been made Professor of History in Paris as early as 1812. He had translated and edited Gibbon and had made use of new historical work, especially German, in order to update the English author's scholarship. When an anti-liberal political movement in 1820 had removed him from government circles he resumed his lectures, choosing the history of representative government as his subject. Like Mably, he sought to find the historical origins of this form of government and like Mably he sought to demonstrate how institutions had been transformed in the early history of France. But unlike Mably he found it necessary to analyse original documents and to consult the work of German jurists and philosophers. The result was a considerable work of scholarship devoted to an old debate which had inspired invention and fantasy rather than learning. Ever since Boulainvilliers, in 1727, had divided the French nation into two races, the defeated Gauls who had lost all their rights, and the conquering Frankish nobility which had maintained a social framework which was capable, at one and the same time, of promoting a liberal organisation of the laws and maintaining an exclusive system of privilege, there had been discussion about the origins of government in France, the role of the monarchy *vis-à-vis* the aristocracy and the other inhabitants of the kingdom. The abbé Dubos, Montesquieu, Mably, and most recently in 1814, a new champion of the aristocracy, Montlosier, had all contributed to this controversy and had discussed the organisation of society amongst the Germanic tribes, the persistence of Roman law in France, or the nature of feudalism, without necessarily having the means to substantiate their assertions. At the same time as Guizot was lecturing on the origins of representative government, a young Aixois, Mignet, submitted an essay for an Academy prize (which he won), later to be published under the title *De la féodalité, des institutions de Saint Louis* in 1821. He too took issue with his eighteenth-century predecessors and sought to grasp the reality of past events. Guizot was among the first to be acquainted with Mignet's work and it may have influenced him in certain ways.

Guizot (and Mignet) did not write history in terms of theory. Nor did they explain what happened as accidents, as the unravelling of the intentions of providence, or as the accomplishment of certain individuals. He explained the necessities which caused Germanic customs to change society. 'Les prééminences sociales ne deviennent légales conquered. Society changed institutions, and institutions then went on to change society. 'Les préeminences sociales ne deviennet légales qu'après avoir été longtemps réelles; c'est seulement quand elles se sont clairement constatées et affermies par la possession qu'elles passent dans les institutions et les lois.' From the one event another arises, since there is an inexorable chain of causation, 'cet enchaînement nécessaire des événements qui fait qu'ils naissent constamment les uns des autres et que le premier jour portait dans son sein l'avenir tout entier'. Ideas and ideologies are affected by this constant development, 'le monde moral a, comme le système des corps célestes, ses lois et son mouvement'. It is therefore the historian's task to study society, in all its complexities. Guizot, with his sense of clarity and system, made his analysis into something which was meaningful and which explained how French society had developed and progressed.

Michelet shared with Thierry his contempt for those historians who had concentrated on the banalities and superficialities of royal and aristocratic splendours, and he shared with Guizot a certain admiration for Mably. Along with Thierry and Guizot too he recognised the necessity of the original documents, as he saw the importance of studying the work of foreign scholars (you will never succeed as a historian, he told a former pupil, unless you learn German). But, paradoxically enough, if he saw himself as working within a certain tradition, yet at the same time he believed that he was to become a unique figure in French historical writing, not simply someone who was going to correct history but somebody who was going to renew it. The tradition he believed in was that inaugurated by Voltaire, especially in the *Essai sur les mœurs* and particularly in his condemnation of Bossuet, and which led to 'toute la grande armée historique, les Mably, les Raynal, les Hume, Gibbon et Robertson, Jean de Müller, etc.'. The uniqueness that he sensed, as he was to explain it in a letter to Lenormant in 1833, and which he was to repeat on various later occasions, was that he found himself between 'l'école pittoresque', which had nothing to say about art, or law, or geography, and 'l'école philosophique', which did not understand that philosophy, religion, art, law, literature, were all living elements that engendered each other. 'Les pittoresques m'assomment de détails, les soi-disants philosophes d'abstractions sans profondeur, sans fécondité. Je ne puis lire . . . d'autre histoire que la mienne.' Michelet was not lacking the enthusiasm for certain of his contemporaries, and amongst his prodigious reading and almost Faustian projects for future writing, he could be generous in his recognition of those who gave him information and insight. But he always saw himself as a solitary figure pursuing a work that was unique to himself.

Of course, these historians had other sources of inspiration. Chateaubriand, a refugee from the Revolution, living in London, published an *Essai sur les révolutions* in 1797. This sought to bring together the history of Athens, of Rome and of France. In 1802 he produced *Le Génie du christianisme*. It has often been said that neither of these books could be considered as historical works. They were constructed in an idiosyncratic manner, they contained much that was inaccurate, they presented no coherent narrative. But they presented the idea that the history of France could be better understood by studying the history of other countries. And they created an enthusiasm for the early Christians and for the medieval. The France of Saint Louis became modish. Seven years later *Les Martyrs*, designed as a pendant to *Le Génie du christianisme*, describes the vicissitudes of two Greek lovers, the one a convert to Christianity and the other a pagan lady who eventually became a Christian. Their story ends with them being reunited in Rome, where they suffer martyrdom. But in the arena where they have died the Emperor Constantine proclaims Christianity as the official religion of the Empire and Christianity triumphs.

As is well known, Augustin Thierry dated his vocation as a historian from his schoolboy reading of the account in *Les Martyrs* of a battle between Romans and Franks.

A mesure que se déroulait à mes yeux le contraste si dramatique du guerrier sauvage et du soldat civilisé, j'étais saisi de plus en plus vivement; l'impression que fit sur moi le chant de guerre des Franks est quelque chose d'électrique. Je quittai la place où j'étais assis, et, marchant d'un bout à l'autre de la salle, je répétai à haute voix et en faisant sonner mes pas sur le pavé: 'Pharamond! Pharamond! Nous avons combattu avec l'épée!'

Guizot too responded enthusiastically to Chateaubriand and was even inspired to send him verse which, he later confessed, was extremely mediocre. But the historical work which was most directly inspired by *Le Génie du christianisme* was undoubtedly Michaud's *L'Histoire des Croisades*, the publication of which began in 1808 and which the author was constantly to revise and to correct.

If Chateaubriand was to incite the historian to exercise his imagination, and to write enthusiastically about the past, the novels of Walter Scott also played an important role. In 1820, after reading *Ivanhoe*, Thierry claimed that there was more 'véritable histoire' in this novel than was to be found in current philosophical compilations, and it is noticeable that six other novels by Scott were translated into French in that year, and several more in 1821. Scott, like Chateaubriand, awakened an interest in periods which had been condemned as backward and in cultures and civilisations which had been written off because they had been suppressed. (Armand Carrel published his *Résumé de l'histoire d'Écosse* in 1825.) This was part of a popular enthusiasm for history, which began to affect the themes of paintings, novels, and biographies, as it encouraged the collection and cataloguing of documents, archaeological remains, monuments and other antiquities.

BEGINNINGS

Thierry, Guizot and Michelet were very different personalities, who enjoyed very different careers. Thierry, who came to history via Saint-

Simonism, political agitation and journalism, was soon stricken by blindness. Guizot, whom Sainte-Beuve described as being the greatest professor of history that France had ever had, described himself as having three careers, one political, one literary, and one religious (connected with his Protestantism). Throughout the 1820s political opposition absorbed much of his activity, from 1830 to 1848 participation in government, sometimes at the highest level, absorbed all his energies, but after the revolution of 1848 enforced leisure (and financial necessity) brought him back to writing historical and religious works. Michelet, who lost his professorial and archival posts after the coming to power of Napoleon III, lived a long life of almost obsessive scholarship, devoted to history, to natural science and to more personal cults. Guizot and Michelet both died in 1874, but there seems little in common between the austere and didactic statesman who was also a historian and the emotional and lyrical writer who sought to encompass all history and life within his visionary intelligence.

Yet as historians they had much in common. They believed in scholarship. They saw the necessity of working with documents. Thierry plunged into the great collections which had been established by the monks of Saint-Maur, Guizot whether as a private individual or as Minister for Public Instruction under the July monarchy, organised the publication of a great documentary series on French and English history, Michelet delved into the archives and with his ready sensitivity trembled before the evidence of human tragedy that he perceived behind the dust of the archives. Yet, whilst accepting and recommending the rigorous discipline inherent in historical enquiry, they were eclectic. They wandered readily into all fields of knowledge. Michelet's reading lists show his voracious appetite for all subjects and it is easy to show how Guizot took his information from a variety of sources (in the *Essais sur l'histoire de France*, for example, he used many of the documents that had been published by Mlle de Lézardière in 1803, although he did not share her opinions). Having demonstrated a variety of facts and opinions, it was their practice to seize upon one single theme, and to make it dominant. In all this there was a vital, underlying assumption, and that was that history was important. History was not for them a diversion, an amusement, a literary exercise. History was, as they saw it, vital for a society. If they never actually used the expression that all thought was historical thought, they might well have done so. And therefore, history had to make sense. History had to teach a lesson and a historical work, or lecture, had to have a point.

All three were bound to history for personal reasons. It could be said that everyone of their generation (Guizot was the oldest, being born in 1787) had been immersed in history, because they had all known the Revolution and the Empire (and Guizot and Michelet were alike in so far as they had not joined in the common admiration for Napoleon and his military victories). Guizot had not only the Protestant sense of the past, but also the knowledge that his father had been guillotined during the Revolution and the memory of his mother going down on her knees to give thanks when she learned of the death of Robespierre. Michelet's father had told him much about the Revolution that was deeply imprinted on his memory. As was often remarked, the Revolution and the Empire changed the nature of historical perspective for a whole generation. They had seen more changes accomplished within the short space of a few years than other generations had known over centuries. Napoleon had reshaped the map of Europe and redistributed the crowns of the continent. It was hardly surprising that as individuals they should feel incapable of understanding the present without consulting the record and the example of the past, and that as historians they should feel confident that their experience qualified them exceptionally to explain the nature of change and progress in history.

Perhaps all historians of this generation, as they looked to the past, also looked back on their own childhood. Chateaubriand was one such, and as he did so he dramatised his appreciation of his life as having been placed between two epochs, like a swimmer who has left the one side of the river but has not yet reached the other. Guizot was to begin his memoirs with the statement that he was one who had been raised up by the Revolution and who would not consent to be reduced. But Chateaubriand's vision of his childhood in the château at Combourg, of his father pacing up and down in the candle-light of the great hall, whilst he and his sister watched him, this is perhaps a recollection of the past which imprints itself on other visions of history.

For Michelet, the lasting childhood impression came from his visits to the collection which Alexandre Lenoir brought together in the cloisters of the Petits-Augustins in Paris, and which came to be known as the Musée des Monuments Français. He saved much that the Revolution had destroyed and vandalised, and his collection, which he opened to the public in Vendémiaire of Year III, saved a great deal which would otherwise have been pillaged or lost. Michelet probably visited it in 1810 (when he was 12) and he was later to write:

C'est là, et nulle autre part que j'ai reçu d'abord la vive impression de l'histoire. Que d'âmes y avaient pris l'étincelle historique, l'intérêt des grands souvenirs, le vague désir de remonter les âges. Je me rappelle encore l'émotion, toujours la même et toujours vive, qui me faisait battre le cœur quand, tout petit, j'entrais sous ces voûtes sombres et contemplais ces visages pâles, quand j'allais et cherchais, ardent, curieux, craintif, de salle en salle et d'âge en âge. Je cherchais. Quoi? Je ne le sais; la vie d'alors sans doute, et le génie des temps. Je n'étais pas sûr qu'ils ne vécussent point, tous ces dormeurs de marbre, étendus sur leur tombes, et quand, des somptueux monuments du XVI siècle éblouissants d'albâtre, je passais à la salle basse des Mérovingiens, où se trouvait la croix de Dagobert, je ne savais trop si je ne verrais point se mettre sur leur séant Chilpéric et Frédégonde.

Elsewhere Michelet recalls the influences upon him of his visits to the cemetery of Père-Lachaise and to the Jardin des Plantes, and he recalls too the effects of the crowded streets and markets of Paris. Once again he saw himself as someone who was different, who had not been influenced simply by the discovery of a book or by the reading of some passage in literature. Possibly thinking of the childhood of Chateaubriand in Combourg he commented, 'C'est quelque chose pour un enfant de commencer par un manoir de famille, par les portraits de ces aïeux, par la longue avenue des chênes qu'ils ont plantés autrefois. Mais c'est quelque chose aussi de commencer par les tombeaux de France.'

This desire to escape from 'ce monde des formules dans lesquelles nous séchons', was accompanied by the sentiment that it was necessary to create a great national history. Michelet expressed it in his own way when he spoke of himself, in the cloître des Petits-Augustins, hearing for the first time, 'l'accord de cette grande lyre, le durable et le progrès dans la personnalité de la France'. But others had the same ambition. Thierry had stressed the need to write about those who were 'les pères de l'indépendance, les pères de la richesse française'; Chateaubriand said that it was necessary for France to re-compose its annals in order to keep in touch with the progress of intelligence; Guizot, justifying for sound intellectual reasons the need to study one particular area of Europe rather than attempt (as he had already done in a preceding course of lectures) to cover the whole of Europe, had no hesitation in choosing the history of France. 'On reconnaît', he explained, 'que la France est le pays dont la civilisation a paru la plus complète, la plus communicative, a le plus frappé l'imagination européenne.'

But it was not to be just any form of national history. The ambition of the new historians was to write a history of France which would give its rightful place to the ordinary people of France. Thierry proclaimed the rights of commoners to be the subject of national histories, Guizot wrote of the need to look to the obscure artisans of the national destiny, and Prosper de Barante suggested that even in those barbarous times when force was supreme, 'la pensée et la voix du peuple exerçaient déjà un immense pouvoir'. But once again it was Michelet who produced the most striking and imaginative formula for this more generalised ambition. 'Nous avons trouvé', said Michelet, quoting to the Collège de France in 1842 the old formula which the public authorities used to use, 'un petit enfant, sanguinolent et qui n'avait point de nom; personne ne connaît ses parents. Cette créature sanglante, qui ne peut rien dire encore, c'est tout un peuple, et le plus nombreux de la terre, le peuple innombrable de ceux qui ont travaillé en silence . . . Nous voulons faire l'histoire de cette pauvre créature muette, dont personne ne s'est soucié, l'histoire de ceux qui n'ont pas eu d'histoire, de ceux qui ont souffert, travaillé, langui, fini, sans pouvoir dire leur souffrance'. The masses sometimes were held down, oppressed, stunned, rendered senseless. All the more reason then, for Michelet to listen to 'les silences de l'histoire', 'ces terribles points d'orgue où elle ne dit plus rien, et qui sont justement ses accents les plus tragiques'. It was the task of the historians of the nineteenth century, when the people had come to prominence and had emerged on to the stage of history, to write about the people, that is to say as Michelet put it, about themselves. 'Ce grand peuple souffrant et silencieux que nous verrons venir à nous depuis l'origine du monde, il n'est autre que nous-mêmes.'

GUIZOT

It was often said that there were two historical schools amongst the French, the 'école analytique' and the 'école narrative' (and it was sometimes claimed that there was a third, the 'école fataliste'). The inadequacy of this division is clearly demonstrated by Guizot. During the 1820s Guizot delivered several courses of lectures at the Sorbonne, on the history of representative government and on the history of civilisation both in Europe and in France. The last-named, which began in 1828, gave him a great reputation and together with his fellow lecturers, Victor Cousin and Villemain, he helped to make the Sorbonne the great intellectual centre of Paris. These lectures, together with the *Essais sur l'histoire de France*, were undoubtedly analytical. Guizot, particularly in his lectures, was addicted to the assertive generalisation, and it could be that the relationship between a lecturer who was a great orator, and an audience which was enthusiastic and ready to be impressed, naturally led to such generalisations. But Guizot was worried that the individual intellectual in France was isolated, and he believed that this isolation could stem from his reluctance to indulge in generalisations. More importantly, Guizot's method as a historian was always to determine the fundamental characteristic of a particular stage of historical development before he had described that development. It could be argued that a particular analysis was imposed upon a historical reality and that because one characteristic succeeded another then a sense of fatalism was imparted to historical change.

Thus Guizot was undoubtedly an analytical historian and could also be accused, on occasions, of belonging to the 'école fataliste'. But he was also a narrative historian. In these same years he published the first two volumes of his *Histoire de la Révolution d'Angleterre* devoted to Charles I, a work which he was to complete in four more volumes in the 1850s, after the 1848 revolution and the establishment of the Second Empire had put an end to his career as a politician and statesman. It could be argued, with some truth, that Guizot was, in the 1820s, a particularly versatile scholar, and that he was bold enough to indulge in different types of history, signalling perhaps the self-confidence of the Romantic historian. But it would be truer to say that Guizot presents, perhaps more clearly but none the less typically, the preoccupation of all historians both with narration and with analysis. The mixture of method could vary according to the intellectual pretensions of the writer, or according to the degree of excitement and colour that he wished to give his account. Sometimes, as was the case with Prosper de Barante, who published his *Histoire des ducs de Bourgogne* from 1824 to 1826, the historian was content to follow the chroniclers and to cite them in order to establish the movement of events, avoiding all personal comment. But other historians, including Guizot and Thierry, even when they concentrated on narrative, often arranged their order of events in order to coincide with the analysis they had made.

When he lectured on civilisation Guizot sought out the distinctive characteristic of European civilisation. For him, this was variety. Outside Europe other forms of society, he believed, were characterised by unity and simplicity, even by monotony. The unity and uniformity of each civilisation expressed itself in politics, religion and literature. Society belonged exclusively to one power which would not tolerate any rival and within this inevitable uniformity all ancient civilisations, for Guizot, included tyranny. But in European civilisation there was both diversity and multiplicity, a confusion and a conflict amongst the different tendencies which were constantly present. All the principles of social organisation existed, theocratic, monarchical, aristocratic, democratic. If one surveyed ideas, then there was the same variety of creeds and beliefs, which were constantly in rivalry and which never ceased to interact amongst each other, challenging, modifying and developing. In terms of sentiment, the insistence upon individuality and independence was met by the pressure of social life, the fidelity of man to man, the tendency of men to submit to authority. In literature and art, Europe affords the same richness and variety.

For Guizot it is the very existence of this diversity and conflict, these systematic antagonisms, which explains the vigour and the progress of European civilisation. Outside Europe one saw religion established upon some single general principle. But in Europe every form of religious society had existed. If one examined the relation between Church and State, for example, one found every possible combination whereby the one or the other was supposed to be predominant. Guizot saw this as an essential factor in the nature of Christianity. It suited his Protestantism (he was to say that his favourite passage in the Bible was that where Jesus said, 'in my Father's house there are many mansions'), his political preference for pluralism, and his intellectual interest in eclecticism, which allowed the historian to exploit the many opportunities which lay before the new history. The Lyonnais Ballanche had understood the situation a few years earlier; 'L'histoire', he had written, 'nous ouvre une carrière immense, c'est presque un monde tout entier à découvrir et à explorer.'

The insistence upon eclecticism led to various conclusions. If there had been only the one principle which led to progress then movements in the past, or present, which offended against this principle would have to be rejected as aberrations, and the historian would become dogmatic, and would fill the role of someone who pronounced exclusions. But Guizot's history was rather conciliatory, one of acceptance, one which accepted all of the past. Another implication was that if progress came from diversity and the play of antagonistic forces, then it was necessary that no single power should obtain any exclusive preponderance in the future. This applied to the power of the Church, or to the power of the crown, or to the power of numbers, that is to say democracy (this last was a principle to be developed by Tocqueville). A third conclusion which arises out of the principle whereby diversity is the source of progress, is that some sort of dialectical process is bound to take place. Various forces, interests and ideas come together in order to produce a government or a society. After a time new forces, interests and ideas arise which contest the existing society. The period of unification is succeeded by a period of dissolution, which in its turn is succeeded by a further period of concentration. From Clovis to feudalism, from feudalism to the monarchy of Louis XIV, from Louis XIV to the French Revolution: the historian records how society is impelled forward, and Guizot noted how the forces of conflict represented various classes in society. Only in Europe, he claimed, did one see a class rise from a low and weak position to one where it absorbed and transformed all around it. But the Third Estate was varied in its origins. Those historians who spoke of the bourgeoisie as if it had always been the same over a long period were mistaken. It was necessary to emphasise how this class had changed and developed and how its power and influence were dependent upon this perpetual progress within itself.

Guizot was obliged to consider the role of the great man in history, since, like his colleagues, he wrote in a self-conscious desire to distinguish himself from those predecessors who had viewed history as the story of great kings and warriors and since, like several generations, he wrote in the shadow of Napoleon. Thus, when he studied Charlemagne, he had Napoleon in mind. For both of them, as for all great men, Guizot described two moments in their lives. In the first, the great man understood more clearly than others what were the needs of his time, and it was this greater perception which formed the basis of his power. In the second, the leader moves away from an understanding of the facts and the exigencies of the moment, and follows more personal and more arbitrary leanings. This is the beginning of egoism which is also illusion. People continue to follow the great man, out of habit, flattery or fear. But they do so with increasing reluctance, and the gulf between them grows wider. Eventually he is abandoned or defeated. The great man cannot effect change contrary to the natural tendencies of his times. He interprets and reinforces. He cannot create, as Charlemagne could not recreate the Roman Empire and as Napoleon I could not create anything which would be lasting or permanent (and this was to be Guizot's comment once Napoleon III had seized power).

Guizot thus spelled out in some analytical detail what Victor Cousin had hinted at when he had alluded to the manner in which the psychology of great men was an expression of their nation's mentality ('Les lieux, les peuples, les grands hommes, voilà les trois choses par lesquelles l'esprit d'une époque se manifeste: ce sont donc là les trois points importants auxquels l'historien doit s'attacher' was his didactic advice, as expressed in his 1828–9 lectures).

And if it was inevitable that Guizot should consider the problem of great men, and their role in history, it was natural that he should also consider the nature of English history. In the 1820s and afterwards, Frenchmen were fascinated by English history. The seventeenth century for England was a time of revolutions and of a civil war which ushered in a period of stability and prosperity, whilst in the person of Cromwell they saw a bewildering personality, a statesman who was soldier, politician and religious leader and an individual who enjoyed victory but who, in the long run, was unsuccessful. Guizot both analysed English history in general and produced an account of the English revolution in particular. He was anxious to underline the differences between English progress, and that of France. In England the conquest had been different from the conquests which had sought to replace Roman rule in France. The similarities between the two societies were such that whereas there was hostility between one society and the other, there was eventually a fusion between the two. In England the conquest meant there was a strong king, and if the nobles were to defend themselves against him, then they had to ally together. The very fact of Norman confederacy, according to Guizot, led to the frequency of assemblies and of charters; the fact of rivalry between a powerful monarchy and a strong nobility led to both sides turning to the knights, the freeholders and the burgesses. Whereas in France centres of power tended to be incomplete, scattered and isolated, in England one needs to see them as a collective whole. Similar forces were compelled to approach one another, and eventually to coalesce and to combine. Different social powers developed simultaneously; local and central institutions tended to advance together, as the Tudor period saw the advance of pure monarchy at the same time as the advance of the parliamentary principle. Thus, according to Guizot, in English history no element perishes completely, so that English government evolved systems of compromise and the English nation qualities of common sense and practical ability.

When telling the story of the English revolution Guizot also pointed to the many-faceted nature of its history. He showed how counties were divided, how Parliament, like the Church of England and the Puritans contained many differing elements, how the forces in conflict faced each other without any overwhelming advantage on either side. And although the method of the narrative, which is impelled forward by the choice of a series of key events, gives the impression of inevitability, it is often suggested that things could have turned out differently. There is no dominating individual, there is a series of competing forces. Perhaps the balance is broken once the king is away from London, and is isolated amongst councillors who give him only the one sort of advice. This break is irretrievable.

Thus even in narrative one can see an analytical mind at work. And it has often been suggested that Guizot's main preoccupation as a historian was to be found in the contemporary political scene. Just as rival politicians had turned to history in order to justify the powers of the king or the privileges of the nobility, so Guizot sought to show the inexorable growth of the Third Estate and the need to curb that which was excessive or exclusive. But as he put it, when history speaks, politics must listen. And when a revolutionary situation developed in 1830, Guizot the politician (he had been a deputy since 1829) was influenced by Guizot the historian who found himself faced by the danger of royal absolutism and by the danger of revolutionary democracy and republicanism. He played a vital role in moderating the revolution and he subsequently refused to give it any special significance. 'Où voulez-vous aller, malheureux jeune homme?' was his question to someone who, in 1830, he judged over enthusiastic, and this was the essential difference between him and historians such as Mignet and Michelet.

MICHELET

It had often been said that the French Revolution had created the need for a new mentality. Victor Cousin claimed to speak for his generation when he spoke, in 1824, of the need to discover the meaning of all the revolutions and changes to which they had been subjected. 'Toutes ces questions, à peu près inconnues à l'Antiquité, commencent à troubler les âmes et à agiter sourdement toutes les têtes pensantes.' It could be said that, although Guizot was perhaps the most accomplished of the new historical school, he never fully shared in the sense of abrupt change and in the need to reassess one's understanding of events. As critics of Guizot have often pointed out, he presents his historical interpretations with such an assurance of logical argument that it precludes dissent or discussion. And behind all his careful marshalling of evidence and his analysis of its significance, he is often dependent upon certain old-fashioned and simple assumptions concerning human nature. He cannot believe or accept a number of possibilities, concerning feudalism, or the ownership of property, or despotism, because he is convinced that they were contrary to principles of human behaviour. This is much what Voltaire believed when he said that what was not in human nature was not in history. The July revolution was to accentuate the way that Guizot's mental furniture appeared dated. Chateaubriand more perceptively showed that he had understood how 'les trois glorieuses', the 27, 28 and 29 July had helped to mature those who had taken part in it. 'Un siècle n'aurait pas autant mûri les destinées d'un peuple que les trois derniers soleils qui viennent de briller sur la France', was his judgment, delivered to the Chambre de Pairs.

Michelet, in his *Introduction à l'histoire universelle*, published in 1831, explains the originality of the revolution as he saw it. Here was the first model of a revolution without a hero, without proper names. An earlier revolution could be summarised in the name of the Maid of Orleans, 'pure et touchante victime qui représente le peuple et mourit pour lui. Ici pas un nom propre; personne n'a préparé, n'a conduit; personne n'a éclipsé les autres. Après la victoire on a cherché le héros, et l'on a trouvé tout un peuple.' In the past, one could find fifty thousand people who were ready to die for a cause; but the 'drapeau tricolore' had expressed the unanimity of many millions. This was new and it was significant.

Michelet had studied and had translated the Italian philosopher Vico, thereby considering the problem of historical inevitability and he had also studied the Germans Herder and Niebuhr, thereby bringing together an acquaintance with philosophy and with scientific history. *L'histoire romaine*, also published in 1831, was notable for the recognition of the nation that existed as Rome, a nation which possessed its own energy and its own powers of creation.

But it was with his *Histoire de France*, six volumes of which were published between 1833 and 1844, taking the story from the origins to the death of Louis XIV, that Michelet really embarked upon his grandiose projects. With Michelet as with Guizot it is inappropriate to place him either in the so-called 'école narrative' or the supposed 'école philosophique'. He endowed his account of events with a drama and a colour that has scarcely been rivalled, but the narration was always attached to certain fixed principles which essentially determined the nature of France's history. He rejected the fatalism, or even at times the importance of races. But he revelled in the geographical conditions within which men evolved. And everything was enveloped in a cloud of enthusiasm and emotion. 'J'ai embrassé la France dans l'unité vivante des éléments naturels qui l'ont constituée', he wrote. He visited the different regions which he wrote about. He even applied for a chair of geography in Paris. But, significantly enough, he did not fall a victim to geographical determinism either. The famous 'Tableau de France' was not placed at the beginning of the *Histoire de France*. Instead, Michelet first surveyed ancient, then Gallic and Latin France, about which knowledge was limited and which were not yet recognisable as France. But when, around the year 1000, he discovers the birth of modern France, it is then that he inserts his Tableau into the history. 'C'est qu'il voit se lever la France, avec son corps, son âme et son esprit, modelés par l'écoulement des siècles', comments the modern historian, Jacques Le Goff, and this is an indication of how Michelet was less a determinist than a 'resurrectionist'.

His attitude to documents is equally revealing of a romantic resurrectionist approach. Writing of his work in the Archives du Royaume, he said, 'Dans les galeries solitaires des Archives où j'errai vingt années dans ce profond silence, des murmures cependant venaient à mon oreille', and more explicitly.

Je ne tardai pas à m'apercevoir dans le silence apparent de ces galeries, qu'il y avait un mouvement, un murmure qui n'était pas de la mort . . . Tous vivaient et parlaient . . . et à mesure que je soufflais sur leur poussière, je les voyais se soulever. Ils tiraient du sépulcre qui la main, qui la tête, comme dans le Jugement dernier de Michel-Ange, ou dans la Danse des morts.

When speaking of the Middle Ages in French history he also referred to the 'étrange dialogue' which existed between him and this history, 'entre moi, son ressusciteur, et le vieux temps remis debout'.

Thus the Middle Ages for Michelet was the period which saw the emergence of France and the triumph of the French language. He was able to personify France, and he was able also to identify the Middle Ages as a living being. With the famous phrase, 'La France est une personne', he sometimes saw France as a succession of individuals. Most clearly there was Joan of Arc, abandoned and alone, a child being burned at the stake, but able to hang on to 'son Église intérieure', her voices. And the Middle Ages themselves were also a child, torn from the very bowels of Christianity, born in tears and lamentations, brought up in prayer and anguish. Joan was the Saviour of France, 'Le sauveur de la France devait être une femme. La France était femme elle-même.' And more than this, the Middle Ages and France had worshipped the Virgin and the martyrdom of purity, France had become a nation, the humble people of France had become important. Joan was thus the synthesis of a whole epoch. 'L'enfant, le peuple, la France, la Vierge . . .' With Joan, Michelet was able to celebrate the emergence of France.

The Middle Ages was also a period of history which Michelet loved, because he was able to indulge in total history. He brought lyricism and enthusiasm together with erudition (as did other Romantic writers, such as Victor Hugo), and he found in this period of French history the opportunity of using as his sources art and architecture, legend and literature, as well as the archives, the charters and the chronicles in which he was steeped. Stone played its part as well as parchment.

Within the nationalism, there was necessarily the cult of the people. 'Il y eut un peuple, il y eut la France.' It could be said that the idea of the people binds together the virtues of the erudite historian and the visions of the prophet, the novelist and the rhetorical militarist. In the 1840s Michelet, together with his colleagues Edgar Quinet and the Polish nationalist historian Mickiewicz, saw themselves as famous Sorbonne lecturers who were the equivalent of their predecessors of the 1820s, Guizot, Cousin and Villemain, and when their lectures were suspended in the 1840s (by the government in which Guizot was the dominating figure) Michelet responded with his book, *Le Peuple*, first published in 1846. Here he was not only the poetic prophet, he claimed also to be the realist, seeing in the peasants those who had preserved the principles of salvation and in the factory workers those who exemplified the principles of fraternity. *Le Peuple* is the climax of Michelet's thought since it is there that he most clearly states that man is born noble and that the popular instinct is the fountain of life. Michelet, like his colleagues, was always influenced by contemporary events, and by 1846 it was natural that he should have expressed these ideas. But already, in the preface to the fourth volume of his *Histoire de France*, he had referred glowingly to the instinct of ordinary, simple people. 'Le peuple des campagnes fera par inspiration ce que la sagesse des villes n'a pu faire; il relèvera la royauté, rétablira l'unité et de cette épreuve où le pays faillit périr sortira, confuse encore mais vivace et forte, l'idée même de la patrie.' Michelet felt deeply and emotionally for those who were poor and who suffered, he felt that their history should be the great preoccupation of the historian; he was able to imagine the factory worker before his machine, listening to its noise which repeated only the one word, 'toujours, toujours, toujours', the brutal condemnation of the worker's life. But the fact of France existing as a nation took priority over these material details. As Ernest Renan was later to put it, expressing Michelet's thought, 'une nation est un principe spirituel'.

When he considered how France emerged as a nation, Michelet demonstrated a method that he had utilised and was to use on many occasions, that of antithesis. Whether this was because politically he was always aware of conflict, or because intellectually he could not discover the unifying features of contemporary society, because as a son he felt personally responsible for the early death of his mother, or because, as a historian of his generation, he felt that he had to give an explanation, however mysterious, for everything, he was always conscious of the antagonism that existed between one element and another and aware of its importance. Thus the east is contrasted to the west, the country to the town, the Old World to the New; the moist is in conflict with the dry, the liquid with the solid; above all, there is the struggle between male and female, mother and son, individual and community, liberty and fatality, life and death. In terms of nationality, it was the invasion of France by the English which created French nationalism and consciousness of nationality. Solidarity might have existed before, but the war against the

English made nationalism a question of will and determination and impelled the population of France forward into a different and distinctive world.

La France jusque-là vivait de la vie commune et générale du Moyen-Âge autant et plus que la sienne; elle était catholique et féodale avant d'être française. L'Angleterre l'a refoulée durement sur elle-même, l'a forcée de rentrer en soi. La France a cherché, a fouillé, elle est descendue au plus profond de sa vie populaire, elle a trouvé quoi? La France. Elle doit à son ennemie de s'être connue comme nation.

Thus the antagonism between France and England bore its fruits.

Like other historians, Michelet had to consider the problem of the role of great men in history, but perhaps this was a problem which he had faced earlier than most of his contemporaries. In 1819, when he was aged twenty-one and when Napoleon was still alive, he had presented his doctoral thesis to the Sorbonne, the subject being Plutarch. He then asked, how could one treat 'ces colosses qui nous effraient dans l'histoire'? And later, under the influence of Thierry and of the German historians, and more particularly under the influence of Vico, he believed that to dwell on the achievements of a great man was to miss what was most fundamental in the movement of history. The revolution of 1830, a revolution without a hero, was a practical confirmation of this notion. Great men were myths and legends, and when a people prostrated itself before some gigantic figure, 'Ce que vous adorez, c'est vous-mêmes, ce sont vos propres conceptions', he wrote in 1831. Much of history as seen by Michelet turned around myths and symbols. It could be that when he worked on Luther, in the mid 1830s, he was forced to modify his views, since he found in Luther someone who was both a real person as well as representing an ideal, someone who was a man of action as well as a man of thought. But as he wrote his history of France, more especially he came to see the great persons in French history not so much in terms of a mythical past as of a mystical past. When Charles VI contemplated a passion play, he was not only a spectator, he was himself a spectacle. 'Le peuple venait voir en lui la Passion de la royauté. Le roi y voyait le peuple misérable, déguenillé, mendiant. Le peuple y voyait le roi plus pauvre encore sur le trône, pauvre d'esprit, pauvre d'amis, délaissé de sa famille, de sa femme, veuf de lui-même et de ses survivants, riant tristement du rire des fous.' The process of Michelet's conversion to a different view of the rôle of the hero in history is through his discovery of a heroine, Jeanne d'Arc. This was not merely a spectacle, a symbol and a legend. It was also reality, because Joan led armies in battle and won victories. 'En elle apparurent à la fois la Vierge et déjà la Patrie.'

It was those developments in Michelet's thought which caused some of his readers both to admire and to distrust him. As his English critic John Stuart Mill put it, Michelet did not appear to be 'altogether as safe a writer as M. Thierry or M. Guizot', in so far as his interpretations of history could not be so accepted as true that those who dislike to explore for themselves could sleep peacefully in the faith that Michelet had done the explorations on their behalf. According to Mill, writing in 1844, Michelet's books did not save the reader the trouble of thinking, they made him boil over with thought. 'Their effect on the mind is not acquiescence, but stir and ferment.'

But the greatest stir and ferment took place in Michelet's own mind. The 'discovery' of Joan dates from 1840; from 1841 he started preparing his work on the French Revolution. In his 1843 lectures on the Jesuit order he expressed his need to recall to France its revolutionary tradition. Above all he experienced his own need to deal with the most heroic and apocalyptic period in French history. He interrupted his plan to write about the Renaissance, and in 1847 he published the first volume of his history of the French Revolution.

THE REVOLUTION

The first studies purporting to recount the history of the Revolution had appeared in the form of 'précis', seeking to set down the principal events of that complicated and intense period. But they had either been produced by actors in the revolution itself, such as Rabaut Saint-Étienne, or by historians who chose to look ironically at so much confusion and wasted effort, such as Lacretelle. A multitude of memoirs were produced, of varying reliability, and the history of France after 1789 tended to be represented as a mixture of tragedy, violence, drama and romance. One notable exception was the *Considérations sur les principaux événements de la Révolution française*, written by Mme de Staël and published (posthumously) in 1818. These volumes justified the Revolution as a necessity, a movement which was the result of what had happened throughout the preceding century. But, as one would expect perhaps from the daughter of Necker, who had become an *émigrée* in 1792, the picture of the Revolution was not one of unmitigated praise. After the achievements of 1789, with the conquest of liberty and the abolition of absolutism, feudalism and clerical privilege, the Revolution became extreme. It lost sight of the principles of liberalism and degenerated into fanaticism, violence, chaos and eventually, Bonaparte. Mme de Staël's *Considérations* sparked off a considerable debate. It was detested by those who disapproved of the Revolution, and it was regarded with enthusiasm by some moderates and liberals. But most significantly it was the occasion for a discussion about history. On the one hand it sought to explain the Revolution, regarding it as a historical event which had to be understood like any other. On the other hand the author treated history in an abstract, theoretical manner, and she appeared to some to be too far distant from the realities of the situation and to underestimate the impact of all the conspiracies, fears, disasters and ambitions with which this period is filled. A former Girondin, Jean-Charles Bailleul replied, also in 1818, with his *Examens critiques des Considérations de Madame de Staël*.

But it was a few years later that two young men from the south, Mignet and Thiers (who happened to be close friends) embarked upon separate projects of writing major works on the Revolution. In 1822 Thiers was hoping that he would soon complete a three-volume précis. But it seems that he became moved by the ambition of producing a more total history, one which would, in his own words, 'unir le poème à la philosophie', whilst still maintaining a place for the factual and for the picturesque. The first two volumes appeared in September 1823, whilst Mignet's completed history in two volumes was published in the spring of 1824. Two further volumes by Thiers were published in December 1824, and the entire work was not completed until 1827. The revolution of 1830, which made Thiers an important politician (he was to be Prime Minister twice between 1830 and 1840) gave an additional lustre to this History, all the more so since Mignet fell largely silent, but it was generally realised that Mignet's was the more important work of the two.

Much of what Mignet wrote was to become the classical version of the Revolution which was to become the subject-matter of countless textbooks. The Revolution, he wrote, was inevitable. By the time the Estates General met, it was 'une révolution déjà faite', and accomplished by the irresistible force of the Third Estate. Its inevitability was proved by the rapidity of its successes. 'Lorsqu'une réforme est devenue nécessaire, et que le moment de l'accomplir est arrivé, rien ne l'empêche et tout la sert.' This was a moment which changed all the existence of the nation. In saying this Mignet realised to what extent he was seeking to protect the Revolution from those who, in the reactionary turn which French politics had taken after 1820, were still hoping to destroy the Revolution, to turn the clock back and to return to something resembling the *ancien régime*.

In these sentiments Mignet resembled Mme de Staël. They were both committed to a Revolution that was natural, liberal and reasonable. But

Mignet was much bolder when he discussed the more violent periods.

For Mignet, the great popular insurrection of 10 August 1792 was comparable to the rising of 14 July 1789. The first had been the revolt of the middle classes against the privileged classes and against absolute power; the second was the revolt of the multitude against the middle classes and against constitutional monarchy. The two revolutions are thus put on the same level, and there are good reasons why they both took place. So far as the second revolution, the popular revolution, was concerned it was the war against France which was responsible for its outbreak, and it was this revolution's heroic defence of France which was its justification. 'Lorsque la société est ainsi remuée dans ses fondements, ce sont les hommes les plus audacieux qui triomphent, et au lieu des réformateurs sages et modérés, on n'a plus que des réformateurs extrêmes et inflexibles.' In this way of thinking Mignet contrasted Lafayette, who was the natural incarnation of the first revolution ('il devint le général de la classe moyenne, il n'eut jamais qu'un but, la liberté, et ne se servit que d'un moyen, la légalité'), to Danton, the chief protagonist of the second revolution (and it was probably his portrait of this 'révolutionnaire gigantesque' that inspired Büchner to write his *Danton's Death*).

Mignet wrote a lively narrative. His account, for example, of the storming of the Bastille, presents the events dramatically, but not over-dramatically. We hear the crowd, from nine in the morning, shouting 'à la Bastille, à la Bastille'; we are told of the old man shouting 'camarades, marchez, suivez-moi'; we are shown the victorious mob returning to the Hôtel de Ville, with the news and the signs of their victory, 'les yeux ardents, les cheveux en désordre, ayant toute sorte d'armes, se pressant les uns les autres et faisant craquer les boiseries sous leur pas'. But Mignet soon passes on to the next incident. We are back in Versailles with the speeches of Mirabeau and the now famous conversation between Louis XVI and the duc de Liancourt ('"C'est une révolte", dit le monarque étonné. "Non, Sire", répondit le duc de Liancourt, "c'est une révolution."'). Nor is the crowd presented in an exclusively noble fashion. The Governor of the Bastille and some of the Swiss guards are put to death 'inhumainement'; one of the victors of the people raises his bloody hand to show some gruesome trophy and Mignet comments: 'chose horrible'.

It is understandable that out of this history, there arose not simply the impression that Mignet was defending the Revolution, because he was critical of the Terror and of the 'épouvantables exécutions' of the Committee of Public Safety, nor that he was merely a nationalist, exalting 'l'immortelle campagne de 1793 et 1794' and 'la civilisation plus avancée de la France', because his accounts of military victories were often muted. More particularly the lesson that was apparently presented was that of fatalism. The Revolution took place because it had to; it became violent and excessive because it was forced so to be by the hazards of war; it could not last because the same war made all its institutions temporary, the necessary result of haste and improvisation; the need to re-establish an ordered society led naturally to Bonaparte, and to his despotism.

This determinism, or fatalism, as Chateaubriand preferred to call it (and which was greatly admired by Engels) in no way led to the suppression of the role of individuals. Louis XVI was 'le meilleur mais le plus faible des monarques', one who might, had he been stronger, have been a successful ruler. Napoleon, rehabilitated in a manner that was deeply shocking to the liberals who had admired Mme de Staël, was the typical despot who at first identified himself with the interests of the people and with the aspirations of the most important sections of the population, in order to concentrate eventually upon himself. Thus Louis was the prisoner of his own weakness; Napoleon the prisoner of his own ambition.

Sainte-Beuve was not alone in finding within this fatalism the premonitory signs of a social history which later generations would call class history. Mignet showed how the middle class was apprehensive of the crowd, 'la multitude'. If the middle class was pleased to accept the support and co-operation of the people in 1789, it was in the expectation of controlling them, of separating them from the process of power by the constitution of 1791, and of fearing them perpetually and exaggeratedly. He saw a class seizing power in a state, as on other occasions an individual would take over the control of a country's government. But this insight was not sustained by any theory of class, or by any real understanding of how economics affected relations between the classes.

There were more details concerning economic history to be found in the works of Thiers. Occasionally too, Thiers showed an emotion as a writer that was not to be found in his friend Mignet. But it is not because Thiers discovered the price of candles and cooking oil, nor is it because he wrote enthusiastically about the 'cocarde tricolore' that he is to be distinguished from Mignet. They seem to have collaborated, and when it came to interviewing those who had taken part in the events which they were describing, such as Lafayette or Talleyrand, they probably shared their information. They both accepted certain developments in the Revolution as necessary. Thiers, for example, believed as strongly as

Mignet, that it was war which had transformed the Revolution. 'La Révolution', he wrote, 'prit enfin le caractère militaire, parce qu'au milieu de cette lutte perpétuelle avec l'Europe il fallait qu'elle se constitue d'une manière solide et forte.' But Thiers, more than Mignet, was drawn to the history of the Empire. Whilst Mignet passes rather rapidly past the story of Napoleon and avoids making any detailed character sketch of him, Thiers was to return to the subject in the 1840s when he withdrew from politics, at the time he was virtual leader of the opposition to the government dominated by Guizot, in order to write his multi-volume history of the Empire. As always he wrote rapidly, made many mistakes, filled many pages with remarks that were ordinary and banal.

It was not the so-called 'fatalism' of Mignet and Thiers that makes them important, although it was echoed by other historians (Sainte-Aulaire, for example, in his *Histoire de la Fronde*, published in 1827, wrote that 'les révolutions ne sont pas l'ouvrage des passions humaines, elles s'accomplissent inévitablement quand l'état de la société les a rendues nécessaires'). It is rather that the framework which they had provided for the Revolution became generally accepted. Mignet, in particular, thanks to his style and to the concise neatness of his narrative, was widely and continuously read.

In the years that followed, the study of the French Revolution made progress, as collections of speeches and other sources were published. It was clear too that attitudes were changing, as it became more common to accept and to praise the more violent aspects of the Revolution, and those who were responsible for them, such as Robespierre. But nothing had made the French public ready for the sensational publication of three remarkable books on the Revolution in 1847. It has always been accepted that the appearance of these three works, all of which tended to glorify the Revolution in its most terrible years, helped to prepare and to influence public opinion in a manner that was directly related to the events of 1848. There can be no doubt that Guizot's government was seriously weakened by this audacious literature, and there was a singular irony in the public challenge which three historians offered to a statesman who had been, and who was to become again, a master of their craft.

The first to appear, in February 1847, was the first volume of *L'Histoire de la Révolution*, by the socialist Louis Blanc (the whole work, in twelve volumes, was not completed until 1862). A week later Michelet published his first volume (the second appeared in November, and all seven volumes were completed in 1853). Then, between March and June

1847, all eight volumes of Lamartine's *Histoire des Girondins* were published.

That which was most easily criticised was by Louis Blanc. It was claimed that he was biased, a politician writing history for political reasons, as he had already written a history of France between 1830 and 1840 in his *Histoire de dix ans* (1841). This was not so much 'l'apologétique du régime révolutionnaire' as 'un panégyrique politique'. But subsequently, it has been pointed out that Blanc had provided a good and accurate guide to the Revolution and that he had written a serious history, not simply a multi-volume pamphlet.

Louis Blanc was nothing if not ambitious. He was very far from seeing his book as a mere pamphlet, or as an appendage to his socialist writings (of which *L'Organisation du travail*, published in 1839 was the most famous). He claimed that the history of the Revolution had yet to be written and he set out to situate the event of the Revolution in its place in world history. For him there were a number of major themes or principles around which history revolved. There was individualism, there was authority, and there was fraternity. The struggle between these three dated back many centuries, and was to be discerned in the histories of John Hus or of Étienne Marcel. The French Revolution at first marked the defeat of authority, and the victory of bourgeois individualism, with its lawyers, its philosophers and its industrial leaders. It was the Jacobins, the Montagnards and the Committee of Public Safety who asserted the principles of fraternity, and who defeated the champions of individualism, who looked back to the traditions of the Reformation and of the Enlightenment, especially of Voltaire, and who were championed by the Constituent Assembly, by the Girondins and by Danton. The heroes of fraternity were Rousseau, then Robespierre and Saint-Just. The 9 Thermidor, with the overthrow of Robespierre and the beginning of a reactionary movement, was the date which marked the failure and the abortion of the Revolution. Thus, contradicting the theories of the liberals, Louis Blanc scorns the so-called first revolution, and praises the second. He accepts violence, and praises those who wielded it as being 'insensibles à la peur, supérieurs aux remords'. In the name of their courage he salutes a revolution which was essentially one of harmony and liberty, and which was overthrown by 'l'ingrate pusillanimité' of certain of their colleagues.

Naturally such an interpretation of the Revolution seemed, at the time, to be biased and even wayward. But few historians would disagree nowadays that the period of the Committee of Public Safety and of Robespierre represented the climax, if not the essence, of the Revolution. Equally many of them would agree that the author, whilst arguing a case, nevertheless was doing so in a careful, well-documented manner. His self-consciousness concerning historical methods was often expressed in his appendices, and whilst arguing in favour of the aspirations of the Revolutionary mentality, he was one of the first to try to understand how it was that dedicated and courageous men fought against the Revolution, in Vendée for example. Just as in terms of socialism, Louis Blanc deserves to be called a 'scientific' rather than an 'utopian' socialist, so, in terms of history, he was scholarly rather than emotional.

The same could not be said of Lamartine. The author of the *Méditations poétiques* (1820) had not contented himself with dreams of a mystical reunion in another world with the only being who was important for him. He had been elected to the Chamber of Deputies in 1833 and had made remarkable speeches on the liberty of the press, on the abolition of slavery and capital punishment. As a journalist too he had written eloquently on his hopes for a society which would have rid itself of self-interest and which would dedicate itself to liberty and social justice. But it was after 1843 that he started his serious bid for political power. Profiting from the absence of Thiers from the political arena of the Chamber (preoccupied as he was with his history of the Empire) Lamartine sought to appear as the leader of the opposition to Guizot. His opposition was significant because it was not an opposition which was ready to content itself with the downfall of the Soult–Guizot government and with the substitution for it of some similar form of ministry, even if he were to be its leader. His opposition was total and he believed in the necessity of some sort of catastrophe occurring before France could find salvation. 'Ce pays est mort', he wrote in 1845. 'Rien ne peut le galvaniser qu'une crise. Comme honnête homme, je la redoute; comme philosophe, je la désire.'

Furthermore, Lamartine was faced with a strategical problem. He knew that he was popular in the country. His speeches found a ready echo in the newspapers, and his political reputation, securely sustained by his standing as a poet and his greatness as an orator, continued to grow. But in the Chamber of Deputies and within the limited circle of the *pays légal* which had the vote and which controlled the official political life that was based in Paris, he was much less successful. There was an easy mockery of 'le facteur de Mâcon' as he was called, and the politicians tended to rely upon each other and to exclude him as an unreliable intruder. It was doubtless in order to affirm his position as a serious political force that, from 1843, he adopted the idea of writing a history of the Girondins. It is a commentary upon the role of the historian at this time that the accepted opposition leader to Guizot, who had made his name as a historian, was Thiers, busily engaged in historical writings, whilst the man who was trying to take on the role of chief opposition leader, Lamartine, should seek for the necessary additional fame, by publishing a large-scale historical work.

It is obvious that Lamartine must have worked with extraordinary speed. He picked up ideas from collections of memoirs, from newspapers which he consulted unmethodically, from conversations with the relatives and friends of the characters whom he was portraying. But once he had assembled his material, then he wrote intuitively, imaginatively, and above all, fervently. 'Il a élevé l'histoire à la hauteur du roman' was the sarcastic comment of Alexandre Dumas, and there were scenes depicted for which the author had little or no evidence and which must have been the result of his creative powers rather than of his scrutiny of documents. But the result was a triumph for Lamartine. His history was the greatest publishing success that had been seen for many a year. And it did not seem to matter that the Girondins had speeches attributed to them which they might never have pronounced, or that they should have figured in episodes which probably did not take place. What did matter was that Lamartine glorified the Revolution, that he exulted in its 'vérités fécondes' and that he found it natural that he should plead its necessity and its greatness. He made Vergniaud, the great Girondin orator, speak the words which justify the role of the historian. 'Les révolutions sont comme ces crises qui blanchissent en une nuit la tête d'un homme: elles mûrissent vite les peuples.' Lamartine's errors may or may not have been important. But his genius was based upon his understanding of what revolution was, and on the eve of the revolution of 1848 he told an excited crowd that his book needed a conclusion. It was they who would provide it for him, he cried.

1848 elevated Lamartine, for a short time at least, into the chief minister of the new Republic, as it made Louis Blanc into the chief organiser of the National Workshops. But neither of them was to enjoy any lengthy success. For Michelet, 1848 was only the occasion whereby he was able to resume his position as a professor (and as a director of the Archives) from which he had been dismissed by Guizot. But the *coup d'état* of Napoleon III drove him from Paris to Nantes, and from there to Nervi, near to Genoa, where he finished his *Histoire de la Révolution*. It was in 1855, in the epilogue to this History, that he defined his work as he saw it. 'Toute l'histoire de la Révolution, jusqu'ici, était essentiellement monarchique. (Telle pour Louis XVI, telle pour Robespierre.)

Celle ici est la première républicaine, celle qui a brisé les idoles et les dieux. De la première à la dernière page, elle n'a qu'un héros: le peuple.'

Because it was to be original, Michelet rejected the existing histories. Reading Mignet in 1843, as part of his preparation for his own projected work, he expressed admiration for many of the details, but thought it false as a whole. Doubtless he found Mignet too detached. He wanted to relive and to remake the sufferings of the Revolution, and as he flung himself into the drama of these tremendous events, so he dramatised his own role in doing this. Every day he asked himself (or so he confided to his *Journal*) if he was equal to the greatness of his subject, if he would be capable of penetrating its mysteries. Later he was to write of his joy in rediscovering those unforgettable days, so that his manuscript seemed intoxicated by his tears.

It is clear that whilst in some respects Michelet, like Lamartine, wished to glorify the Revolution, his determination to resurrect the past places his history in a different category of historical writing. It is as if the French nation was such a driving force that it is useless to point to the mistakes or the weaknesses of those régimes which were overthrown by the Revolution. This means that if Michelet is far from being favourable to the *ancien régime*, he nevertheless recognises the role that it played in establishing national unity, and he applauds those monarchs who had overthrown the powers of the great feudal lords or who had protected the people against the tyranny of the seigneurs. 'La justice royale fut bénie pour sa rigueur. Le Roi apparut terrible, dans ses Grands Jours, comme le Jugement dernier, entre le peuple et la noblesse, le peuple à droite, se serrant contre son juge, plein d'amour, de confiance.' But what happened, was that the monarch had ceased to play this role. Instead, the monarch governed in the name of the privileged class, and the people ceased to invest him with their power. Hence Louis XVI was overthrown and guillotined.

It is no accident that in 1847 Michelet noted in his *Journal* that Louis-Philippe, who had been invested with power by the heroic insurgents of July 1830, was now governing only in the name of the rich. Louis XVI had believed that he was a god. 'Mais ce mot Dieu, il n'y a rien compris. Être Dieu, c'est vivre pour tous.' The condemnation to death of Louis XVI was not simply the execution of an individual, of someone who would be replaced. It was rather 'la condamnation éternelle de l'institution monarchique'.

Thus Michelet solves the problem of the hero in history. When the people give their life-force to an individual, then that individual is elevated. Dumouriez, on the eve of the battle of Valmy, was an ordinary officer in the French army. But on the day of the battle he was seized by the Revolution, adopted by it, and raised above himself. Even Marat, whom Michelet had compared to a frog, with his green clothes and his grey and yellow eyes, was transformed by the generosity of 'ce bon peuple de France'. The nearer the hero is to the simple people of France, then the truer is his transformation. Thus Danton, 'la voix même de la Révolution et de la France', is close to the peasants of Champagne and to the cunning compatriots 'du bon La Fontaine'. It is an obscure representative from Lyons who incarnates most purely the people. When he spoke he was not a man: 'c'est une ville, un monde souffrant . . . La profonde boue des rues noires, jusque-là muette, a pris voix en lui. En lui commençent de parler les vieilles ténèbres, les humides et sales maisons jusque là honteuses du jour; en lui la femme souillée . . .'

In the great *journées révolutionnaires*, the people were themselves inspired. Not only were they brave, with a courage which was in defiance of ordinary common sense or of any calculation of risk, but their actions were spontaneous, in no way foreseeable, or even explicable. On 14 July 1789, 'Une idée se leva avec le jour, et tous virent la même lumière. Une lumière dans les esprits et dans chaque cœur une voix: Va, et tu prendras la Bastille! Cela était impossible, insensé, étrange à dire . . . Et tous ouïrent néanmoins. Et cela se fit.' In the other great days of the Revolution, when the struggle was less intense and the physical combat absent, then it was fraternity and solidarity which triumphed amongst the people who were now sovereign, whose unity no longer needed to be symbolised by a person, by a king. Michelet wrote of 'l'union des cœurs, la communauté de l'esprit, le profond mariage de sentiments et d'idées qui se fait de tous avec tous'. Egoism was replaced by patriotism and by concern for 'le genre humain'.

But there remained difficulties. Could the people not be mistaken, could they not be betrayed? It was obvious that the great hopes of the Revolution, and of other revolutions, were disappointed. 1789 degenerated into Bonaparte, 1830 was seized by the King and by the bankers, 1848 led to repression and to the reign of another Bonaparte. 'Mon seul héros, le peuple, l'ai-je flatté?' asked Michelet. He replied, 'Point du tout. J'ai montré et ses heureux élans et ses promptes rechutes.' Who, he asked again, could claim that the people was never mistaken? The victories of the people are contrasted to the people's errors, in Michelet's didactic manner.

These errors arose for many reasons. The people could be manipulated (as were the peasants of Vendée who were used by nobles and priests in a senseless struggle against the Revolution). The people could become inert, could fall back into the rituals of monarchy, could take refuge in obscure and furtive silence. And the people could be betrayed, especially by a hero who was aloof from the natural simplicity and poetry of the masses. Such a personage was Robespierre. Michelet believed that his supposed virtue, his claim to be incorruptible, his assertion of revolutionary faith, were all unconvincing. His simplicity was affected, his puritanism isolated him, his culture placed him in a world of mediocrity. He was, in fact, for Michelet, a man of principle, that is to say someone who would sell his country or the people in the name of these principles.

There was a further difficulty for Michelet. His personal identification with the revolutionary masses was complete. He believed that his vocation was to write the history of the Revolution, the story of the taking of the Bastille. He claimed that all his historical work was in preparation for this great day. 'Que vous avez tardé, grand jour . . . J'ai vécu pour vous raconter.' But was this appropriate? Was he not, like Robespierre perhaps, a man of principle, a man of culture and learning which separated him from the people? He was not, like Lamartine (whom he admired, calling him 'le premier des premiers') a man of action. He could not, like Lamartine, say of the revolution of 1848 'nous vivons la plus sublime des poésies'. His self-dramatisation led to self-doubt. Years later he expressed the problem as he saw it. 'Être vieux et jeune, tout à la fois, être un sage, un enfant . . . Là, j'ai senti notre misère, l'impuissance des hommes de lettres, des subtils. Je me méprisais.'

CONCLUSION

One of Michelet's closest friends, with whom he had shared the experience of Germany (and whose translation, with a preface, of Herder's *Idées sur la philosophie de l'histoire de l'humanité*, which appeared in Paris in 1827, was one of the most profound influences on French Romanticism), published a work between 1848 and 1852, which showed how there was a similarity between historians, even when the subject was not the dominant national subject of France. Edgar Quinet's *Les Révolutions d'Italie* sought to find 'l'âme d'Italie'. Quinet visited Italy; he discovered the reality of the Italian people as he contemplated the churches and the frescoes, the palaces and the statues. He then studied the chronicles and the institutions, the literary and the religious changes, as well as those that affected politics and diplomacy. With a view to describing 'une nation qui se cherche' he wrote as a scholar, whose work was based on a solid documentation, and as a prophet, who imagined that he could foresee the future of Italy (as, in another work, *De l'Allemagne et la Révolution*, 1832, he had with some accuracy, foretold the future of Germany).

Some years later Quinet was to discuss the destiny of France. After his work on *La Philosophie de l'histoire de France* (1854), he published, in 1865, *L'Histoire de la Révolution* (although much of it had been written many years earlier). For Quinet, however much the Revolution had promised a new moral and social order, which would be the natural climax to a long period of gestation and development, it had ended (as had the revolution of 1848) with political servitude for the French people. For Quinet, more surely than for Michelet, what one had to understand was failure. He suggested that the Revolution never had the audacity to put forward a new religion (comparable to the Protestantism of the sixteenth century). Furthermore it had not been able to rid itself of the old trappings of absolutism, whether Roman, monarchical or Jacobin. Robespierre was a later version of Richelieu, and he was the harbinger of Bonaparte. Whereas Michelet had been able to contemplate the possible, occasional failures of the people, Quinet, by linking Jacobinism to Bonapartism, threw into question the whole nature of the Revolution.

In this he must be compared to his contemporary, Alexis de Tocqueville, who died prematurely in 1859. Like most of his fellow historians, Tocqueville was deeply involved in politics, becoming a deputy for the region in Normandy where his family were the local seigneurs. His father, a prefect, was the somewhat dilettantish author of a *Histoire philosophique du règne de Louis XV*, and it was perhaps inevitable that after Tocqueville had gone to the United States of America in order to study its penitentiary system, he should write, in 1836 and 1839, a book on *La Démocratie en Amérique*. But it was not inevitable that this book should have an enormous success at the time of its publication and that it should continue to be regarded as one of the great essays in contemporary history. It was not surprising that one of the most perceptive, and prophetic, critics of the Guizot administration should, after the 1848 revolution, have been elevated, for a short time, to be Minister of Foreign Affairs. But it could not have been expected that he should then have written the most original work on the French Revolution to have been published since Mme de Staël's *Considérations*, his unfinished *L'Ancien Régime et la Révolution* (1856).

Tocqueville always sought, by a lucid, objective analysis to establish what was the social and political character of the nation that he was studying, what were the principles which guided its existence and how the spirit of government was dominated by a certain ethic. His was the work of a moralist, who contemplated with dismay the lack of feeling and purpose within society. His was also the work of a perceptive historian who saw continuity where others had seen a dramatic and meaningful break and who described this continuity in a style that was concise and plain. It was the work of a writer who was more interested in society than in French society and who was concerned to show how French society was showing in miniature all the individualist traits of the democratic society which interested him.

Tocqueville, like Michelet, sought to discover 'l'âme d'un peuple', but both by temperament and by ambition he went about it in a different way. Perhaps one can say that Tocqueville became the alternative to Michelet, just as one can see how he had been influenced by the historical analyses of Guizot, the race theories of Thierry and the geographical surveys of Michelet. He was modest in his ambitions, more interested in recording the long traditions of beliefs and customs than in denouncing them or in announcing their demise. In a historian such as Fustel de Coulanges, whose great work, *La Cité antique* was published in 1864, one can see the influence both of Michelet and of Tocqueville, but it is the latter who predominates.

The list of French historians who began to establish their celebrity with the works of Chateaubriand, Thierry, Guizot and Mignet and who reached their *apogée* with Michelet, Quinet and Tocqueville is very varied. 1848 forms the natural break. It was then that Chateaubriand died and that the blind Thierry (whose *Récits des temps mérovingiens* had been published between 1833 and 1840) ceased to write. Louis Blanc, Michelet and Quinet were soon exiled. Guizot, like Thiers and eventually Tocqueville, suffered a personal and political exile from within France which brought him back to the writing of historical works.

All these historians were fervently conscious of the importance of history. They knew about scholarship, but they were immensely ambitious, voraciously eclectic, and determined to make history play its role in the life of the French nation which dominated their preoccup-ations. But they were also varied. If the distance between Michelet and Tocqueville as historians is great, the distance between Guizot and Tocqueville at times seems slight. Yet politically speaking each of the three was vastly different from the other.

It is inevitable that it should be Michelet who should be thought of as closest to the poets and novelists of his time, since it was he who most emphatically achieved a synthesis of literature with science and social consciousness. But it is appropriate that even Michelet should have remained essentially a historian, conscious of the exigences of his craft. In his exile at Nervi he looked back to the excitements of *Hernani* and to the development of 'le romantisme effaré', as he called it. He found a great deal of noise, but little in the way of ideas or creation or reality. 'Je plantai dès lors ma tente à part, ou plutôt contre toute cette littérature.'

But Michelet underestimated the manner in which his writings can be compared to those of the writers of whom he disapproved. He also, like other historians, failed to see the impression that history made in the real world. Here it is wiser to take Tocqueville as one's guide. When, in his *Souvenirs*, he recalled the great days of February 1848, with the duchesse d'Orléans in the Chamber of Deputies pleading that her nine-year old son should be declared the rightful king of France, he wrote:

Nos Français, surtout à Paris, mêlent volontiers les souvenirs de la littérature et du théâtre à leurs manifestations les plus sérieuses; cela fait souvent croire que les sentiments qu'ils montrent sont faux, tandis qu'ils ne sont que maladroitement ornés. Ici, l'imitation fut si visible que la terrible originalité des faits en demeurait cachée. C'était le temps où toutes les imaginations étaient barbouillées par les grosses couleurs que Lamartine venait de répandre sur ses *Girondins*. Les hommes de la première révolution étaient vivants dans tous les esprits, leurs actes et leurs mots présents à toutes les mémoires. Tout ce que je vis ce jour-là porte la visible empreinte de ces souvenirs; il me semblait toujours qu'on fût occupé à jouer la Révolution française plus encore qu'à la continuer.

BIBLIOGRAPHY

The history of the study of history in France in the first half of the nineteenth century is to be found in several excellent works. Perhaps the best known is by Louis Halphen, *L'Histoire en France depuis cent ans* (A. Colin, 1914), and perhaps the most incisive is by Pierre Moreau, *L'Histoire en France au XIXe siècle: état des travaux et esquisse d'un plan d'études* (Études Françaises, Cahier 35, Les Belles Lettres, 1935). Georges Lefebvre, himself one of the greatest of French historians, lectured on the subject at the Sorbonne, during the academic year 1945–6, and his lectures have been published, with an introduction by Guy Palmade, under the title *La Naissance de l'historiographie moderne* (A. Colin, 1971) (they are primarily concerned with France). Camille Jullian published an anthology of French historians in *Extraits des historiens français au XIX siècle* (Hachette, 1896) with a long introduction entitled 'Notes sur l'histoire de France au XIX siècle' which has recently been reprinted as an independent publication (Paris–Geneva, Ressources, 1979). Although he is more concerned with the period after 1850, Charles-Olivier Carbonnel, *Histoire et Historiens: Une mutation idéologique des historiens français* (Toulouse, Privat, 1976) has many interesting things to say about the writing of history in France, whilst B. Reizov, *L'historiographie romantique française 1815–1830* (Moscow, undated) is disappointing. Stanley Mellon, *The Political Uses of History: A Study of Historians in the French Revolution* (Stanford University Press, 1958) and Jacques Barzun, 'Romantic Historiography as a Political Force in France', *Journal of the History of Ideas*, 11 (June 1941), both study special aspects of the subject.

Historians

On individual historians there are many good specialised books. For Chateaubriand there are two studies which are still valuable although they were written a long time ago: A. Dollinger, *Les Études historiques de Chateaubriand* (Les Belles Lettres, 1932), and Marie-Jeanne Durry, *La Vieillesse de Chateaubriand* (2 vols., Le Divan, 1933). Thierry has been studied more recently by Rulon Nephi Smithson, *Augustin Thierry: Social and Political Consciousness in the Evolution of a Historical Method* (Geneva, Droz, 1973), and before that by Kieran Joseph Carroll, *Some Aspects of the Historical Thought of Augustin Thierry (1795–1856)* (Washington, DC, Catholic University of America Press, 1951).

For Guizot one should consult Ch. Pouthas, *Guizot pendant la Restauration* (Plon, 1923); Douglas Johnson, *Guizot: Aspects of French History 1787–1874* (London and Toronto, Routledge and Kegan Paul, 1963); and the session devoted to Guizot's historical writings in the meetings which were held to commemorate the centenary of his death in *Actes du Colloque François Guizot 22–25 octobre 1974* (Société de l'Histoire du Protestantisme Français, 1976). The principal speakers were Charles-Olivier Carbonell, Olivier Lutaud, René Rémond and Michel Richard.

On Michelet there has been a tremendous literature, and Michelet studies have been reinvigorated by the complete edition of his works which is being published by Flammarion in Paris, under the general editorship of Paul Viallaneix. It is he who has written *La Voie royale* (Flammarion, 1959, new edition 1971) which is a study of the idea of *le peuple* in Michelet's work. Gabriel Monod, *La Vie et la Pensée de Jules Michelet* (2 vols., Champion, 1923), remains a classic, but Lucien Febvre, *Michelet* (Geneva, Les Trois Collines, 1946) and Roland Barthes, *Michelet par lui-même* (Seuil, 1954) have more recently become classics. There was a special number of the *Revue d'histoire littéraire de la France*, vol. 74 (September–October 1974) devoted to Michelet, as was *L'Arc*, no. 52 (1973). J.-L. Cornuz, *Jules Michelet, un aspect de la pensée religieuse du XIX siècle* (Geneva, Droz, 1955), and José Cabanis, *Michelet, le prêtre et la femme* (Gallimard, 1978) are more specialised studies.

Mignet is the subject of an excellent thesis by Yvonne Knibiehler, *Naissance des sciences humaines: Mignet et l'histoire philosophique au XIXe siècle* (Flammarion, 1973), but, whilst there have been many studies of Tocqueville as a political thinker and as a sociologist, one still awaits a study of him as a historian. His *Œuvres complètes*, the definitive edition, edited by J.P. Mayer, which has been published by Gallimard since 1951, contains all his historical writings and will include all his correspondence.

IX · *The visual arts*

WILLIAM VAUGHAN

A NEW TYPE OF ARTIST

'Ungrateful fatherland, you shan't have my work!' These words are uttered by a painter in a cartoon by the great French graphic artist Honoré Daumier (illustration 5). The print itself shows the unfortunate man in the process of destroying his 'masterpiece' after it had been sent for exhibition and been rejected. There had been pictures of poor and unsuccessful artists before this time. But never had they expressed the arrogance and self-destructive disdain manifested here. What Daumier has captured is the image of a new kind of artist, the 'Bohemian'. Unkempt, contemptuous of the materialism of the bourgeoisie, he is fundamentally at odds with the society in which he lives, and sees himself as possessing superior values to it.

We are so familiar with this image of the artist, that we sometimes forget that it does not reach back further than the Romantic period. Before that time painters were less insistent on their uniqueness and the elevated nature of their vision. Like other highly skilled professionals, they were more concerned with achieving the status of gentlemen.

This change in the view of the artist did not originate in France. It can be found already in Germany in the 1770s, amongst members of the *Sturm und Drang* movement. Not long after, it emerged in England, personified by William Blake. The French were not innovators in this matter. But what they did do was bring a sense of permanence to it, turning scattered occurrences into a tradition. The individual rebels and breakaway groups in England and Germany had no immediate followers. In France, on the other hand, they led to the establishment of an ongoing avant-garde. The Bohemia of Romantics became that of the Realists, and then of all the other movements and 'ism's that followed.

It is difficult to give a precise account for why this should have happened. Yet there are a number of important factors that appear to have contributed to it. The first is that 'official' art received far greater support from the government in France than it did elsewhere in Europe.

Ever since the time of Louis XIV the upper echelons of the French art world had been carefully monitored by the State. The key institution in this system was the Academy of the Fine Arts. This body controlled the education of artists through its own school and through the *Prix de Rome,* the prize that provided the means for an artist to complete his training in Rome. It also regulated the public exhibition of pictures through its biennial show, the Salon. At one time, indeed, in the 1780s, artists were prevented from showing their works in any other place.[1]

During the middle years of the eighteenth century the rule of the Academy had been relatively benign. However it tightened its grip again

5. Honoré Daumier, *'Ingrate patrie, tu n'auras pas mon œuvre!'*

in the later eighteenth century, partly as a result of the desire of reformers to restore positive government in France. After the Revolution of 1789 the system was temporarily disrupted. But it was reinstated in all its essentials by Napoleon, and strongly reinforced by the Bourbon government after the Restoration of the monarchy in 1814. Undoubtedly an important reason for this was the desire to foster a form of 'official' art that would either be overtly propagandist or would support a sense of hierarchy and order. In the early years of the Restoration monarchy there was a vast programme of government commissions for historical and devotional pictures supporting the legitimacy of the Bourbon dynasty and the authority of the Catholic church.[2]

However, it was precisely in this period that tension began to build up between the interests of artists and the requirements of the State. In the pre-Revolutionary period the status of artists had been such that they were less inclined to question the judgments of those who patronised them, particularly if they happened – as was most often the case – to be royalty, or members of the aristocracy. During the Revolutionary period such traditional patronage had vanished and the artists found themselves – like other members of professional and artisan classes – more their own masters. Their patrons tended now to come increasingly from the bourgeoisie, from a section of society which they regarded as their equal. After the Restoration this situation persisted. Even though royalty and aristocracy returned once more into the field of patronage, they no longer held the same kind of authority.

This situation not only led artists to adopt less obedient attitudes to their patrons, it also encouraged them to rely increasingly on uncommissioned work, for which they would endeavour to find purchasers by means of public exhibition. It is revealing that the number of artists who made use of the Salon to exhibit their works increased rapidly during the early years of the nineteenth century. The historian Benoit showed that between 1791 and 1812 the number of exhibitors at the Salon rose from 166 to 430.[3] This tendency was to intensify, and the pressure for exhibition became such that, in 1830, the Salon changed from being a biennial to an annual event.

The artist became a man of greater independence, and as he did so, he became as well a man of greater intellectual pretensions. Malcolm Easton has pointed out that this was the period when the visual artist began to feel himself on a par with the writer – something that would never have been tolerated amongst the *philosophes* of the Enlightenment.[4] It is symptomatic of this change that the artist should begin to make his area of habitation in Paris in the *quartier latin*, that area around the Sorbonne that was the traditional haunt of scholars. It was in this area that the celebrated 'Bohemia' emerged, that state of life that became the subject of Henri Murger's *Scènes de la vie de Bohème* (1847–9). For the most part this was peopled by the casualties of the new independence, those artists who had sought to address the world in the new, liberated manner, and found no audience. If all outsider artists had simply been people with no talent the situation would not have been so explosive. But often they were artists who were excluded from the Salon because they had moved too far away from the conformist norms that the Academy still tried to maintain. Ultimately it was the continued presence of this norm that was to keep the alternative tradition, that of the disaffected artist, alive.

A NEW TYPE OF ART?

On the face of it, it might seem a simple matter to make a correlation between the disaffected Bohemian artist, full of his originality and genius, and a new 'Romantic' style of painting. Certainly it is easy enough to show that the more painterly manner that began to be adopted by a growing number of French artists in the early years of the nineteenth century was associated with those outside official circles. In the 1820s critics and commentators commonly characterised 'classic' artists as those who conformed to academic standards and painted in a severe, dispassionate manner, and 'Romantics' as the rebels who sought to overthrow the existing aesthetic order and paint impassioned, unregulated pictures. But the more closely these identifications are examined, the less satisfactory they appear. Delacroix, the most extreme of the 'painterly' artists (artists, that is, who emphasise the more sensuous qualities of paint, its colour, richness and texture) was frowned upon by the Academy; but he was no Bohemian. He was elitist and conservative in his outlook, and received an impressive amount of state patronage. Furthermore, there were Bohemian artists who worked in a meticulous and detailed manner more commonly associated with classicism.

A further complexity emerges in the apparent lack of correlation between the painterly 'Romantic' style and the types of emotive and exotic subject matter normally regarded as Romantic. The painter Ingres, who was considered to be a bastion of classicism, and painted in a precise linear manner, regularly depicted medieval and exotic subjects. Conversely Delacroix would frequently paint scenes from classical antiquity.

It is perhaps more fruitful to look upon Romanticism as opening up a new series of possibilities which were explored in different ways by different artists. Once again the common characteristic would seem to be individualism. Just as the artist was asserting greater independence in his career and way of life, so he was manifesting greater individualism in his work. To some extent the growth in the practice of exhibiting pictures encouraged such a development. For it was necessary for an artist's work to have a clearly identifiable persona to be recognised and appreciated in the public market-place of the Salon.

However, the variety of choices made by artists in this period should not lead to the assumption that anarchy prevailed: rather it points to a complex network of considered choices. Nor should this complexity lead to an abdication of the discussion of the problem of pictorial style. The growing habit in recent years of categorising the art of the period thematically is illuminating in many respects. But if taken too far, it can endanger the understanding of the new modes of perception that were developing in the Romantic era. Romanticism in pictures was not simply a case of the illustration of certain themes and attitudes. It also involved a rethinking of the whole nature of the visual arts. Greater emphasis was placed on qualities regarded as innately pictorial – on colour, texture, and the enigmatic, symbolic potential of imagery. Such changes can be found even amongst the non-painterly artists of the period. One of the features that distinguishes the work of Ingres from that of his classical predecessors is the extent of the part which colour and texture play in his pictures, and the degree to which these manifest linear rhythms, distorted forms and other devices that emphasise the two-dimensional nature of the surface on which they are depicted.

This concern for the essential pictorial nature of the visual arts was preceded by the development of a new theoretical position. This was the notion of the autonomy of art, the idea that art appealed on its own account and not for any associations that it might have with other interests. Eventually this was to lead to the doctrine of 'art for art's sake' adopted by such aesthetes as Théophile Gautier after 1830. It did not originate in France. It came from Germany, where it was first authoritatively expounded by Immanuel Kant in his *Critique of Pure Reason* (1790), and was popularised by the critic A.W. Schlegel and others. The popularised version came to France via Mme de Staël's *De l'Allemagne*. Later the French philosopher Victor Cousin was to explore its implications in a more profound manner. But Mme de Staël remains the most accessible source for the layman. Significantly it was her book that Delacroix referred to when discussing the nature of painting in his journal in 1824: 'Je retrouve justement dans Mme de Staël le développement de mon idée sur la peinture. Cet art, ainsi que la musique, *sont au-dessus de la pensée*; de là leur avantage sur la littérature, par le vague.'[5]

In fact, as with the notion of the artist as independent genius, one finds that the theoretical and practical exposition of a new pictorial practice is largely imported from abroad. The theory of 'art for art's sake' was inspired by the example of German philosophy. The development of a more spontaneous, painterly and direct manner was inspired by English artists, particularly such painters as Constable, Lawrence, Turner and Wilkie. But once again these elements became developed in France into something more consistent and probing. Romantic painting may not have originated in France, but it was in France that it was explored most extensively and became incorporated into a tradition. Constable and Turner had no immediate followers in England. In France, on the other hand, the explorations of Delacroix were to provide a stimulus for the Impressionists and for many subsequent groups.

This relating of Romanticism to a tradition can be seen in the continuing prestige of history painting during the period. History painting – the representation of great men at great moments – was the form of art considered to be of the highest importance by the Academy. It was also the form of art that was most assiduously supported by the State – often because of its propaganda potential.

It would be misleading to suggest that official support for history painting led to the exclusion of all other art. In fact history painters were at all times in a minority. A glance at any Salon *livret* – or catalogue – will show that most of the pictures exhibited there were of a less ambitious kind. They were portraits, views, domestic scenes, still-life paintings. But the point is that it was the history painter who received the prestigious treatment. His works were discussed first and most extensively by the critics. He was the person who would receive large state commissions and the rewards and honours that accompanied them. There was only one way for a French painter of the early nineteenth century to reach the top of his profession, and that was by making his name with some grand historical picture. For the French Romantics this was the type of art around which the battle was principally to be fought. The picture that effectively launched the movement – Géricault's *Radeau de la Méduse* (illustration 11) – was as vast and heroic in its style as anything produced by his classical predecessors. Delacroix – the central figure in French Romantic art – remained a history painter first and foremost throughout his life.

However, if the French Romantics did not abandon the genre of

6. J.-L. David, *Le Serment des Horaces*

history painting, they did subvert its principles. In their hands it was no longer a vehicle for representing public virtues in a clear and idealised manner. It became instead a means for conveying more complex and private emotions, often questioning rather than reinforcing conventional morals.

The different ways in which this occurred will, it is hoped, become clearer in the latter part of this chapter when individual cases are discussed. At this point, however, it will perhaps help to underline the distinction by making a comparison.

Undoubtedly the most celebrated classical history painting of the period preceding the Romantics was (and still is) David's *Le Serment des Horaces* (illustration 6). This picture – the outcome of a government commission – shows three Romans swearing to fight to the death in the defence of their country. Painted in 1784 it reflected and helped inflame the mood of strengthening resolve that was to precipitate the Revolution five years later. The picture is a highly emotive one. The raised arms of the brave warriors create a climax of excitement which is contrasted to the sorrow of the wilting female relatives in the background. But despite this, the emotion is not allowed to get out of hand. The warriors are subjugating their private feeling to reason. They are prepared to lay down their lives for the good of their country. Their nobility and resolve are intimated by the clear and spartan appearance of the picture. Even the spatial structure seems to bear out the message. The scene takes place in a box-like courtyard, set against three simple arches. It is clear, logical and direct.

Nothing could be further from this forceful argument in favour of public virtue than Delacroix's *La Mort de Sardanapale* (illustration 7). Exhibited at the Salon in 1827 it was one of the most notorious of all Romantic paintings; so notorious in fact that he was warned by the government of the day not to paint anything of a similar kind again if he wished to receive any further state commissions. Vast in scale and classical in its subject-matter, *Sardanapale* conformed to the format of traditional history painting. Yet its message was anything but heroic. It shows the ancient Assyrian King (whose name has become a byword for luxury and self-indulgence) at the end of his tyrannical rule. As his palace is broken into by insurgents (just visible in the top right-hand section of the picture) he is committing suicide by having himself burned on a pyre together with his goods, slaves and concubines. Delacroix has not only chosen a subject of dubious morality. He has also represented it in a way that emphasises its senselessness and barbarism. He has made a feature of the struggling protesting concubine who is being stabbed by a slave in the foreground. The confusion of the incident is brought out by the violent, clashing colours and the ambiguous space that seems to cause the figures to tumble out towards us. The only moment of calm in the picture is that provided by the form of Sardanapalus himself. He reclines on his bed regarding the carnage with what appears to be total indifference.

While history painting in the grand manner remained the dominant art form in France during the Romantic era, there were a number of other forms which began to assume a greater importance. Alongside the grand history painting there developed the small-scale intimate representation of domestic moments from the past. Such pictures were concerned less with the teaching of moral lessons than with providing an evocation of the sense of a historical period. They built upon that nostalgia for the past so keenly felt at the time, and catered for in the novels of Walter Scott and his followers. Delacroix painted many such

7. E. Delacroix, *La Mort de Sardanapale*

small-scale historical genre pieces, as did his associate the Anglo-French painter Bonington (illustration 14). Another related development was the growing importance given to the painting of scenes from contemporary life. Géricault did this most challengingly by depicting topical events on a scale normally considered appropriate only for heroic historical themes. However it was left to a later generation – that of Courbet and the Realists – to follow his lead and make the large-scale painting of contemporary and domestic subjects a central issue in French art.

The fascination with exploring a wider range of moods and experiences affected the interpretation of the 'lesser' genres as well. Those types of art which had traditionally been looked down upon for merely copying nature and having no 'subject' – such as portraiture, animal painting and landscape – now took on a growing importance. For they seemed capable of conveying experience in a direct and compelling manner.

Portraiture had always been a widely practised art since the time of the Renaissance. But in the Romantic period its traditional roles of purveying official images and recording the features of well-to-do individuals became supplemented by the desire to record moods and emotions. There emerged a fashion for portraying figures revealing their feelings – as in the case of Girodet's portrait of the writer Chateaubriand meditating in unkempt state before the ruins of Rome (1808; Saint-Malo, Musée). At times this was simply a matter of posturing, but it could also lead to the most moving of studies – notably the portraits of insane people in the grip of their obsessions by Géricault (illustration 12). In animal painting – notably in the works of Géricault, Delacroix and Horace Vernet – there developed a taste for wild and ferocious themes. Partly this was an interest in the exploration of the extremes of nature, and partly an interest in finding in the behaviour of animals analogues for the sensory and instinctive side of human personality.

Both these developments were peculiar to the Romantic period. But the change in attitudes towards landscape painting was to have more far-reaching consequences. Like the portrayal of contemporary life, it was to become a type of painting more fully developed by the Realists. As with portraiture and animal painting, the stimulus for a growing interest in landscape painting in France appears to have been the vivid treatment of such subjects by the English. There had been, it is true, a glorious tradition of landscape painting in France. In the mid eighteenth century the vivid and dramatic scenes of Claude-Joseph Vernet had been the most celebrated in Europe. But during the neo-classical period the genre had been subjected to a sterner discipline and also to a loss of status. With the success of such English artists as Constable and Bonington in France in the 1820s, landscape painting began to take on new significance as a means of exploring the moods of nature. It was in this period that landscapists of the stature of Corot and Rousseau emerged in France.

So far the discussion of Romantic art has been undertaken almost exclusively in terms of painting. This is because painting was the visual art form most extensively affected by Romanticism. The reason for this would seem to lie in the innate qualities of painting – its concern with colour, effects of light and shade, textures, the potential for evoking vast spaces. Certainly the theorists of Romantic art – from A.W. Schlegel in 1802 to Théophile Gautier in 1866[6] – held painting to be the visual art most compatible with Romanticism on account of its vivid and evocative properties. Sculpture, by contrast, was the least Romantic. Dealing with the realisation of form it was considered to be quintessentially classical. It would be a mistake to set too much store by the pronouncements of theorists. But it is certainly noticeable that sculptors of the period had greater problems in abandoning the dominance of classical forms than did the painters. Only in the field of animal sculpture – where there were relatively few prototypes from antiquity – can this be said to have been fully achieved. For the rest Romanticism rarely went beyond the illustration of 'Romantic' themes using classically inspired figures.

The graphic arts – as might be expected – followed more closely the situation in painting. A number of technical developments – notably the invention of lithography[7] – enabled the introduction of more painterly effects into the production of prints (illustration 5). Both lithography and wood engraving – another innovation of the period[8] – allowed for the production of cheaper and more rapidly executed prints. As a result illustration was able to play a full part in the vast expansion in publishing during the period. The illustrated journal became a commonplace, and illustrations were more frequent in books of all kinds. Graphic artists therefore found themselves in a position to engage increasingly in the depiction of contemporary events and of contemporary literature. The careers of such figures as Raffet – the illustrator of Napoleonic subjects – and Daumier grew out of this situation. It is also noticeable that many painters – for example Géricault and Delacroix – made use of the technique of lithography, with its potential for spontaneous and painterly effect, to illustrate literary and contemporary subjects.

The position in architecture is more problematic. It can certainly be shown how Romanticism affected its practice in a number of ways. While classically derived forms remained the norm in French architecture throughout this period, they became more floreate and decorative. One striking development in this direction was the experimentation with polychromy by the architect Hittorf.[9] This was a revealing event, not only because it suggested a revision of classicism in the direction of more pictorial effects – something that can be seen in classical painting and sculpture of the period – but also because it showed a new concern for archaeological exactitude. Hittorf pioneered the use of colour in classical buildings because it had been discovered that such colour actually had been used on Ancient Greek buildings. He became less concerned with the following of a timeless classical norm, than in imitating a precise historical event. With this shift the whole basis of classicism was in effect undermined. It was being replaced in architecture as elsewhere with historicism, with the resurrection of the styles of past periods in order to evoke the characteristics of those periods. Gradually the range of historical styles emulated expanded to include Renaissance and medieval forms, though this never occurred to the extent that it did in England, where a full-scale gothic revival got under way. In France the gothic revival was a small and feeble affair. Only in the field of archaeological reconstruction did it really flourish. This was particularly the case with the brilliant restoration of Notre-Dame in Paris and other medieval monuments by Viollet-le-duc. It is significant that in the discussion of Romanticism in architecture in the Larousse dictionary of 1869 only archaeological reconstructions were mentioned.[10]

In all these fields, therefore, there is a slowness and caution in the adoption of Romantic attitudes and practices in France that contrasts with the relatively precipitate action that can be found in England and Germany in the early nineteenth century. It is probably true to say that the French Romantics were not so much seeking to overthrow a tradition as to revitalise it, to save French culture from the dead hand of academicism and restore its relevance to contemporary experience. This would certainly seem to have been the opinion of Delacroix when he gave the following definition of Romanticism to his friend the landscape painter Paul Huet: 'Le romantisme fut une réaction contre l'école, un appel à la liberté de l'art, un retour vers une tradition plus large: on voulut rendre justice à toutes les grandes époques, même à David.'[11]

THE CLASSICAL TRADITION

Delacroix's genuine admiration for the art of David emphasises that the Romantics had no quarrel with the art of the arch-classicist in itself. Their objection was to mindlessly repeating its formulae in an age for which it no longer had a relevance. Their opposition was directed towards the pupils of David who seemed to be engaged in this activity. And one of the few things that they held against David was the accusation that his method of training had destroyed his pupils' individuality. As Clément, the biographer of Géricault, wrote: 'David avait coulé ses élèves dans un moule uniforme.'[12]

When one looks at the variety of art produced by these followers, one might doubt whether this was in fact the case. There does not, after all, seem to be much of the 'uniform mould' about the bravura of Gros (illustration 8), the bizarre fantasies of Girodet, or the subtle archaism of Ingres (illustration 9). In fact there seems to be about as much to distinguish the work of these artists from each other as there is to separate out the works of the Romantics of the 1820s. But it is true to say there had been a change of attitude. For the earlier generation of artists there was still the notion of conforming to a classical norm; whilst for the later generation individualism was the key word. Furthermore, by the 1820s the pupils of David were closing ranks, trying to emphasise the conformity in their art in the face of the new school that was threatening to undermine their world. Thus Gros – whose early works were inspiring the Romantics to explore more colourful and exotic effects – was constantly insisting upon the norms of Davidian classicism to his students. 'It is not me who is speaking to you', he would tell them. 'It's David, David, always David.'[13]

ART OF THE EMPIRE

As Gros's example suggests, the pupils of David had in fact been exploring a kind of proto-Romanticism in the early years of the century. It was a tendency much encouraged by Napoleon after his meteoric rise to power. Politically he had inherited the impetus of the French Revolution, but now sought to confirm his position by aligning himself with traditional institutions, re-establishing Catholicism as the official religion of France in 1801 and crowning himself as Emperor in 1804. In the visual arts he favoured a similar modification, favouring a form of florid classicism that was capable of suggesting the dignity and grandeur of Empire without undermining a sense of classical values. In architecture this was provided by Percier and Fontaine, who devised and publicised a rich decorative style as well as carrying out many building works for the Emperor himself. The French sculptors of the period – Bosio, Chinard, Chaudet – also practised a decorative and senti- mentalised form of classicism which was much appreciated by members of Napoleon's court. In painting he encouraged David and his followers to paint in a direct heroic manner that would reinforce the virtues of his régime. This can be seen most strikingly in the large number of modern historical subjects he commissioned. David himself was chosen to celebrate the coronation ceremony. But the more exotic and dramatic events of Napoleon's military campaigns were entrusted to other artists who were prepared to compromise their classicism with a greater degree of bravura.

Undoubtedly the most successful of these was Antoine-Jean Gros (1771–1835), an artist who became something of a military expert after winning a competition in 1800 to paint a subject from Napoleon's Near East campaign, *Le Combat de Nazareth*. Over the next decade he was to paint five more large-scale scenes from Napoleon's wars, and then received a commission to decorate the Pantheon in Paris with patriotic themes.

8. A.-J. Gros, *Bonaparte visitant les pestiférés de Jaffa*

Although trained under David, Gros had subsequently developed a taste for such colouristic and dramatic artists as Titian and Rubens. In his Napoleonic scenes he took care to emphasise the exoticism of the subjects. His most celebrated pictures are *Les Pestiférés de Jaffa* (1804; illustration 8) which is set in a moorish style of building in Palestine, and *La Bataille d'Eylau* (1808; Louvre) which shows Napoleon and his troops in the frozen wastes of Northern Europe.

It is not hard to see why such pictures should have interested the Romantics so strongly. For not only do they exploit painterly effects, but they also show extremes of emotion and suffering. Yet they still differ from the works of the Romantics in their objectives. The strong emotional appeal in these pictures is used to reinforce, rather than subvert, authority. *Les Pestiférés de Jaffa* is a notorious example of this. It shows Napoleon visiting those of his troops who had succumbed to plague at one point in his Near Eastern campaign. Much emphasis is given to the lurid depiction of sufferers in the foreground. But the main point of the picture is the action of Napoleon, who is courageously visiting the plague house and is fearlessly touching the wounds of one –

a gesture that conjures up the image of Christ as healer. He is the bringer of hope and order in a distressed world. As in any classical history painting, he occupies the centre of the stage in a clearly defined area. There are no spatial ambiguities in the picture. Everything is organised according to a well-established hierarchy.

Such works were intended as propaganda statements. In private, Napoleon was able to accommodate more complex manifestations of Romantic sensibility. The love of the primitive, medievalism, wild nature and melancholy all occur in works painted for his court circle and for his private house at Malmaison. Once again such sentiments stayed within well-defined limits. As can be seen from his treatment of the writers Chateaubriand and Mme de Staël, he would not tolerate any art form that might seem to be subverting his authority. In the case of the fine artists he had nothing to fear. Only Anne-Louis Girodet (1767–1824) came anywhere near using his art for critical purposes; and he was never so foolish as to make Napoleon the target for one of his attacks. Even before the Empire Girodet had built up a reputation for exotic themes. One of his earliest pictures *Le Sommeil d'Endymion* (1792; Louvre) shows strong mystical and erotic tendencies in the way it treats the classical legend of the shepherd boy who was beloved by the moon goddess. During the Empire he painted disaster scenes, such as the *Scène de Déluge* (1806; Louvre) and subjects from fashionable writers – notably Chateaubriand's *Les Funérailles d'Atala* (1808; Louvre). An awkward moment occurred when Girodet exhibited his portrait of the disgraced Chateaubriand in 1810 (Saint-Malo, Musée). But Napoleon passed it off with a remark that the melancholy and unkempt author looked 'like a conspirator who had just crawled down a chimney'.[14] Before this time Girodet had pandered to Napoleon's own fantasies. For his house at Malmaison he had painted a fantasia based on the Emperor's favourite author, Ossian. Ossian – the fictive Celtic bard whose poetic works had been forged by the Scot Macpherson in 1762–3 – enjoyed an enormous success in France at that time. Its combination of Nordic, wild subject-matter with the classical structure of a Homeric epic seemed perfectly suited to the tastes of the Empire. For Napoleon the simplistic descriptions of heroic deeds and strong sentiments proved irresistible. He commissioned several artists to paint Ossianic subjects for him. Girodet, however, was the only one who brought the covert identification of the French Emperor with the mythic bard's world. His picture showed modern French generals – the fallen of the Revolutionary wars – being received into heaven by Ossian.

Gros's pictures appear to graft exotic pictorial effects on to a classical structure. Girodet seems to proceed from the opposite principle, for his wild and fantastic themes are clothed in a meticulously smooth surface. Curiously, despite his attempts to suggest ethereal and dramatic light effects, he showed little interest in colour or textures, and from this point of view his firm, rounded forms could almost be classical statues. An artist who was close to Girodet in this respect, as well as in his willingness to portray fashionable, literary subject-matter was François Gérard (1770–1837). Gérard's manner was softer and more flattering than Girodet's. Appropriately he became exceedingly successful as a portrait painter. He combined both kinds of expertise in his portrait of Mme de Staël in the role of her heroine, *Corinne au Cap Misène* (1819; Lyons), for the authoress's admirer Prince Auguste of Prussia.

All these artists could be described as producing modifications of Davidian classicism. There was only one major artist at work at the time who could be considered to have provided an alternative. This was Pierre-Paul Prud'hon (1758–1823), an artist who had never been a student of David's. Prud'hon's artistic heroes were the high Renaissance artists Leonardo and Correggio. His own work developed from them a soft and poignant treatment of light effects. A favourite painter of the Empress Josephine, he portrayed her seated in a melancholic pose before a stream (Louvre), endowing the work with a moving sensibility that seems to penetrate beyond fashionable effect. Even in his public works Prud'hon pursued his particular brand of poignant feeling. His most famous work, *La Justice et la Vengeance poursuivant le Crime* (1808; Louvre), which was painted for the Cour Criminelle of the Palais de Justice, uses gloomy light-effects to convey the horror of the subject. Yet once again the sentiments of the picture fall within the bounds of conventional morality. For there is no doubt about the guilt of the criminal or the rightness of the vengeance being visited upon him.

'LES PRIMITIFS'

Prud'hon's art was different, but it was not sufficiently forceful to present a serious challenge to the Davidian school. The strongest challenge came in fact from within the master's camp, from a generation of students younger than those already considered, who were coming to maturity around 1800. This was a group who were known as 'Les Primitifs'. As their name suggests they advocated adhering to an even more rigorous form of classicism than David himself. Their leader, Maurice Quai, was by all accounts a charismatic figure. Dressing in Grecian robes he immersed himself in the world of Homer. His other passion, revealingly, was Ossian. For although the *Primitifs* advocated the emulation of Grecian art, they saw the primitive as a universal virtue to be found in all archaic societies.

The little work by Quai which survives suggests he was an indifferent painter. He seems to have belonged to a new brand of artists – typical of the Romantic era and soon to be found in abundance in 'Bohemia' – whose ideas outstripped their performance. His name would probably not have been remembered at all had he not affected the work of a number of artists of more tangible talents, notably Jean-Auguste-Dominique Ingres (1780–1867).

Ingres has become so well known for his defence of classicism against Romanticism that it is necessary to remind oneself that he performed this function only in the latter part of his life. During the Empire he was the most radical and deviant of artists, and the brilliantly inventive archaic manner that he devised was to remain the mainspring of his art throughout his life.

Ingres's earliest success was *Les Ambassadeurs d'Agamemnon*, (Paris, École des Beaux-Arts) with which he won the *Prix de Rome* in 1801. It shows a concern for two-dimensional rhythm – based on the study of Greek vase paintings – that was far more 'primitive' than anything attempted by David. In the succeeding years his art began to show as well the impact of gothic art. In this he was following the rapid developments taking place in the taste for the primitive. With Napoleon's restoration of Catholicism, the publication of Chateaubriand's *Génie du christianisme* (1802) and the establishment of the Empire, the medieval past took on a new significance. It became an age in which French culture was felt to be rooted, and was venerated as such. The Empress Josephine was particularly interested in this cult, and favoured those artists who started to paint medieval scenes in a minute manner based upon illuminated manuscripts, notably Fleury Richard (1777–1852). The development of the medieval cult was greatly aided by the presence of the Museum of French Monuments that had been set up by the National Assembly in 1790 and which, under the inspired directorship of the artist Alexandre Lenoir, had gathered together medieval monuments pillaged from churches by the Revolutionaries. Added to this was the vast collection of art works gathered together by Napoleon as a result of his campaigns, which included medieval works from Italy and Flanders, including Van Eyck's masterpiece *The Adoration of the Mystic Lamb*.

The taste for depicting scenes from the Middle Ages in a miniaturist manner gradually gained the nickname 'style troubadour'. It was to

9. J.-A.-D. Ingres, *Napoléon Ier sur le trône impérial*

survive into the Restoration period where it served equally well to reinforce the claims of the Bourbons. Ingres painted several 'style troubadour' scenes throughout his life, but this was far from being the full extent of his gothicism. For he was also looking closely at fifteenth-century painting and combining its qualities with those that he had adapted from the Greek art. This can be seen in his impressive portrait of *Napoléon Ier sur le trône impérial* (illustration 9). The image combines suggestions of the Greek god Zeus with reminiscences of God the Father in Van Eyck's *Adoration of the Mystic Lamb*. Together with the neo-classical concern for outline is a concern for texture and vivid colours. Above all, it suggests the primitive as a potent, living force – something that might well have pleased Napoleon.

In fact Ingres managed to bring the primitive alive in his art in a quite remarkable way. Perhaps it was because he was essentially an artist who relied upon direct observation. His most convincing works are usually his portraits and those works – like his paintings of nudes – which involved the depiction of real rather than imagined people and events. Later in the century Ingres was to be admired by many of the Realists for his precision and control. But in his early years there were few who attempted to follow his complex art. Perhaps this was partly because he was absent from France for eighteen crucial years between 1806 and 1824, living in Italy. When he returned he found the revolt of the Romantics in full swing. His subtle primitivism had been overtaken by more excessive forms of medievalism and sensuality. By contrast he now appeared a 'classic' and found himself falling into the position of the defender of academic norms.

THE RESTORATION

It was under the Restoration monarchy of Louis XVIII that a fully fledged Romantic movement came into being in France. In the visual arts this was preceded by a division of ranks, a separation of establishment and non-establishment artists. The Bourbons had every bit as much need of propagandist art as had Napoleon. The Salon of 1817 – the first to be held under the new régime – was full of pictures commissioned to show the good deeds of the family. The 'style troubadour' painters were much in evidence. Fleury Richard, for example, showed a picture demonstrating the benevolence of Louis XVI's sister, *Madame Élisabeth de France distribuant du lait* (Versailles). But other stalwarts of the Napoleonic court, such as Gros and Gérard, were also enlisted to support the renewed monarchy.

10. T. Géricault, *Portrait équestre d'un officier de chasseur à cheval*

Whether it was the case that these artists were now past their prime, or whether it was the case that they found it less easy to give the conviction to the celebration of their new master that they had to their old, the outcome was that these artists produced works that were on the whole lacklustre, and far more conformist than the works that they had painted in the Napoleonic period. But, at the same time that they were painting, there were artists on the fringe of the establishment who were producing new developments. In some cases these artists were outsiders for overt political reasons. In particular there were the Bonapartists. The most prominent of these was Horace Vernet (1789–1863), the painter of military scenes whose works were refused at the Salon of 1822 on account of their anti-monarchical leanings. His acquaintances included the illustrators N.-T. Charlet and D.-A.-M. Raffet who, like him, employed the new technique of lithography to celebrate the exploits of the *Grande Armée* in a vivid, forthright manner.

The very existence of these 'opposition' artists suggests the complexity of the new situation in France, where a restored monarchy had not in any way halted the growing power of the bourgeoisie or managed to suppress the discontent of the old supporters of the Emperor, or the liberals. Significantly Vernet and his circle were not at a loss for patrons. Vernet himself was supported by the Duke of Orleans, the man who, after the revolution of 1830, was to come to power as the 'bourgeois' monarch Louis-Philippe.

It was in the circle of Vernet that the most remarkable painting of the period was created, a picture that used the full resources of the grand historical manner to present a powerful and moving censure of the government, Géricault's *Radeau de la Méduse* (illustration 11).

THÉODORE GÉRICAULT

Unlike Vernet, Géricault (1791–1824) had no explicit political message. But he was committed to giving clear and sincere expression to the events of his age. In this sense he was a follower of David, and of the Gros of Napoleonic times. In fact he intensified the modernity of these artists, for he rarely depicted anything that was not a contemporary subject. Coming to maturity during the last years of the Empire he had trained first under Carle Vernet – the father of Horace – an animal painter who was producing celebrations of Napoleonic battles at the time. From this artist he acquired the taste for dramatic modernity. His next master, the history painter Guérin, instructed him in the rudiments of painting in the grand manner. Such expertise was to be crucial to him in the preparation of his masterpiece.

Géricault's first exhibited works already demonstrate his brilliance and his ability to choose themes of telling topicality. His *Portrait équestre d'un officier de chasseur à cheval* (illustration 10) was exhibited in the year that Napoleon marched on Moscow. It surpasses all other military portraits of the period in its evocation of action. The turning movement of the officer and the rearing horse reintroduced a sense of dynamic energy that had been absent since the days of the seventeenth-century masters of the Baroque. The vivid reds and subtle atmospherics convey a mood that is heroic, but fraught with danger. Two years later Géricault was to provide a pendant for this work, the *Cuirassier blessé quittant le feu* (Louvre). Exhibited in 1814, it was the perfect image for a country that had just lost a war. The fire and action of the previous work has been replaced by sombre, leaden tones and restrained forms. It is hardly surprising that the early work was greatly praised and the later sternly condemned by the critics. They complained at its lack of colour and the fact that it had inflated a 'genre' subject to the scale of a history painting. They did not wish the defeat of France to be treated as a serious matter.

It was five years before Géricault exhibited another picture – his celebrated *Radeau de la Méduse*. During this period he was constantly working towards the production of a grand heroic work. Going to Rome in 1816 – partly to complete his artistic education and partly to escape from a destructive liaison with the young wife of his uncle – he toyed for a time with depicting the popular 'Race of the Riderless Horses' that took place annually in the *corso*. However, when he returned to France he lost interest in the project, perhaps because of its lack of topicality. His second choice of theme 'The Fualdes Affair', certainly had that quality. It was based on the story of the murder of a former Napoleonic provincial magistrate by what was suspected to have been a royalist gang. This theme certainly suggests the influence of the circle of Horace Vernet which he was now frequenting. In the end, however, he seems to have felt that the subject was too specific and partisan. It lacked the epic dimensions, the pitting of man against fate and nature, that the story of the raft of the Medusa could provide.

The story of the shipwreck of the Medusa had even more serious political implications than the Fualdes affair, for it suggested government incompetence. The *Méduse*, flagship of a convoy carrying French soldiers and settlers to the colony of Senegal, had run aground off West Africa, largely as a result of the ineptitude of the captain, a returned royalist *émigré*. As there had been insufficient lifeboats, 149 men and one woman were forced to board a makeshift raft, which it was intended would be towed by the lifeboats. However, the crews of these, in their eagerness to reach the shore, cut the raft adrift. There followed fifteen

11. T. Géricault, *Le Radeau de la Méduse*

days of terrors, which included mutiny, cannibalism and a bitter moment of false hope at the sighting of a ship from their convoy, the *Argus*, which failed to notice them. When the raft was eventually found by the *Argus*, only fifteen of the 150 were still alive. At first the government tried to cover the whole incident up, but two of the survivors – who had been dismissed from government service when they applied for compensation – published an account of the disastrous event, which became a sensation throughout Europe.

Géricault's choice of such a theme suggests an audaciousness previously not encountered in visual artists in France. It was a gesture magnified by the scale on which he made it; for the picture itself is vast and is treated in the grand heroic style of the history painting. Normally such pictures would only have been commissioned by the government itself – or would have been bought for the State on exhibition.

Yet the picture should not be seen primarily as an anti-government gesture. For Géricault is more interested in the incident as a human tragedy. When exhibited, the picture was simply described as the scene of a shipwreck, without any reference to the *Méduse*. He wished it to have a universal relevance, to question fundamental assumptions about experience. Its true subversiveness lay in the way it undermined the notion of history painting as the celebration of positive moral action. There are no heroes in the *Méduse*, only sufferers. The unfortunates on the raft are victims of circumstances beyond their control for which they were in no way responsible. The disaster that had led to their shipwreck had been the fault of their incompetent captain. Furthermore, the picture offers no hope of relief. The crescendo of forms culminates in the man waving his shirt to attract the attention of a distant ship. But it is evident that no one in that ship would be able to see anything as small and low in the water as this raft. Géricault did in fact deliberately choose to represent the moment in the ghastly saga when the *Argus* passed the raft at too great a distance to notice it. The hope that seems to lift the composition to a pinnacle is in fact a false one. The picture is subversive in the way it makes hoplessness and senseless suffering the subject of a history painting. Yet it is, despite this, far from being a negative work. For with its powerful design and heroic treatment of forms it provides an image of dignity and humanity persisting even in despair. It is this that makes it one of the most beautiful and moving paintings of the nineteenth century.

In the five years of life left to him, Géricault did not produce another *grande machine* for the Salon. Perhaps he sensed the heroic was no longer an appropriate mode for describing the experiences of contemporary life. But he did not lose his commitment as an explorer of modernity. A visit to England in 1821 – where the *Méduse* was successfully exhibited – stimulated him to produce a series of lithographs of London life. In these the disturbing, dehumanising effects of a modern metropolis are movingly intimated. The visit also brought him into closer contact with English artists, whose spirited naturalism he greatly admired. His late paintings of horses – either racing or in tempestuous mood – show the influence of such English animal painters as Stubbs and Ward.

Géricault's greatest achievement as an observer in these years was his series of portraits of insane people made for his medical friend Dr Georget (illustration 12). Apparently they were commissioned in order to demonstrate the relation between certain physical characteristics and explicit forms of derangement. Yet they exceed the bounds of medical illustration as much as the *Méduse* exceeded that of pictorial journalism. It is the sympathy with which they evoke people preoccupied and debilitated by their own inner obsessions that is their most striking feature. The attitude that they convey is a reminder that this was the period when a new view of madness was emerging, when it was

12. T. Géricault, *Le Kleptomane*

beginning to be seen less as a misdemeanour to be punished, and more as a disease that required treatment. It is also a reminder that post-Napoleonic France was a time when incidents of derangement increased dramatically – frequently as a result of people trying to maintain in their imaginations the grandeur and pretensions of the vanished Empire.

In his obituary in 1824 Géricault was described as a 'Romantic'. He was, indeed, the first visual artist to be accorded the epithet in France.[15] Certainly it seems an appropriate term – especially in view of the recent characterisation of Romanticism by Stendhal in *Racine et Shakespeare* (1823) as the fearless exploration of reality, addressing the age in the terms most relevant to it. And yet it would be a mistake to believe that there were any direct connections between Géricault and the self-styled literary movement. Géricault had little interest in such matters. His way of painting, furthermore, had been fully formed before the writings of Victor Hugo and his contemporaries began to appear. However those painters who were to profit from the new pictorial dimensions that Géricault had opened up were susceptible as well to the influence of the new literary school, and their relationship with it is far more problematic.

DELACROIX AND THE ROMANTICS

There is no doubt that these artists – who were, for the most part, born around 1800 – formed a loose-knit group in the 1820s which bore striking parallels to the new tendencies to be found in the predominantly literary salons. Like Victor Hugo and Alfred de Vigny, such artists as Delacroix, Delaroche and Scheffer could be seen to be taking a stand against the classical norms of the Academy, and to be looking outside the traditions of recent French culture for their inspiration. Both writers and artists took a new interest in the art and society of the Middle Ages, and in those historical masters whose vividness, freedom and imaginative vigour seemed to be the antithesis of classicism (Shakespeare for the writers; Caravaggio and Rubens for the artists). Both looked to the contemporary cultures of Germany and England, absorbing the aesthetics and metaphysics of the former and the sensationalism and naturalism of the latter. Similarly, both can be seen to engage in a series of brushes with officialdom. The battleground of the artists was the Salon. From 1822 – when Delacroix exhibited *La Barque de Dante* (Louvre) – the forces gradually increased. 1824 was the year when the importance of contemporary English art was acknowledged. 1827 was the year of extremism and defiance, when Delacroix exhibited his shocking

La Mort de Sardanapale (illustration 7), Boulanger his *Mazeppa*, and Eugène Devéria triumphed with his *La Naissance de Henri IV* (Louvre) – having a bonfire of casts after antique statues ignited in his honour. 1831 was the year of final acceptance, performing much the same function for the artists that the conflict over the staging of Hugo's *Hernani* had done for the writers a year before.

Yet despite these parallels, direct connections between the two are remarkably few. On the whole it was only the minor visual artists who can be found frequenting the *cénacles* of Hugo and of Gautier. There were figures like Louis Boulanger (1808–67), the illustrator of Hugo, who Gautier felt had been ruined by the master's praise and advice; Eugène Devéria (1805–65) who – despite his success in 1827 – was never capable of being more than delicate and charming; the sculptor Jean Duseigneur (1808–66), whose *Orlando Furioso* was described as the equivalent to Hugo's *Préface de 'Cromwell'* when it was exhibited in 1831, but who came to little afterwards.

By contrast Eugène Delacroix (1798–1863), the artist who was by far the most gifted painter of this generation, disparaged all attempts to connect him with the literary Romantics. As early as 1826 he was being described as the pictorial counterpart of Victor Hugo.[16] Eventually he got so fed up with this habitual comparison that he retorted that he was a 'pur classique'. Later Gautier – who clearly felt betrayed by Delacroix's dissociation – accused him of adopting his position as a form of exaggerated dandyism.[17] But there was more to it than that. Delacroix was wishing to separate himself from all the politics and posturing, the red waistcoats, military metaphors, the cheap confusion of individuality with exhibitionism. He wished to emphasise the seriousness of his own pictures, which he saw as attempts to continue the grand traditions of art – in contrast to the arid formalism of the academic classicists of his day. But if he was right to reject 'programme' Romanticism, he was wrong to associate Victor Hugo with it. For Hugo – like Vigny and the other major writers of his generation – was also disdainful of such posturing and was attempting to align himself to a grand tradition.

There was, however, another reason for Delacroix to reject the comparison. This was his concern for the innate qualities of the visual arts. He did not wish picture making to be seen in any way as subordinate to literature or dependent upon it. As has already been mentioned,[18] he saw pictures, like music, as being 'higher than thought'. The musical analogy is a telling one. Such an association was, of course, not new,[19] But its presence in Delacroix helps to draw attention to his obsession with the abstract qualities of art.

This concern distinguished him strongly from Géricault, who always seemed to be using painting not as an end in itself, but as a means of presenting and clarifying an actual event or circumstance. In his book *Icarus: The Image of the Artist in French Romanticism*, Maurice Shroder distinguishes two types of Romantic artists, one basically a 'hero', the other an aesthete.[20] Géricault might be characterised as the former, Delacroix as the latter. He was always fastidious and withdrawn, and his pictures – no matter how violent their subject-matter – never lost sight of the purely pictorial thrill of brilliant paint surfaces and vibrant colour harmonies.

Nothing better expresses the difference between Géricault's and Delacroix's attitudes than the younger artist's début at the Salon, *La Barque de Dante* of 1822 (Louvre). This picture, which shows Dante and Virgil crossing the 'murky pool' to the infernal city in Phlegias' bark, pays homage to the *Méduse* in its air of nautical disaster. Yet instead of choosing a controversial catastrophe, Delacroix selected instead a fashionable literary source, one that had been habitually used by artists since the English sculptor Flaxman's book of engraved drawings, *Outlines to Dante*, of 1792. Furthermore, the darkened tones of this picture are made far more attractive than the lurid greys and greens of the *Méduse*. The fiery city of Dis provides a rich glow in the background; the greens of the foreground are enlivened by the reds of Dante's headdress and the russet of Virgil's cloak; and the whole of this central area is brought into a chromatic balance by the shaded blue of the cloak of Phlegias. Small wonder that this work – which was bought by the government – should have been hailed by Gros as the work of a 'subdued Rubens'.

Delacroix's next major exhibit, at the Salon of 1824, was awarded a gold medal (second class) and was acquired again by the government. But there was more to disturb in it. Called *Scènes des massacres de Scio* (illustration 13) it was based upon a gruesome humiliation of the Greeks in a recent incident in their struggle for independence against the Turks. It was a topical subject – but hardly a subversive one – for sympathy for the plight of the Greeks was widespread in France as in other Western European countries. What was disconcerting about it was its negativism. The defeated Greeks await death, or slavery, with indifference. There is not even the heroic despair of the *Méduse*.

The muted lethargy of this picture is perhaps a commentary on the vagaries of fate. At a later date in his life Delacroix wrote in his diary of 'cette nécessité éternelle . . . de se soumettre aux arrêts de la sévère nature', adding that, 'la maladie, la mort, la pauvreté, les peines de l'âme,

13. E. Delacroix, *Scènes des massacres de Scio*

sont éternelles et tourmenteront l'humanité sous tous les régimes; la forme, démocratique ou monarchique, n'y fait rien'.[21] Whether this is the case or not, it is remarkable that this picture should have aligned its dispassionate treatment of horrific suffering with a new form of technical experiment, emulating the art of the newly fashionable English painters. Shortly before the opening of the Salon, Delacroix saw the *Haywain* of Constable, a work that was to become a sensation when it was shown in Paris that year. The sight of this fresh view of the Suffolk countryside excited Delacroix so much that he reworked part of his Greek massacre, using patches of broken colour to enliven the foreground and other areas.

Delacroix's interest in the brightness and informality of English art was enhanced by his own acquaintances in Paris, notably Richard Parkes Bonington (1802–28; illustration 14). Although trained in France, Bonington was valued by his French contemporaries as a representative of English art, particularly on account of his immense facility with watercolour. Delacroix later wrote to Théophile Thoré about him: 'Personne dans cette école moderne, et peut-être avant lui n'a possédé cette légèreté dans l'exécution, qui, particulièrement dans l'aquarelle, fait de ces ouvrages des espèces de diamants dont l'œil est flatté et ravi, indépendamment de tout sujet et de toute imitation.'[22]

Delacroix's fascination with the formal qualities of English art during this period led him to follow in Géricault's footsteps and visit England. Yet the inconveniences of life there displeased him, and he kept his admiration after that on a strictly artistic footing. This spread to a taste for the works of Scott and Byron. The latter fascinated him also for his ironic stance – something that fitted in with Delacroix's own dandyism. Yet the French artist surpassed even the English milord in his sang-froid when he painted *La Mort de Sardanapale* (illustration 7). This subject was based on a scene from Byron's play about the Assyrian sybarite and tyrant. But Byron is prepared to portray Sardanapalus as a hero, who seeks only to bring peace and plenty to his land. His suicide after failing to achieve this is a gesture of honour. He leaps on to the funeral pyre alone, and then is joined in death voluntarily by Myrrha, his favourite concubine. Delacroix changes all this. As has already been mentioned (p. 315 above), he shows Sardanapalus presiding over an orgy of destruction with uninterest. Once again this shocking theme is set off with the most brilliant treatment, the daring juxtapositions of reds and orange, the maelstrom of tumbling forms that he manages still to keep under control.

Delacroix never painted so controversial a theme again. Apparently

14. R. Bonington, *François Ier et Marguerite de Navarre*

he received an official warning; but the rejection of extremes seems also to have accorded with his own personal development. From now on he was to use ambiguity and irony for more evasive purposes.

There could be few more neatly balanced gestures from this point of view than that of the large painting that he submitted to the Salon of 1831, *Le 28 juillet: la Liberté guidant le peuple* (illustration 15). The subject here is a celebration of the revolution of the previous year, which had led to the régime of the 'bourgeois king', Louis-Philippe. There were twenty-three other pictures concerned with these events in the same Salon, so there was nothing unusual about Delacroix's choice of theme. He was alone, however, in his lack of idealisation. Even the figure of Liberty, as she rushes forward in her Phrygian cap with a gun in one hand and the tricolour in the other, is no frigid allegory. What was more disconcerting to most people was the rabble she was leading. Delacroix was taken to task for having taken his models 'from the populace rather than from the people'. There were no figures in the work that the genteel visitor to the Salon could have identified with; even the man in the top hat is clearly no gentleman. Implicit in the work was an unpleasant reminder: the revolution that benefited the bourgeoisie was fought by a less fortunate class.

The ambiguities of this work are an indication that Delacroix himself viewed the revolution with mixed feelings. He was an elitist and a Bonapartist.[23] He was glad to see the Bourbons go, and the tricolour restored as France's national flag. But he had severe misgivings about the new philistine society that was now so clearly in the ascendancy.

The new government met Delacroix's gesture with a similar ambiguity. He was appointed to the Légion d'honneur and the picture was bought. But it was hidden away from public view and did not re-emerge until after 1848.

AFTER 1830

Nevertheless Delacroix's public fortunes continued to thrive under the bourgeois monarchy. His old friend and supporter, the critic Thiers, was now Minister of the Interior, and was in a position to arrange for him to be well supplied with government commissions. Delacroix started with the Salon du Roi in the Palais Bourbon (1833–7), and then went on to paint the library of the Palais Luxembourg (1840–7), the ceiling of the Galerie d'Apollon in the Louvre (1849–51) and the Salon de la Paix in the Hôtel de Ville (1850–3). Finally he painted the Chapelle des Anges at Saint-Sulpice, a work that was completed in 1861. While painting these vast schemes Delacroix moved further and further away from the Romantics, seeking to align himself with the great masters and avoid the topical and sensational. His technique changed significantly. He replaced the glittering surfaces and strident colours of his early work with a more sober treatment, firmer handling and more subdued tonalities.

However, this should not be seen as a retreat. It was in fact a continuation of the exploration of pictorial effect already to be discerned in his works of the 1820s. A visit to North Africa in 1832 had opened his eyes to the effects to be obtained by a purer use of colour. He had also been impressed by the 'timeless' way of life of the Arabs, believing he had found there a natural dignity equivalent to that of the Greeks and Romans. His *Les Femmes d'Alger* (illustration 16) brings both these qualities together. It shows how colours could be made effective without the cacophony of a *Sardanapale*. Here they float in half-shadow. The door in the background, with its juxtaposition of complementaries of red and green, creates a powerful base for the rose and dull gold tints of the women. He seems to have become concerned in this picture with the creation of a surface pattern of colours which would mutually intensify each other and in which both lighted and shaded areas would have a positive effect. Later such usage was to become systematised by the neo-Impressionists, who openly confessed their debt to Delacroix.[24] For Delacroix himself, however, colour usage remained a matter of personal sensibility. Nor, indeed, did the concern for colour effect ever become independent of association. In the *Femmes d'Alger* it suggests a heightened sensuality, tinged with a Baudelairean sense of *ennui*. It may seem strange at first that Delacroix should endow those classically reposing figures with such sentiments. Yet they do in fact fit in with his own view of classicism, which combined a vivid sense of harmonious existence, of *gravitas*, grace and decorum with a resigned pessimism. In his later years he was continuously to express his misgivings at the modern world, which seemed to him to move further and further away from civilisation, while exhorting himself to practise the stoicism of Marcus Aurelius and other late classical authors. This feeling comes out most poignantly in one of his last exhibited works, *Ovide exilé parmi les Scythes* (1859; National Gallery, London), in which the classical author is shown reclining amongst the barbarians that he had been condemned to live with. The cool tonalities and tender rhythms of this picture bear out the message: gentle sorrow and resignation, like a meditative piece of music.

No other French artist developed the aesthetic potential of Romanti-

15. E. Delacroix, *Le 28 juillet: la Liberté guidant le peuple.*

cism with the profundity of Delacroix, but it is noticeable that, in the 1830s, most of them were moving away from the programme Romanticism of the 1820s. In different ways they were painting in a more subdued and sober manner. In the case of Horace Vernet this led to a more detailed and factual way of painting – evident in the vast military paintings he executed for Louis-Philippe at Versailles. Ary Scheffer – who had always had a penchant for Germanic metaphysics – purified his style, emulating the German medieval revivalist artists, the Nazarenes. Other artists began to achieve success with their depiction of Romantic subject-matter in a realistic style. The painter Léopold Robert (1794–1835) painted scenes of brigands in the Roman Campagna in such a manner, and Alexandre-Gabriel Decamps (1803–1861) Arab scenes from North Africa.

In part this new sobriety can be related to their new position. With the advent of Louis-Philippe the Romantic artists had become officially

16. E. Delacroix, *Les Femmes d'Alger*

respectable. The monarchical and governmental patronage of Delacroix and Vernet has already been mentioned, but there were many other projects on which the radicals of the 1820s became employed. Most notable is the Galerie des Batailles at Versailles – a series intended to reawaken a sense of national pride.

However, there was more than state patronage behind the new mood. There was also a widespread desire to make the July monarchy a means of reconciling the warring factions of French society to achieve a new synthesis. This desire – inspired by the positivism of Auguste Comte – encouraged a search for the *juste milieu* in the visual arts, in which the best of classicism and Romanticism could be combined. For a time this seemed to be met by the eclecticism of Paul Delaroche (1797–1856). A former pupil of Gros, Delaroche had set out in the 1820s to paint vivid historical tragedies in an impassioned, painterly manner. In the 1830s he continued to paint historical pictures of great psychological complexity, but gave them a new 'objectivity' by treating them in a sober and

17. P. Delaroche, *Cromwell et Charles Ier*

meticulous manner with painstakingly researched historical detail. Such pictures as *Cromwell et Charles Ier* (illustration 17) – which caused a sensation in the Salon of 1831 – seemed to offer a reasoned disquisition on the processes of history, providing the lessons that were so eagerly being sought. Interestingly, Delaroche's art began to fall out of fashion in the late 1830s – at much the same time that it was becoming clear that Louis-Philippe's régime would not provide the healing liberal forum that was required.

Other forms of art that could be associated with the more naturalistic side of Romanticism began to emerge at this time. Landscape painting began to assume a new importance. In the 1820s the English painters – particularly Constable – had had their imitators. But none of these – not even Delacroix's friend Paul Huet (1803–69) – had been able to offer a convincing alternative to classical landscape painters like Valenciennes. Nor had they been able to shift the generally accepted view of landscape as an essentially inferior genre. It was only in the 1830s that a new evaluation began to emerge. It was the artists who began to move to the

18. T. Rousseau, *Le Val du Saint-Vincent*

Forest of Fontainebleau, to surround themselves with the marshes and woodlands in the neighbourhood of the village of Barbizon, who established the significance of the direct recording of local nature. The most dominant figure in this loosely-knit group, Théodore Rousseau (1812–67) drew upon Romanticism when describing his perception of nature to be guided by 'that which is within us'. Exhibiting first at the Salon of 1831, his naturalism was still too challenging and vigorous to be accepted (illustration 18). Only after 1848 did he achieve official acceptance. Yet the work of his less dramatic associates began to appear and to popularise the depiction of a simple unaffected nature. Even artists trained in the classical tradition began to move in this direction – notably Jean-Baptiste-Camille Corot (1796–1875). Returning from Rome in 1828, he began to augment his classical repertoire with views of French scenery. Altogether his art shifted away from grandiose expression towards an almost Franciscan love for common nature, recorded in a straightforward, workmanlike manner.

It could be argued that the growing acceptance of studies of 'simple' nature in the 1830s reflected the desire for an increasingly urban society to be reassured about the endurance and reality of rural life and the natural world. Certainly these painters shifted increasingly away from charged, emotive description towards an apparently objective technique.

A more curious development of the 1830s was the final emergence of a form of sculpture that was 'Romantic' in technique as well as subject-matter. This is the more striking because it was in France alone that a few sculptors dared to break with the commonly held assumption that their art was essentially classical and emulate the effects of Romantic painters. The most daring was Pierre-Jean David d'Angers (1788–1856), who exclaimed that 'sculpture is a religion' and entertained mystic concepts about his materials. As early as 1816, in fact, he was planning a statue of the *Grand Condé* showing him in his actual seventeenth-century costume and swaggering in a most un-classical manner. However he was constantly censured for his excesses. Despite being considered by Victor Hugo to be the greatest sculptor of his age, his talent was only really appreciated on the level of the small-scale portrait medallions that he made after the famous figures of his day. These works, with their spirited virtuoso recordings of the features of genius, provided an attractive kind of high-class journalism that reinforced popular misconceptions about the potential of physiognomy for revealing character. Attempts to apply a more vivid and tactile treatment to ideal figurative groups were consistently disfavoured. David d'Angers's pupil Auguste Préault (1809–79) exhibited a number of reliefs showing such tendencies in the early 1830s. His *Tuerie* (1834; Chartres, Musée) has figures expressing fear and horror with a violence previously only found in painting. But Préault remained a marginal figure – partly on account of the lack of official patronage and growing exclusion of his works from the Salon. The greatest French sculptor of the age, François Rude (1784–1855) – who didn't suffer such extreme censorship – practised a form of eclecticism, in which a certain modernity and verve is used to enliven heroic classical forms – notably in his celebrated group for the Arc de Triomphe, *Le Départ* (1835–6).

Such limitations on expression contrast to the success of Antoine-Louis Barye (1796–1875). After he had exhibited *Tigre dévorant un gavial* (illustration 19) in the Salon of 1831, this sculptor became immensely popular as the modeller of violent and dramatic animal subjects. It would seem that there was no taboo on the Romantic sensibility here, where no challenge to the classical canon of the human form was posed. Significantly Barye returned to antique models when sculpting human forms – as he did for the Pavillon Denon of the Louvre.

However, popular though they were, even Barye's works were excluded from the Salon when they were considered to have gone too far in expression or freedom of handling. Only in private works can untrammelled exploration be said to have flourished during these decades, notably in the modelling that certain painters and draughtsmen (such as Géricault and Daumier) resorted to.

There was only one art form in which the extravagance of the 1820s continued to flourish. This was in graphic art – particularly illustration. Victor Hugo must take the credit for producing the most extreme essays in this genre. However, his work drew its strength from a kind of inspired amateurism. It abounds with suggestion, which never has to be developed beyond a certain point. His imaginative vigour was also a stimulus to professional illustrators. His protégé Louis Boulanger (1807–67) produced his best works not in the field of painting, but in lithographs such as *La Ronde du sabbat* which were inspired by the master's work. Another favourite of Hugo, Charles Meryon (1821–68) produced precisely worked views full of foreboding (*Etchings of Paris*, 1852), which continued the Romantic vision of the city into a new age.

The licence of fantasy also gave a new lease of life to political commentary after the lifting of censorship in 1830. The new 'armoury' that the exaggeration of form and effect had given the political cartoonist had already been employed in England by Gillray and his associates.[25] Now a generation of French illustrators developed the genre further. Honoré Daumier (1808–79) was the most notable of these, using the technique for such devastating satires as his celebrated transformation of the head of Louis-Philippe into the shape of a pear. After the reintroduction of censorship the graphic artists had to disguise their criticisms as social satire (illustration 5). This was a genre in which the subtle observation of Paul Gavarni (1804–66) flourished. For one illustrator, Grandville (1803–47), such censorship became the stimulus for a new form of extravagance. He turned to a world of make-believe where one thing is constantly turning into another. In *Un autre monde* (1844) the viewer is presented with a topsy-turvy reality in which the ingenuity of the game seems to have taken over from any kind of satirical commentary that had originally been intended (illustration 20).

Finally – in this brief survey of developments after 1830 – it should be noted that this was the period that first saw a challenge to classical norms in architecture. Hittorf's notorious publication drawing attention to the polychrome decoration that originally existed in Greek temples appeared in 1829.[26] In the subsequent decades a creeping historicism could be found in architecture in France – leading to the production of gothic and romanesque churches, and chateaux in the styles of the fifteenth and sixteenth century. Louis-Philippe took some interest in the notion, ordering a gothic remodelling of his family mausoleum by P.B. LeFranc (1795–1856) in 1839. However, this remained a relatively minor affair.[27] It in no way rivalled the rich and often fantastic development of historical and exotic styles that can be found in Britain in the early nineteenth century. It is symptomatic of the relatively cautious response of the French to historicism in building that the greatest triumphs of the movement can be found in the field of the restoration of ancient monuments. This is particularly the case with the work of Viollet-le-duc (1814–79). Indeed, it could be argued that his refurbishing of Notre-Dame in Paris was France's greatest contribution to Romantic architecture; especially since the undertaking had been inspired in the first place by Hugo's *Notre-Dame de Paris*. Certainly the touches of picturesqueness and fantasy that he added – including a new pinnacled chapter house (1847) and the addition of gargoyles and a *flèche* – make the building conform more to a Romantic vision of gothic than to anything that might have been conceived in the Middle Ages.

LEGACIES

Such considerations emphasise that Romanticism was, as Baudelaire remarked, primarily a 'way of feeling'. It is as a way of feeling that it has

19. A. Barye, *Tigre dévorant un gavial*, bronze

20. Grandville, *Les métamorphoses du sommeil*, wood engraving

remained most pervasively with us, colouring our perceptions of landscapes, ruins and exotica in incalculable ways. But there were more specific legacies as well. In French art the image of the independent creator retained its potency and guided future generations of breakaway groups. The critical writings of Baudelaire – starting with his Salon review of 1843[28] – reaffirmed many of the tenets of Romanticism at precisely the moment when they were becoming utterly outmoded. He rescued the notion of the 'painter of modern life' and emphasised as well the exploration of pictorial effect – the technical and associative properties of colour. In the 1840s it was the issue of modernity that most engaged the younger generation of painters – particularly Courbet and his associates. Significantly this was a time when Géricault's work was coming once more into prominence.[29] Courbet himself was following in the footsteps of the *Méduse* when he painted his vast canvases of modern life subjects such as *Un Enterrement à Ornans* (1850) and *L'Atelier du peintre* (1855).

The exploration of colour effect appealed more to a later generation. Here Delacroix's influence was crucial – particularly the understanding of him that was gained from a reading of the adulatory commentaries of Baudelaire. The Impressionists' adoption of a palette of pure colours already shows a debt to the Romantic master. But a later generation – that of Van Gogh and the Symbolists – became involved as well in Delacroix's use of colour associations and emotive expression.[30]

It would be misguided to overstate such influences, or to suggest that an art form should be assessed primarily in terms of the impact that it has on subsequent developments. But the existence of such connections does help to emphasise that Romanticism in the visual arts in France was more than some temporary aberration. Rather, it was a critical moment of reassessment. By searching beyond the normal boundaries of French art such figures as Géricault and Delacroix were able to revitalise a tradition and maintain its fruitfulness and validity for subsequent generations.

NOTES

1. A. Schnapper, *David – témoin de son temps* (Fribourg, Office du Livre, 1981), p. 15.
2. *De David à Delacroix* (exhibition catalogue, Grand Palais, 1974), p. 233.
3. F. Benoit, *L'art français sous la Révolution et l'Empire* (L.-Henry, May 1897), p. 243.
4. M. Easton, *Artists and Writers in Paris. The Bohemian Idea 1803–1867* (London, Edward Arnold, 1964), p. 41.
5. A. Joubin (ed.), *Journal d'Eugène Delacroix* (3 vols., Librairie Plon, 1960), I, 50.
6. For further discussion of this issue see W. Vaughan, *Romantic Art* (London, Thames and Hudson, 1978), pp. 267–8.

7. By Senefelder in Bavaria in 1798. See M. Twyman, *Lithography* (Oxford University Press, 1969), pp. 3ff.
8. Pioneered as a high quality technique by Thomas Bewick in the late eighteenth century, this form of engraving became widespread in France in the 1820s. See A. Dobson, *Thomas Bewick and his Pupils* (London, Chatto and Windus, 1884).
9. In 1829 Hittorf published vivid polychrome impressions of the temples at Selinus. Later reconstructions of the temples at Paestum were considered so outrageous by Viollet-le-duc that he held them culpable of 'disrupting the State, religion and the sanctity of the French family', *Colour* (London, Mitchell Beazley, 1980), p. 403.
10. M.I. Larousse, *Grand dictionnaire universel du XIX siècle* (17 vols., Larousse, 1869), IV, 403.
11. R.-P. Huet, *Paul Huet* (Librairie Renouard, 1911), p. 75.
12. C. Clément, *Géricault* (Didier, 1867), p. 5.
13. In M. de La Combe, *Charlet, sa vie, ses lettres* (Paulin et le Chevalier, 1861), p. 61.
14. *The Romantic Movement* (exhibition catalogue, London, Tate Gallery and Arts Council, 1959), pp. 149–50.
15. P. Courthion (ed.), *Géricault raconté par lui-même et par ses amis* (Geneva, P. Cailler, 1947), p. 274.
16. L. Johnson, *The Paintings of Eugène Delacroix. A Critical Catalogue 1816–1831* (2 vols., Oxford, Clarendon Press, 1981), I, 47.
17. T. Gautier, *Histoire du romantisme* (2nd edn, Charpentier, 1874), p. 47.
18. See note 5 above.
19. For a succinct discussion of the history of this association see H. Honour, *Romanticism* (London, Allen Lane, 1979), pp. 119ff.
20. M.Z. Shroder, *Icarus: The Image of the Artist in French Romanticism* (Cambridge, Mass., Harvard UP, 1961), pp. 37–9.
21. Joubin, *Journal d'Eugène Delacroix*, I, 189.
22. To Thoré, 30 November 1861. A. Joubin (ed.), *Correspondance générale d'Eugène Delacroix* (5 vols, Librairie Plon, 1935–8), V, 247.
23. Johnson, *The Paintings of Eugène Delacroix*, p. 146.
24. See especially P. Signac, *D'Eugène Delacroix au néo-impressionisme* (H. Floury, 1899).
25. E.H. Gombrich, 'The cartoonist's armoury' in *Meditations on a Hobby Horse* (London, Phaidon, 1963), pp. 107–9.
26. See note 9 above.
27. H.R. Hitchcock, *Architecture. 19th and 20th Century*, Pelican History of Art, Z 18, 2nd edn (Harmondsworth, Penguin Books, 1963), pp. 107–9.
28. Especially the Salons of 1845, 1846, 1849. See C. Baudelaire, *Curiosités esthétiques*, ed. H. Lemaître (Garnier Frères, 1962).
29. F. Haskell, *Rediscoveries in Art* (Oxford, Phaidon, 1976), p. 63.
30. H.R. Rookmaaker, *Synthetist Art Theories* (Amsterdam, Swets and Zeitlinger, 1959), pp. 14–26.

BIBLIOGRAPHY

Most of the general books on Romanticism pay no more than passing attention to the visual arts. H. Honour, *Romanticism* (London, Allen Lane, 1979) provides an invaluable account of the visual arts in terms of the broader cultural ramifications of the movement. Jean Clay, *Romanticism* (Oxford, Phaidon, 1981) discusses Romanticism more in terms of pictorial types – and provides an excellent compendium of well-reproduced images. W. Vaughan, *Romantic Art* (London, Thames and Hudson, 1978) provides a general history of the art associated with the movement. Other accounts can be found in W. Hofmann,

Art in the Nineteenth Century (London, Faber and Faber, 1961) and F. Novotny, *Painting and Sculpture in Europe, 1780–1880*, Pelican History of Art, Z 20 (Harmondsworth, Penguin Books, 1960). L. Eitner, *Neoclassicism and Romanticism*, Sources and Documents in the History of Art Series (Englewood Cliffs, NJ, Prentice-Hall, 1970) is an excellent annotated anthology of writings by artists and theorists of the period. The exhibition catalogue to the Council of Europe exhibition *The Romantic Movement* (London, Tate Gallery and Arts Council, 1959), contains valuable entries on individual works.

Two of the older studies specifically devoted to French Romantic painting are still important. These are L. Rosenthal, *La Peinture romantique; essai sur l'évolution de la peinture française de 1815 à 1830* (Albert Fortemoing, 1900) and W. Friedländer, *David to Delacroix* (Cambridge, Mass., Harvard UP, 1952). The catalogue to the exhibition *De David à Delacroix* (Grand Palais, 1974) contains valuable essays by P. Rosenberg, A. Schnapper, and R. Rosenblum, and highly informative biographies of artists and catalogue entries.

For sculpture L. Benoist, *La Sculpture romantique* (Larousse, 1927) is recommended.

For architecture see H.R. Hitchcock, *Architecture. 19th and 20th Century*, Pelican History of Art, Z 18 (Harmondsworth, Penguin Books, 1958), and L. Hautecœur, *Histoire de l'architecture classique en France* (5 vols., J. Picard, 1955), vol. IV.

There are several useful studies of movements and topics relating to the visual arts in France in the early nineteenth century. M. Easton, *Artists and Writers in Paris. The Bohemian Idea 1803–1867* (London, Edward Arnold, 1964) and M.Z. Shroder, *Icarus: The Image of the Artist in French Romanticism* (Cambridge, Mass., Harvard UP, 1961) are both concerned with the changing social position of the artist. F. Haskell, *Rediscoveries in Art* (Oxford, Phaidon, 1976) contains much discussion of changing tastes in France during the period. The exhibition catalogue *Le Style Troubadour* (Bourg-en-Bresse, 1971) has helpful information about the vogue for medievalism in France. A. Boime, *The Academy and French Painting in the Nineteenth Century* (London, Phaidon, 1971) provides an authoritative account of the role of the official art institution. T.J. Clark, *The Image of the People* (London, Thames and Hudson, 1972) and *The Absolute Bourgeois* (London, Thames and Hudson, 1973) are concerned primarily with French Realism, but they contain much important discussion of the relationship of this movement to Romanticism.

For criticism and the visual arts see A. Brookner, *The Genius of the Future* (London, Phaidon, 1971), D. Wakefield, *Stendhal and the Arts* (London, Phaidon, 1975) (extracts – with a lengthy introduction), C. Baudelaire, *Curiosités esthétiques*, ed. H. Lemaître (Garnier Frères, 1962), J. Mayne, *The Painter of Modern Life* (London, Phaidon, 1964) (translations of writings by Baudelaire, with introduction).

For studies on individual artists see the following:– *Barye* (exh. càt., Louvre, 1956). *Corot*: G. Bazin, *Corot* (2nd edn, Tisné, 1973); P. Courthion (ed.), *Corot raconté par lui-même et par ses amis* (Geneva, P. Cailler, 1946). *Daumier*: O.W. Larkin, *Daumier* (New York, McGraw Hill, 1966). *Delacroix*: A. Joubin (ed.) *Correspondance générale d'Eugène Delacroix* (5 vols., Librairie Plon, 1935–8); A. Joubin (ed.), *Journal d'Eugène Delacroix* (3 vols., Librairie Plon, 1960); L. Johnson, *Delacroix*, (London, Weidenfeld and Nicolson, 1963); L. Johnson, *The Paintings of Eugène Delacroix. A Critical Catalogue 1816–1831* (2 vols., Oxford, Clarendon Press, 1981); G.P. Mras, *Delacroix's Theory of Art* (Princeton University Press, 1966); M. Sérullaz, *Mémorial de l'exposition Eugène Delacroix* (Editions des Musées Nationaux, 1963); J.J. Spector, *Delacroix: The Death of Sardanapalus* (London, Allen Lane, 1964).

Delaroche: N.D. Ziff, *Delaroche*, Outstanding Dissertations Series (New York, Garland, 1974). *Géricault*: C. Clément, *Géricault* (Didier, 1867); P. Courthion (ed.), *Géricault raconté par lui-même et par ses amis* (Geneva, P. Cailler, 1947); L. Eitner, *Géricault's*

Raft of the Medusa (London, Phaidon, 1973); *Géricault* (exh. cat., Los Angeles County Museum, 1971); *Géricault* (exh. cat., Rome, 1978). *Girodet*: P.A. Coupin (ed.), *Œuvres posthumes de Girodet-Trioson* (Jules Renouard, 1829); *Girodet* (exh. cat., Montargis, 1967). *Gros:* J.B. Delestre, *Gros et ses ouvrages* (Jules Labitte, 1845); *Gros, ses amis, ses élèves* (exh. cat., Petit Palais, 1936).

Ingres: *Ingres* (exh. cat., Petit Palais, 1967–8); R. Rosenblum, *Ingres* (London, Thames and Hudson, 1967). *Prud'hon*: J. Guiffrey *L'Œuvre de P.P. Prud'hon* (Picard, 1924). *Rousseau*: *Barbizon Revisited* (exh. cat., San Francisco, 1962); A. Sensier, *Souvenirs sur Th. Rousseau* (Durand-Ruel, 1872); *Rousseau* (exh. cat., Sainsbury Centre, Norwich, 1982). *Rude*: L. de Fourcade, *François Rude* (Librairie de l'Art Ancien et Moderne, 1904); M. Legrand, *Rude, sa vie, ses œuvres, son enseignement* (Dentu, 1856).

X · *Music and opera*

HUGH MACDONALD

Romantic music enjoys a privilege not shared by music of other epochs or other persuasions since it rides comfortably and complacently on the general belief that music, at least in its more romantic manifestations, is superior to other arts. This was first stated by German writers whose quest for the inexpressible goals of man found music to be a well-nigh ideal vehicle for transporting them to remote worlds unreachable by mere words or mere representational images. The apparent meaninglessness of music provided a key to the beyond or the divine, and the evident pleasure, even ecstasy, palpably derived from music suggested that this other world might be heaven itself.

Musicians were always sceptical of these alluring, largely literary notions, mainly because to them their art was all too mundane and matter-of-fact; Kapellmeisters were not noted for their ecstatic submission to a state of bliss when listening to each other's compositions. Mendelssohn, in a famous letter, remarked that music was too precise in meaning, not the opposite. It was much more commonly writers and critics who gave tacit (and sometimes explicit) support to music's capacity to command the human soul. The independent supremacy of music seemed to be reinforced by Beethoven's superhuman achievements in sonata and symphony and by the corresponding decline, however hard to measure, in the importance of song and opera in the early nineteenth century. It remained an article of faith only lightly disturbed by Wagner's theoretical equalisation of the arts in the *Gesamtkunstwerk*; the music-dramas themselves seemed only to reinforce the notion, not to threaten it.

Many Romantic ideas crossed the Rhine from Germany, but this was not one of them. Indeed French Romantic music is striking for its failure to acknowledge (with one or two notable exceptions) how powerfully music can act upon the human system and how easily tears and emotion can be drawn by it. The French, in fact, showed a certain reserve towards the more powerful manifestations of music and clung tenaciously to traditional balances and collaborations which gave music an important role in the theatre, in the concert hall, in the home, in church and in state ceremonial, but only rarely in the heart. Abstraction, so alluring to German minds, found no support in France, where music continued to be allied to words in opera, song, and dramatic symphony, preserving its literary dimension and throwing it open to all thinking men to discuss and enjoy. French Romantic music is thus not so much a specimen of fashionable ideas as a conveyor of them; it is not the supreme product of a great artistic movement but an essential adjunct or ingredient in a complex literary and philosophical network. Opera, consequently, is the most representative musical genre of the period, though not necessarily the most Romantic. The smaller, more intimate forms were abundantly cultivated, but again not always in the sense we would think of as obviously Romantic. These uneven factors need to be investigated more closely.

It is tempting to focus on the 1830s as the period most fertile in works and ideas and most expansive in the cultivation of music. But it must not be forgotten that the 1790s produced a new musical genre, the serious brand of *opéra-comique*, which swept Europe in the wake of the Revolution. Operas with spoken dialogue and a serious political or moral message were a typically French product, best illustrated by works by Cherubini such as *Lodoïska* (1791), *Élisa* (1794) and *Les Deux Journées* (1800), and by Méhul such as *Euphrosine* (1790), *Horatius Coclès* (1794) and *Ariodant* (1799). None of these works is heard today except in courageous specialist revivals, yet they were parents to Beethoven's *Fidelio*, a work with the clearest declarations about liberty and constancy derived from a French libretto, Bouilly's *Léonore, ou L'Amour conjugal*, set by Gaveaux in 1798. Spontini's and Lesueur's operas, composed for Paris and exported throughout Europe in the early years of the new century, gave French ideas and French librettists a commanding lead even though not all the composers (notably Cherubini and Spontini) were French.

Napoleon's musical tastes were narrow; he liked the new grandiose style of opera which the Revolutionary type soon assumed and he welcomed the spread of French opera in the train of military conquest. But a more characteristic posture for French opera was import, not export. It had always been so, since the time of Mazarin and Lully, and foreign musicians continued to seek fame and success in Paris. Cosmopolitanism is by far the most striking aspect of French music at the height of the Romantic period. This too is in strong contrast to German attitudes, Weber and Schumann taking a firm stand against dangerous Italian mannerisms, and Wagner obsessed with his Germanness and his dedication to a national art. Perhaps after 1815 the French were tired of patriotism and empire; perhaps they were seeking, as always, the latest fashionable artists and were happy to welcome foreigners to their circle. At all events this period is more than usually dominated by foreign musicians, a state of affairs unthinkable in literature and poetry, but familiar in music from the precedents of Lully and Gluck both of whom held sway at the Opéra in their time. The Romantic period is sometimes referred to as 'l'époque de Rossini et Meyerbeer', recognising the dominant influence of an Italian and a German at the Opéra under, respectively, the Restoration and the July monarchy. In the Paris salons much the same could be observed, the most sought after artists being a Pole and a Hungarian, each to play a greater part in the development of the art, and in particular the pianoforte, than any of their contemporaries: Chopin and Liszt.

What of the French themselves? The leading musician in this cosmopolitan company was unquestionably Berlioz, with no rivals among his compatriots. René Dumesnil[1] regarded Félicien David as the only French composer who could even be considered in the same breath, yet his achievement, though significant and full of interest and charm, is certainly that of a *petit maître*. And Berlioz was himself so much of an individualist, keeping fashionable movements so intuitively at arm's length, that he is never easy to align with currents of the epoch. Even though he embodied many characteristics of Romanticism he is still far from being a typical Romantic composer.

THE OPÉRA

The Opéra was the central musical institution in a politically centralised nation and therefore it attracted the closest attention. Writers, politicians, social climbers, *petits bourgeois*, artists and musicians were all fully aware of what the Opéra had to offer. Its performances were widely reported in the press at home and abroad, and it commanded the greatest singers of the time. Its successes made fortunes, its failures led to bankruptcy. It was adored and hated, applauded and derided, but no one could escape its magnetism. No civilised Frenchman in the 1830s could admit to not having seen *Robert Diable*; when Balzac made a discussion of its merits a central episode in his *Gambara* he could assume that his readers knew it well. The enormous works which made up the Opéra's repertory drew on all kinds of Romantic subject-matter and fed a taste for great outpourings of passion – religious, political, amorous, epic, patriotic – characteristic of its time, but its practitioners were not so much originators of a new art-form as skilful architects who knew their own capacities and their audience's preferences and were able to devote unprecedented resources to matching one to the other. French grand opera is thus 'An Art and a Business', to cite the title of William L. Crosten's history of the genre, with the emphasis as often on the latter as on the former. Feeling and imagination are to be found in abundance, but an art form which marshalled so many people and consumed so much artistic energy had to rely as much on generalship and efficiency as on inspiration.

The following table sets out the leading works played at the Opéra between 1800 and 1850:

Date	Composer	Title	Librettist	Acts
1804	Lesueur	*Ossian, ou Les Bardes*	Dercy	5
1807	Spontini	*La Vestale*	Jouy	3
1809	Spontini	*Fernand Cortez*	Jouy	3
1813	Cherubini	*Les Abencérages*	Jouy	3
1826	Rossini	*Le Siège de Corinthe*	Soumet & Balocchi	3
1827	Rossini	*Moïse*	Jouy & Balocchi	4
1828	Auber	*La Muette de Portici*	Scribe & Delavigne	5
1828	Rossini	*Le Comte Ory*	Scribe & Poirson	2
1829	Rossini	*Guillaume Tell*	Jouy, Bis & Marast	4
1831	Meyerbeer	*Robert le Diable*	Scribe & Delavigne	5
1833	Auber	*Gustave III*	Scribe	5
1835	Halévy	*La Juive*	Scribe	5
1836	Meyerbeer	*Les Huguenots*	Scribe	5
1838	Halévy	*Guido et Ginevra*	Scribe	5
1838	Berlioz	*Benvenuto Cellini*	Barbier & de Wailly	2
1840	Donizetti	*Les Martyrs*	Scribe	4
1840	Donizetti	*La Favorite*	Royer & Vaëz	4
1841	Halévy	*La Reine de Chypre*	St Georges	5
1843	Halévy	*Charles VI*	Delavigne & Delavigne	5
1849	Meyerbeer	*Le Prophète*	Scribe	5

Some striking facts emerge from this table. Firstly, although this was a great period in the history of a celebrated art-form, not one of these twenty works remains in the repertory today, with the exception of *Le Comte Ory*, which is in any case a comic opera; its appearance at the Opéra was an exception. The modern rehabilitation of Berlioz has brought *Benvenuto Cellini* to several stages in recent years, although it is by no means typical of operas of its time and paid the price of failure in 1838. Revivals of Spontini, Meyerbeer and Halévy are exceedingly rare, in contrast to the worldwide success of works like *Les Huguenots*, *La Juive* and *Le Prophète* in the last century. Just as a Beethoven work is the only surviving representative of the Revolutionary type of French opera, so also we are familiar with French grand opera only through its offspring by Wagner and Verdi, and thus only in reflection. There are certainly French borrowings in *Tannhäuser*, perhaps also in *Lohengrin*, while *Aida* has sometimes been facetiously regarded as the greatest of all French grand operas. *Un Ballo in Maschera* and *Don Carlos* are also demonstrably of the same family.

Secondly, of the nine composers represented, only four were French. Cherubini and Spontini both lived in France for the greater part of their long lives. Rossini settled in Paris in 1824 and remained until his death forty-four years later. Meyerbeer's greatest successes were in Paris and he spent many years there, even though he always regarded Germany as his home.

Thirdly, two librettists dominate the repertory: Étienne de Jouy in the early part and Eugène Scribe from 1828 onwards. In fact Scribe's first operatic success was at the Opéra-Comique in 1825 with Boïeldieu's *La Dame blanche*. Both were productive men of letters with many plays to their credit as well as operas. Jouy's adventures having taken him to distant lands and very nearly to the guillotine, a taste for the sensational and spectacular became a prominent feature of his work. *La Vestale* is a tale of conflict between love and duty in a Roman setting, while his *Fernand Cortez*, also set by Spontini, involved battles and shipwrecks on an epic scale and introduced horses for the first (but no means the last) time to the stage of the Opéra. This taste for sensation is found also in Scribe's librettos, which fearlessly introduced a ballet of incorporeal nuns (*Robert le Diable* – illustration 21), a skating scene (*Le Prophète*) or a ship in cross-section (Meyerbeer's *L'Africaine*, 1865). In the classic Scribe libretto great deeds are done against a backdrop of national or tribal upheaval, with personal feelings, filial or amorous passion, generally in conflict with epic movements which render mere individuals powerless in a grand chain of events. The plots are often spring-loaded with past events, so that the carefully timed revelation of unknown facts creates a *frisson* marvellously suited to operatic expression as a grand ensemble on which to bring down the curtain Halévy's *La Juive* provides a good example, since the Jewess Rachel discovers that her lover, whom she knows as 'Samuel', is (a) a Christian, not a Jew; (b) married; and (c) Prince Leopold, of royal blood. Each revelation generates great dramatic tension which the music ably serves, the highest climax coming at the final curtain when Rachel, put to death in a boiling cauldron for the sake of her faith, is revealed to be not a

21. The Paris Opéra, playing Meyerbeer's *Robert le Diable*

Jewess at all but the secret daughter of her Christian inquisitor.

Such sensational dramaturgy was brilliantly contrived and given a variety of settings, usually in precise historical locations (*La Juive* is set in Constance in 1414). The verse is resourceful but repetitive and lapses constantly into doggerel, rendering the musician's task difficult if he is to escape the monotony of balanced phrases. Meyerbeer and Halévy were both unable to disguise the sing-song quality of Scribe's verse, plentiful though their invention was. In the great Act iv of *Les Huguenots*, after the thunderous 'Bénédiction des poignards' and a love-duet of great intensity, the lovers part, knowing that they are doomed. Scribe provides the hero, Raoul, with the following lines:

> Plus d'amour, plus d'ivresse,
> Ô remords qui m'oppresse,
> Je les vois et sans cesse
>   Égorger à mes yeux!
> Mes amis vont m'attendre,
> Je ne dois plus t'entendre,
> Et je cours les défendre
>   Ou mourir avec eux!

If these lines are read at some speed with a regular pulse in the voice, they lapse into jingle, aided by the caesura in every line. Meyerbeer's music does nothing to disguise this here. If anything, the obviousness of the metre is underlined by the setting, producing an appalling banality at the one point in the drama where some subtlety is required. The predictability of Meyerbeer's music is its most severe shortcoming; it never sounds unfamiliar, even when it is.

Subjects were chosen to provide opportunities of local colour (both in scenery and the music), religious or political conflicts, and a strong dramatic framework. There was clearly some borrowing from Romantic drama, from Hugo, even from Schiller (as in *Guillaume Tell*), but nothing discernible from Shakespeare. Véron, director of the Opéra in the early 1830s, wrote that Scribe 'never wanted to play the role of a man of genius; he never posed as an innovator; . . . he never wrote a preface, something that is rare in these times'.[2] Scribe is an unromantic figure but his products were regarded as up to date by his bourgeois audience if not by more discriminating critics. He freely exploited the latest mechanical resources of the Opéra. Cicéri's brilliant effects of staging, using three-dimensional scenery and panoramic views were supported by Daguerre's ingenious visual inventions, creating illusions of movement and perspective previously unknown in the theatre.

Musical instruments were similarly exploited for novelty and effect: the bass clarinet, with its sombre colour, indispensable in later music from Wagner onwards, made its bow in *Les Huguenots* in 1836, followed swiftly by *Benvenuto Cellini*. Chromatic brass were first heard in Halévy's *La Juive*. The same opera used an on-stage organ at the opening of Act I, an effect copied in many later operas, notably *Die Meistersinger*. Bells to evoke the chime of midnight, usually to sinister effect, are found in nearly all these operas, from *Guillaume Tell* onwards, indeed bells often toll in French operas of the earlier period. The harp is recurrently required to evoke tenderness, reflection, heavenly bliss or sometimes remote Celtic peoples, as in Lesueur's *Ossian*. In *Les Huguenots*, Meyerbeer gave a solo to a 'viola d'amore', although his belief, shared by Berlioz, that the instrument could become popular, was unfounded.[3]

The chorus, too, takes a prominent part. The 1837 registers record a strength of 29 sopranos, 27 tenors and 20 basses, a generous provision by any standards, although for many works they were certainly needed. When conflicting peoples come into confrontation a double chorus is required. In Act III of *Guillaume Tell* the Swiss patriots cry 'Anathème à Gesler!' while a chorus of soldiers reply 'Vive Gesler!', and huge forces would be required to do this scene effectively. In the wedding scene in *Les Huguenots*, Act III, there are three choruses: a 'chœur de la noce' of mixed voices, a group of 'seigneurs' and a third group of students and soldiers. These many-layered choral masses, often supported by off-stage wind instruments, gave the composer considerable scope for ingenious musical dialogue and contrapuntal skill, although a stolid style in block harmony was the norm for each individual choral group or for the whole chorus if treated as a single unit.

There is a perceptible move towards the epic in this period. Lesueur's operas had focused on great racial conflicts, and his *Mort d'Adam* of 1809 involved the whole human race. *Fernand Cortez* takes a grand historical perspective, and the very title of *Les Huguenots* suggests that individual heroism gives place to the fortunes of the sect. The most truly epic grand opera was Berlioz's *Les Troyens* (1856–8), in which the destiny of the Trojan people, and ultimately of the Romans as well, is the mainspring of the action; the stories of Cassandra, Aeneas and Dido are only incidental to this larger plan.

The *corps de ballet* at the Opéra was even larger than the chorus, with 29 solo artists and 83 in the *corps*, plus 44 student dancers and seven 'supplémentaires'. Ballet alternated with opera, and had its notabilities, such as Taglioni and Fanny Essler, as well as its balletomanes, such as Gautier. Adam's *Giselle* was first staged at the Opéra in 1841. All the larger operas had ballets of some length, contrived to celebrate a scene of pageantry or exoticism, with an opportunity for virtuosity or special effects in the orchestra. Many devotees of opera were said to enjoy the dancing more than the singing. When Wagner's *Tannhäuser* was mounted at the Opéra in 1861, the great stumbling-block was the management's insistence that a ballet be inserted in the second act, regardless of dramatic considerations. Wagner's refusal incurred the implacable hostility of the notorious Jockey Club, even though he was happy to write a ballet scene for the Venusberg at the beginning of Act I. The curious thing is that it was certainly not *de rigueur*, nor even traditional, to place the ballet in Act II: Acts I and III include ballets as often as Act II in this repertory, though there is an understandable rarity of ballets in Act V. Favourite settings were Tyrolean, Bohemian, Spanish or 'African' (the setting of Scribe and Meyerbeer's *L'Africaine* is actually India). Marches, waltzes, polonaises, and a profusion of 'chœurs dansés' are also found.

Whatever the adulation paid to ballerinas, great singing was the mainstay of the Opéra in the Romantic era as in any other. Voices had changed considerably since the eighteenth century, especially in power. The most remarkable achievement, still unchallenged today, was the emergence of the tenor voice as the true bearer of heroism. A tenor as hero and a baritone or bass as villain is the rule in Romantic opera, strengthened by the careers of one or two notable exponents. Nourrit, Duprez and Roger in turn occupied the tenor throne at the Opéra during this period, and an equivalent glory was bestowed on the great sopranos, such as Cinti-Damoreau, Dorus-Gras, Falcon, Stoltz and Viardot.

THÉÂTRE-ITALIEN AND OPÉRA-COMIQUE

The one sphere where the Opéra was seriously challenged was in the brilliance of its singing stars, for one had only to step from the Rue Le Peletier, where the Opéra then stood, across the Boulevard des Italiens (the name was significant) to the Théâtre-Italien, where a feast of great singing, in a quite different repertory, was to be heard. It was here that

Bellini's *I Puritani* was first played in 1835, the cast including such stellar names as Grisi, Rubini, Tamburini and Lablache. Rossini had been the theatre's director and was then its *éminence grise*. Works by Rossini, Bellini, Donizetti and eventually Verdi were played, and the traditions of *bel canto* lovingly sustained. French critics were divided, as they had been many times in the past, on the subject of Italian music. For Stendhal and his fellow dilettanti it was the purest source of delight; Castil-Blaze, on the *Journal des débats*, adored it and never ceased to berate French music for being tuneless in comparison. Others were less impressed. The Théâtre-Italien was outgunned by the Opéra in lavish staging and fashionable attractions, and was persistently attacked by Berlioz and others for the facile style of its repertory and its dependence on over-elaborate singing. Meyerbeer had worked in Italy for many years and had picked up, in his characteristically eclectic way, a number of obvious Italian mannerisms such as a passion for coloratura, yet he knew as well as Berlioz that greater subtleties of expression and colour were to be derived principally from the orchestra, from its widening palette and from an increasingly sophisticated use of instruments. Donizetti knew this too, even though Berlioz was unwilling to credit him with any such discernment.

The Théâtre-Italien was not the Opéra's only rival. The Opéra-Comique, with its tradition of spoken dialogue, scored success after success. Those who insisted on melody as music's first priority were even happier there than at the Italiens, and a succession of composers emerged with a happy gift of satisfying the not very demanding tastes of the bourgeoisie. Many of these works drew on the same Romantic set-pieces as the Opéra: conflicts of love and duty, midnight assignations, double-dealing with witchcraft and sorcery, fatal passions of many kinds. Stories of country folk distressed, confused or rescued by supernatural agencies such as potions or hermits, were common. The knots were invariably untied at the end with everyone sent away happy. Scribe was a master of this genre as of its more inflated brother, with a permanent success to start off his operatic career in Boïeldieu's *La Dame blanche* (1825), based on Scott's *The Monastery* and *Guy Mannering*. Ghosts appearing on castle walls could safely be shivered or laughed at in the theatre now that centuries of real witchcraft had finally come to an end.

The 1830s saw the production of a great many *opéras-comiques* that remained in the repertory for the rest of the century, and can still be heard occasionally today in piano or brass band arrangements. Auber, despite his great gifts and the success of *La Muette de Portici* at the Opéra, concentrated on *opéra-comique* and produced *Fra Diavolo* (1830), *Le*

Philtre (1831), *Le Cheval de bronze* (1835), *Le Domino noir* (1837), *Les Diamants de la couronne* (1841), and many others. Hérold, a fertile specialist in the form, provided *Zampa* (1831) and *Le Pré aux clercs* (1832); Halévy's success was *L'Éclair* (1835); Adam's was *Le Postillon de Longjumeau* (1836); even Meyerbeer scored a hit with *L'Étoile du nord* (1854). At the heart of the Opéra-Comique lay the split which the later nineteenth century would force wide open, for it was still possible for a serious composer to seek success in both higher and lower forms, and many did. It was not thought demeaning for the Director of the Conservatoire or the Permanent Secretary of the Institute to be writing catchy tunes to a libretto about village boys and girls. By the time that Offenbach came rapidly to public attention, during the Exposition Universelle of 1855, this was no longer the case, and the cheeky melodies he wrote in such torrents for the Bouffes-Parisiens mark the birth of the true light music composer, a breed earlier obscured by the higher aspirations that all composers were expected to nourish. Even so, Offenbach, like Sullivan, craved serious success, and with his half-finished *Contes d'Hoffmann* (1881) almost achieved it.

TWO OPERATIC SCENES

Let us look at two operatic scenes as illustrations of the repertory. The finale of Act I of Auber's *La Muette de Portici* (1828, libretto by Scribe) became a model for many later grand operas. Set in Naples in 1647, when the fishermen rose against their Spanish oppressors, the opera generated revolutionary sympathies and even sparked off the movement for Belgian independence in 1830. Just before her marriage to Alphonse, the Viceroy's son, Elvira learns the story of Fenella. Fenella is a deaf-mute, and she explains in mime how she is searching for a faithless lover who has deserted her. The literal expressiveness of Fenella's mime provides a wonderful opportunity for descriptive music and clever acting. Elvira is called to the ceremony, and a bridal chorus in solemn, churchy tones allows a procession of some splendour.

> Ô Dieu puissant, Dieu tutélaire
> Nous t'implorons à genoux,
> Daigne exaucer notre prière,
> Et bénis ces heureux époux.

Against the stately tread of the chorus, in a striking musical *combinaison*, soldiers have to hold back the importunate Fenella; the women do so also with greater dignity. To much livelier, briefer music the full chorus greets the pair, now united. Elvira, in a sprightly rhythm, turns immediately to Alphonse and declares her pity for the unfortunate girl who is trying to approach them. The music modulates freely and rapidly as Elvira tells of Fenella's plight. A crash and 'ô ciel!' from Alphonse mark the moment of dramatic crisis, followed by silence out of which a big ensemble can grow. Here, as in most such ensembles, the beginning is slow and disjointed. Elvira leads off in hesitant phrases:

ELVIRA: Quel est donc ce mystère?
            Parlez, répondez-moi!
ALPHONSE: Ô funeste mystère!
            C'est elle que je vois!

A chorus of soldiers and another of the people respond in overlapping blocks, culminating in a cadence and pause, the slowness of the music's pace emphasising the static horror of the scene. Elvira returns to a faster pace and questions Fenella: 'Do you know Alphonse?' Fenella's music replies (the libretto informs us): 'It is he who deceived me', 'It is he who betrayed me'. The ensemble resumes, now in fast tempo, the choruses muttering in turn, the two principals (soprano and tenor) proclaiming their horror (Elvira) and shame (Alphonse). The orchestral activity is tremendous with recurrent climaxes. On a pause Fenella escapes; everyone else remains on stage, motionless, then the music becomes even faster and more furious for the final curtain ensemble.

This kind of scene was reproduced with many variations (not, of course, the dumb mime) in Meyerbeer's and Halévy's operas, and also in Verdi. The first act of Berlioz's *Les Troyens* has an ensemble of frozen horror more sophisticated than this but belonging to the same dramatic genre. The exaggerations of gesture and response, and the breadth of the action, discouraging any subtlety or nuance, are typical of Scribe. Although the music eventually moves at a fast tempo, the dramatic pace remains stolid.

For a contrast let us consider the beginning of the second scene of Berlioz's *Benvenuto Cellini* (1838, libretto by Auguste Barbier and Léon de Wailly). The curtain opens on Cellini alone singing an aria inserted purely because the tenor felt he had too little of prominence in the role. To a long, lightly accompanied melody he sings:

La gloire était ma seule idole;
Un noble espoir que je n'ai plus
Ceignait mon front de l'auréole
Que l'art destine à ses élus.

After two verses, a conventional cadence invites applause. The goldsmiths, Cellini's colleagues and workers, enter and call for wine. They begin a drinking song, but Cellini interrupts and persuades them to sing a nobler song, to their art – which they do, with a certain elaboration and splendour, almost a formal set-piece. Having done so, they call for wine again. The innkeeper, a 'Juif grotesque à la voix nasillarde', refuses to serve more until the bill is paid, and in a character piece of comic purpose (the orchestration is deliberately grotesque) he lists the wines they have drunk but not paid for. The rowdy goldsmiths are about to rough him about when Cellini intervenes and suggests they wait for his apprentice Ascanio, who is due to arrive with money provided by the Pope to commission the statue of Perseus from Cellini. Ascanio does duly arrive, and the music which has been highly disjointed settles into a broad ensemble as Ascanio (a trouser role for mezzo-soprano) explains the high purpose of the commission. The effect is, as always, static, while the music grows warmer and broader. At its conclusion Cellini suggests moving off to the Piazza Colonna for their next escapade, so with a reprise of the goldsmiths' hymn to their art they all leave.

This scene advances the plot very little. It simply illustrates Cellini's devotion to his art and the goldsmiths' guild fraternity and their fondness for youthful pranks. Ascanio is introduced for the first time and the commission of the Perseus is explained. Yet the scene is highly coloured and comic in the best sense. *Benvenuto Cellini* is an 'opera semi-seria', combining the scale of grand opera with the livelier character-isation of *opéra-comique*, and allowing some departures from the more contrived norms of Scribe's serious librettos. It was above all the libretto of *Benvenuto Cellini* that was held responsible for its failure in 1838.

OTHER INSTITUTIONS

Let us not forget that music then played a far greater part in all theatrical experience than now. The somewhat exaggerated mode of acting then in favour in Romantic theatre would have been heightened by incidental music played at frequent intervals. Full orchestras were maintained by the Théâtre du Vaudeville, the Théâtre des Variétés, the Gymnase Dramatique, the Théâtre du Palais-Royal, the Gaïté, the Ambigu-Comique and the Porte St-Martin. Smaller bands were found at the Théâtre du Panthéon, the Gymnase des Enfans, and the Porte St-Antoine. Casual engagements were offered by the Folies-Dramatiques and the Cirque Olympique. Large concert orchestras were engaged by the Société des Concerts, the Athénée Musical, the Gymnase Musical and the Concerts Musard; there were a dozen military bands and no less than four orchestras made up of blind musicians. Even allowing for much overlapping of individuals from one orchestra to another, this is an astonishing commitment to active music-making in a city of less than a million inhabitants, comparable to the outpouring of books and journals in feverish literary activity. By the late 1830s Paris was publishing three weekly music journals.

Statistics and institutional history alone do not define the spirit of the age, but they do provide evidence of artistic activity spurred on by the twin forces of commercial expansion and artistic novelty. The theatre and the opera were favourite avenues for speculative directors who knew little about art; grand opera is thus perhaps merely an updated application of commercial enterprise to the traditional French *grand spectacle*. Yet the gift for expressing human passion revealed by Gluck and Spontini was inherited, however faintly, by Rossini and Meyerbeer, and the *diablerie* of Weber's *Der Freischütz* (first heard in Paris in 1824) introduced a taste for *Schauerromantik* which was admirably suited to French musical styles of the time.

THE ROMANCE

The music of individuals was equally subject to commercial forces and to changes in personal taste. Throughout the period the pianoforte gained ground as a domestic instrument at the expense of the harp and the guitar, both of which contributed to one of the most characteristic genres of the age, the *romance*. Under the Revolution and Empire far more people owed their musical experience to the *romance* than to any other musical form, especially in the provinces. Simple strophic songs with accompaniment for harp or guitar, on a sentimental text by, say, Florian, were published in hundreds. Boïeldieu, Loïsa Puget, Romagnesi and Monpou were the favourite composers of a form which allowed a certain quiet passion, with titles that betray their character: 'Le Rêve de Marie', 'L'Exilé du pays', 'La Bénédiction d'un père', 'La Mère du matelot'. The music was melodious and singable, with simple accompaniments repeated unchanged for each verse. Journals issued *romances* as bonuses for their subscribers and the cover illustrations were themselves examples of an art form that flourished throughout the century on a taste for touching, exotic or evocative vignettes (illustration 22).

22. Title-page of an early edition of Niedermeyer's *Le Lac*

The wider imagery of Romantic poetry, the importation of Schubert's songs and the growth of Berlioz's genius led to the emergence of the *mélodie*, a worthy match for the German *Lied*. Gounod, Bizet, Delibes, Lalo and above all Fauré and Duparc contributed to a corpus of songs that closely reflects the phases of Romantic feeling; their music is permitted the maximum subtlety of expression in striking contrast to the over-emphatic manner of the Opéra.

THE SALON

Songs of these generally modest dimensions were mainly for private use. They were not often to be heard in fashionable salons where the preference seems always to have been for operatic excerpts and virtuoso performances on the piano or the violin. Unlike public concerts and operas, salon performances were for the most part unrecorded by the daily press and are therefore less easy to estimate in importance or frequency. Such records as we have pick on the finer specimens. Marie d'Agoult's *Souvenirs* give a description with an interesting sociological sidelight:

Les compositeurs et les chanteurs gardaient encore une place à part; ils ne paraissaient dans les salons, en dépit de l'empressement qu'on mettait à les y avoir, que d'une manière subalterne. Voulait-on, par exemple, donner un beau concert, on s'adressait à Rossini qui, moyennant une somme convenue, assez minime, quinze cents francs, si j'ai bonne mémoire, se chargeait du programme et de son exécution, ôtant ainsi aux maîtres de maison tout embarras du choix, tout ennui des répétitions, etc. Le grand maestro tenait le piano toute la soirée. Il accompagnait les chanteurs. D'ordinaire, il leur adjoignait un virtuose instrumentiste, Herz ou Moschelès, Lafon ou Bériot, Nadermann, le premier harpiste, Tulou, la première flûte du roi, ou la merveille du monde musical, le petit Liszt. Tous ensemble, ils arrivaient à l'heure dite, par une porte de côté; tous ensemble, ils s'asseyaient auprès du piano; tous ensemble, ils repartaient après avoir reçu les compliments du maître de la maison et de quelques *dilettanti* de profession. Le lendemain on envoyait à Rossini son salaire et l'on se croyait quitte envers eux et envers lui.

Mme de Girardin's *Lettres parisiennes* (1844) give further glimpses of this vanished society; she recalls Chopin's playing for princesse de Vaudemont, maréchal Lannes, comte Apponyi, baron Rothschild, prince Radziwill and, of course, her own celebrated receptions.

THE ROMANTIC VIRTUOSI

The piano still had the aura of newly patented machinery. Lured by Erard's double escapement action and streamlined methods of production more and more bourgeois homes equipped themselves with pianos

Godschalk. Prudent. Listz. Henri et Jacques Hertz.

23. Nadar, *Five Virtuoso Pianists (Gottschalk, Prudent, Liszt, Henri and Jacques Herz)*

and purchased some of the dozens of *études*, variations and fantasies that poured from the engravers. Even so, the piano's extrovert qualities easily upstaged its superb utility as a domestic instrument, and the generation of virtuosi (illustration 23) that came to Paris in the 1820s and 1830s exemplified a style of glamorous public achievement which many a poet and painter envied. As in opera, it was Paris's easy receptivity, not to mention adulation, of foreign artists that drew Kalkbrenner, Moscheles, Herz, Field, Thalberg, Halle, Hiller, Heller and many others not to mention Liszt and Chopin – to the capital. Liszt was only twelve when he first played in Paris in 1823 and his flamboyant personality coupled to an astonishing technical facility drew upon himself the legend of the Romantic virtuoso, which he was only too happy to encourage. Legouvé, in his *Soixante ans de souvenirs*, recalled Liszt's attitude at the piano, comparing it to that of a pytheness, with lips quivering and nostrils palpitating. He also pointed out the histrionic style of his mannerisms. 'Constantly tossing back his long hair, his lips quivering, his nostrils palpitating, he swept the auditorium with the glance of a smiling master. He had an actor's mannerisms.' His style was often compared to that of the great tragic actors, for the effect on his audience was similar: the expert showman courting adulation. The sensational appearance of Paganini in Paris in 1831 profoundly affected Liszt, not as inspiration to further exhibitionism but as an example of consummate virtuosity which spurred him to even greater study of his instrument and to a deepening perception of his own role as composer. Paganini, unlike Liszt, had little of the Romantic in his nature; in this respect he was closer to his compatriot Rossini. He seems to have taken no interest in literature and nourished no exalted view of himself as a creative artist. He was simply the supreme technician of the violin in a long tradition of professional Italian virtuosi, supplying his own music for the purpose. He was astute enough to exploit an image of himself as a man of mysterious origin with unspecified dark deeds in his past, a suspicion of satanism and a striking physiognomy of extraordinary thinness. He was, in the eyes of the public, the Romantic virtuoso *par excellence*, and there is no doubt that his ability on the violin was quite out of the ordinary. As an inspirer of hero-worship, imitators, gossip, parody and suspicion he had no rivals. His appearances were not confined to France, of course, but it was the close-knit circle of artists in Paris that relished his strange personality the most, and apart from Schumann it was Liszt and Berlioz whose music was most affected by him.

Chopin had heard Paganini in Warsaw in 1829. He at once wrote a *Souvenir de Paganini* which reveals a poetic touch where one would least expect to find it. But then Chopin, who arrived in Paris in late 1831, never allowed virtuosity to bury the tender, poetic quality which all his music exhibits. If Liszt at this stage of his career exemplifies the titanic artist, huge in achievement and aspiration and heroic in the public view, Chopin is the lyricist whose playing and whose compositions elicited the quieter emotions. Both Liszt and Chopin were accepted in the French cultural milieu, both had famous affairs with celebrated ladies of letters, respectively Marie d'Agoult and George Sand, and both were composing, in the 1830s, works of seminal importance which have lost none of their stature today. Liszt is more obviously a Romantic figure, drawing inspiration freely from landscape and literature, overtly emotional in expression and challenging the limits of the possible in virtuosity. Although he wrote many songs in many languages, it was the wordless expressiveness of music that most appealed to him. Settings of three Petrarch sonnets made in 1838 exist both as songs and as piano solos and are more admired in the latter version. Recitative, in which a solo voice traditionally divests itself of melody and approaches close to speech, is frequently found, as in *Vallée d'Obermann* (1836), where the percussive voice of the piano has the most articulate expressive utterance, even though its meaning is not stated:

Lento

The pieces published in 1840 as *Album d'un voyageur* (later regrouped as *Années de pèlerinage*), and the *Harmonies poétiques et religieuses* (1834) represent a peak of Romantic expression in Liszt's work never dependent on technical virtuosity for its own sake. Even his *Études* (1838) embrace an illustrative purpose, with titles like *Feux follets, Wilde Jagd* and *Paysage*. Liszt's later achievements in programmatic orchestral music were based on these early ventures at the keyboard, and his influence on Wagner and the later nineteenth century was inestimable. He had, from the first, a vivid feeling for advanced modern harmony, and in this he was alone of his generation with Chopin. Both thus contributed strongly to Wagner's mature language.

Chopin's single-minded devotion to the piano and his sensitive, frail personality reflect a familiar image of the doomed, consumptive artist. He displayed none of Liszt's or Berlioz's literary flair and was not the least interested in opera or grand Romantic subjects such as *Hamlet* or *Faust*. He was at pains to disclaim programmatic or literary sources for his pieces and remained an intensely private man averse to the public display of emotion. His passionate identification with Poland was an exception, made plain in the Mazurkas and Polonaises, but elsewhere his abundant feeling is articulated only in the notes themselves. A glorious gift of melody, loosely derived from Italian opera, a wholly unconventional view of structure, intricate chromatic harmony, and physical dependence on the fingers and their faculties are the dominant properties of Chopin's music. His personality is largely mysterious, made the more inscrutable by the legends that quickly accumulated around him. At his funeral at the Madeleine in 1849 all Paris gathered to mourn the passing of one whom they instinctively regarded as one of their number, as if he were the archetypal French Romantic artist.

BERLIOZ

That label has more often been attached, in later years, to Berlioz, who stands pre-eminently among French musicians as the single composer worthy of comparison with foreign musicians like Schumann, Liszt and

Chopin on the one hand and French writers like Hugo and Balzac on the other. His stature as the leading French composer between Rameau and Debussy is unchallenged, and he does stand as a representative symbol of many (though by no means all) aspects of French Romanticism. He was, firstly, completely cosmopolitan in outlook. From 1821 to his death, Paris was his home; he never seriously considered living anywhere else despite alluring offers from Dresden and London. His friends and colleagues were drawn from the refugees, exiles and expatriates that made up the musical fraternity in Paris; he never regarded French music as inherently superior to that of any other land, although a prejudice against Italian music implanted at an early age turned him against Rossini and Bellini and prevented his appreciation of Donizetti and Verdi. His favourite literature was Shakespeare, Goethe and Virgil, his most admired composers Gluck, Spontini, Beethoven and Weber, not one of them French. He knew some Italian and a little English but never mastered any foreign language even when he was travelling frequently abroad. His marriage to the Irish actress Harriet Smithson, which was in itself a supremely Romantic act, foundered, we may surmise, largely on their lack of a common fluency in either English or French, but his adoration of Shakespeare, with which his adoration of Harriet was hopelessly entangled, permitted no barriers of language or culture to stand in its way. He saw himself as a participant in a world culture transcending differences of nationality or period, although such a grandiose view was never so crudely articulated.

The Harriet Smithson affair does have the dramatic *élan* of fiction, the passionate young composer transfixed by an ideal beauty on stage, his Ophelia and his Juliet. Many of his contemporaries were overwhelmed by her beauty and her art, but none persisted as he did in the face of every discouragement. The *Symphonie fantastique* was composed early in 1830, two and a half years after his first sight of her, and it exorcised a passion which had consumed him incessantly in that period but had then turned sour. Convinced she was worthless, he was able to close his symphony in a violent paroxysm as if to dismiss her from his consciousness and consign her to hell's flames. The *Ronde du sabbat*, the last movement, is as spectacular a piece of musical *diablerie* as any ever composed, drawing partly on Weber but mostly on his own fervid imagination. It exposed his command of a large modern orchestra for the first time and it gave an ingenious twist to the format of Beethoven's symphonies, on which the symphony as a whole is based, by concluding in a black rage rather than in the confident optimism which was Beethoven's usual gesture. Berlioz could not then have known that he would meet Harriet for the first time two years later and quickly propose marriage. If ever any man has married an imagined ideal rather than a creature of flesh and blood, it was Berlioz. It was an ideal, furthermore, which he had already violently excoriated in his music.

A similar predominance of imagination over reality guided his passion for Estelle Dubœuf, a pretty eighteen-year-old when Berlioz, then twelve, first fell for her. He felt drawn to her again over thirty years later and they exchanged letters; when he was a widower of sixty and she a widow of sixty-six he reverted to this childhood image and fell at her feet, oblivious of the intervening years. Their monthly exchange of letters was the principal solace of his last years, when he had outlived two sisters, two wives and his adored son Louis.

Berlioz's imagination was the mainspring of his art, not simply as a creative force such as any composer or writer requires, but as a guiding principle in the format and medium of his music. He never accepted rigid categories such as symphony or cantata or even opera. Elements from one always overlap another. Miscellaneous groupings are found in the *Neuf Mélodies irlandaises* (1830), for example, with songs and choruses side by side, or the *Huit Scènes de Faust* (1829) which range from chorus and orchestra to solo voice with guitar. More pertinent are the concert works in which a dramatic subject is presented without visible action: *Roméo et Juliette* (1839), *La Damnation de Faust* (1846) and *L'Enfance du Christ* (1850–4). The last two of these have stage directions even though there is no stage, and extensive passages for the orchestra alone where action or a stage picture is to be imagined, evoked by the music alone. In *Roméo et Juliette* neither of the lovers have sung words; they are impersonated solely by the orchestra, whereas Mercutio and Friar Laurence have singing roles in the manner of an opera. The chorus is prominent in all three, sometimes as narrator, sometimes as commentator, sometimes as protagonists as when they divide into two groups as Montagues and Capulets. In his operas Berlioz makes extensive use of off-stage effects, as he does also in his symphonies and choral works, as if he preferred things to be heard and not seen. The immense Wooden Horse in Act I of *Les Troyens* (1856–8) is not actually seen onstage even though its arrival is the dramatic and musical climax of the act. It is difficult to picture Scribe or Meyerbeer missing an opportunity of this kind, and indeed no modern producer has ever taken Berlioz literally here. His vivid imagination actually inhibits his command of operatic craft in instances such as this, despite the supreme achievement of *Les Troyens* as the climax of a lifelong devotion to Virgil and as the epic offspring of a long line of French classical opera from Rameau, Gluck and Spontini.

Berlioz was an idealist who could see all too clearly a perfect musical world in his mind. Indeed he described it in a *nouvelle* entitled *Euphonia* (1844), later published in *Les Soirées de l'orchestre* (1852). Here an entire city is devoted to the service of music with a street of piano tuners, a street of sopranos, and so on. There is high comedy here, of course, but Berlioz's painful awareness of the shortcomings of Parisian music drove him to give concerts more and more abroad. *Euphonia* is actually situated in Germany, 500 years in the future, for it was in the old-fashioned German courts thàt Berlioz found the kind of lavish patronage of music, with orchestras and theatres at the composer's complete disposal, that he dreamed of. A similar dream of unlimited resources colours the final pages of his *Grand Traité d'instrumentation* (1844), a pioneering textbook on orchestration. Eventually his frustration with the corruption of Parisian musical life and the rapid decline of taste in the 1850s drove him into a black disillusionment from which he never emerged, his ideals all pitifully unrealised. In this sense, for all his positive achievements in many spheres as conductor, critic and composer and for all his wit, Berlioz is a profoundly tragic figure, subject to merciless attack by critics who found his enthusiasm and commitment offensive and who felt that his music 'lacked melody'.

In the Postscript of his *Memoirs* Berlioz put it as follows:

La principale raison de la longue guerre qu'on m'a faite est dans l'antagonisme existant entre mon sentiment musical et celui du gros public parisien. Une foule de gens ont dû me regarder comme un fou, puisque je les regarde comme des enfants ou des niais. Toute musique qui s'écarte du petit sentier où trottinent les faiseurs d'opéras-comiques fut nécessairement, pendant un quart de siècle, de la musique de fou pour ces gens-là. Le chef-d'œuvre de Beethoven (la IXe *symphonie*) et ses colossales sonates de piano, sont encore pour eux de la musique de fou.

A little later there follows a famous passage describing his own music:

Les qualités dominantes de ma musique sont l'expression passionnée, l'ardeur intérieure, l'entraînement rythmique et l'imprévu. Quand je dis expression passionnée, cela signifie expression acharnée à reproduire le sens intime de son sujet, alors même que le sujet est le contraire de la passion et qu'il s'agit d'exprimer des sentiments doux, tendres, ou le calme le plus profond.

Here lies the key to Berlioz's music, indeed to all Romantic music, since expression was universally held to be its highest purpose before any notions of abstraction or pure structure came to supplant it, a development which can loosely be dated to the publication of Hanslick's *Vom Musikalisch-Schönen* in 1854. With an unbroken tradition of literary allusion in French music from the Pléiade through *tragédie-lyrique* to the *romance*, Berlioz was simply accepting the equivalence of music and feeling and bringing to it the resources of the modern orchestra. All his music relates to a text, a programme, an image or to personal experience. It is not simply 'programme music', offering narrative or pictorial description, but music which reflects the movement of the mind in the same way that prose or poetry does. No composer has woven his own life so intricately into his music. *Harold en Italie* (1834) reflects his experiences in Italy with a Byronic gloss; the *Symphonie fantastique* evolved from one love-affair, as we have seen, its sequel *Lélio* (1831) from another. His greatest works spring from his passion for literature, principally Shakespeare, Goethe and Virgil, and there are pieces based on Byron, Scott, Fenimore Cooper and other fashionable figures of the day. His sacred music is a response to the dramatic and expressive qualities of Latin texts, as in the *Grande Messe de morts* (1837) and the *Te Deum* (1849). These large choral works belong to a category he termed 'architectural' since they are grand in the manner of the great ecclesiastical monuments. He had no particular interest in architecture as an art form, but St Peter's, St Paul's and the Hôtel des Invalides all contributed to that numinous sense of space when he asks unusually large choral and orchestral forces to fill an unusually large sacred building, whether in pianissimo or fortissimo. Heine compared Berlioz's music to 'the hanging gardens of Semiramis, the marvels of Nineveh, the mighty constructions of Mizraim, as we see them in the pictures of the English painter Martin'. Not only John Martin among painters had an affinity with Berlioz; he is also close to the Belgian Antoine Wiertz whose monumental canvases touch on Berliozian subjects, *Le Carnaval romain* for instance. A comparison with Delacroix yields similar common ground especially in their earlier years, with the additional element of an acquaintance (no more) one with the other and of Delacroix's aspirations as a musician. His *Mort de Sardanapale* (1827) preceded Berlioz's cantata of the same name by three years and his Hamlet and Faust studies reflect a shared enthusiasm; Delacroix was also inflamed by the Odéon Shakespeare performances in 1827.

With the great writers of his time – Hugo, Balzac, Vigny, Dumas – Berlioz was on familiar terms. Although he found Hugo unsympathetic ('il trône trop'), he drew on *Le Dernier Jour d'un condamné* and his *Ronde du sabbat* for the *Symphonie fantastique* and turned two of the *Orientales* into ravishing vocal works: *La Captive* and *Sara la baigneuse*. Vigny was clearly a close confidant of Berlioz in the years 1832 to 1835; he seems to have proposed the subject of Benvenuto Cellini as an opera and taken a hand in its libretto. As a writer himself Berlioz deserves more than passing attention, provided that no claim is made for him other than as *feuilletoniste* and *nouvelliste*. Even his incomparable *Mémoires*, prepared like Chateaubriand's for posthumous publication, consist almost entirely of articles written for the press at various stages of his career, skilfully edited. As regular music critic for the *Journal des débats* and the *Revue et gazette musicale* for over thirty years, his writing brought him constantly to the centre of Parisian music and also helped to pay the bills, but it was ultimately counterproductive not only because he failed in his self-appointed task of winning readers to his views but also because his fame as a critic gradually impeded his role as composer even if it had not stolen precious time from his preferred task. His writings can be read with pleasure for their musical judgments, for their dry and often sarcastic wit, and for a fantastic quality akin to that of E.T.A. Hoffmann, whose tales he read in Richard's translation, published in 1830. Like many German writers, Berlioz had a penchant for setting his music criticism in a fictional framework, the best example being the collection *Les Soirées de l'orchestre* (1852), a series of stories, gossip, biography, criticism and fable presented as the idle chit-chat of musicians in an opera orchestra (illustration 24). Most evenings, since the repertory is generally feeble and worthless, they sit around and swap stories, but when a masterpiece is being played, by Beethoven, say, or Weber or Gluck, they all attend devotedly and lovingly to their duties.

OTHER FRENCH COMPOSERS

Two French composers must be considered alongside Berlioz as making individual though significantly lesser contributions to the movement. Félicien David (1810–76) joined the Saint-Simonian movement early in 1832, long before he enjoyed any fame as a composer. He became the leading musician of that group of utopian social thinkers in their retreat at Ménilmontant and composed numerous hymns and songs for their rituals. When the community broke up in 1833 David left on a mission to the Middle East where the second phase of his career opened up. In Smyrna and Egypt he composed a number of *Mélodies orientales* for piano whose modest success on his return to Paris in 1836 paved the way for more adventurous pieces in an oriental idiom. *Le Désert*, of 1844, was a runaway success, spawning a number of imitations and confirming the French taste for Eastern colour so evident in operas of the later part of the century. The vast wastes of the desert, the muezzin's call and a mildly exotic background are evoked by orchestra and men's chorus, with a reciter to introduce each of the four movements in a novel dramatic fashion. Echoes of *Le Désert* are to be heard in Berlioz's *L'Enfance du Christ* (1854), Bizet's *Pêcheurs de perles* (1863), Meyerbeer's *L'Africaine*

24. Honoré Daumier, *L'Orchestre pendant qu'on joue une tragédie*

(1865), Massenet's *Le Roi de Lahore* (1877), Delibes's *Lakmé* (1883), and in many other French works. David himself never equalled his own success, although he continued to pluck the oriental lyre for many years, most successfully in his opera *Lalla Roukh* (1862). Auber's wry comment was, 'I wish he'd get off his camel.'

In complete contrast to David and indeed to all his contemporaries was the Jewish piano virtuoso Alkan (1813–88), an enigmatic and neglected figure whose misanthropic ways and reclusive career shielded him from public attention in his own lifetime and ever since. A number of impulses meet in his music. His early works are brilliant in the conventional style of 1830 but they soon took on extravagant proportions at the same time as Liszt's concert studies opened the way to a more poetic and more grandiose style. Some of Alkan's pieces make superhuman demands on the technique and stamina of the performer; the first movement of the *Concerto* (1857), for example, lasts half an hour alone. Some of his music is bizarrely evocative in its colour or titles: the *Chant de la folle au bord de la mer*, or the piano sonata entitled *Les Quatre Âges* (1847), representing man at the ages of, respectively, twenty, thirty, forty and fifty in its four movements, the last three of which bear the subtitles *Quasi-Faust*, *Un Heureux Ménage* and *Prométhée enchaîné*. Much of it relates to Hebrew or classical learning; many pieces reproduce eighteenth-century styles; and behind the Satanic mask which has led him to be compared, somewhat inappropriately, with Berlioz there lies a strain of rigour and exactitude revealed in inflexible harmonic patterns, a rejection of rubato of any kind and the deliberate concealment of his personality (and indeed his person, for many years).

THE EPOCH AND ITS CLOSE

No French composer of the Romantic age completely fits the conventional image. None showed much interest in the chivalric tone that delighted Weber, Schumann and Wagner, nor in folk or patriotic material. Things medieval had little appeal for Berlioz and his only attempt at a gothic opera (*La Nonne sanglante* on a Scribe libretto after Lewis's *Monk*) came to nothing. Only Berlioz believed in the supremacy of feeling as the composer's guide, the rest yielding to other priorities such as dramatic construction, pictorial evocation or commercial demand. Music nonetheless played a vitally important part in French culture and drew the constant attention of writers and critics. Beethoven acted as the ideal image of the inspired creator, Liszt and Paganini as the supreme virtuosi. It was an age of enthusiasms and passions that were more evident in music's admirers, for the most part, than in its executants. France has always preferred to discuss and argue about music than to perform it and listen to it and the Romantic age was no exception. Genuine admirers of the *Symphonie fantastique* and *Roméo et Juliette* were numerous, but they were as nothing compared to the admirers of Meyerbeer and Auber. We thus confront a serious difficulty in attempting a balanced appraisal of a society whose tastes differed so radically from our own: we equate Berlioz with Haydn and Schumann and Debussy while ignoring Meyerbeer's music altogether. This gaping chasm between their world and ours cannot be simply explained away by condemning the *habitués* of the Opéra as men of little taste or learning, ignorant of what was really good in their midst. French society was as complex then as it has ever been, full of artistic sympathies of which we have no understanding today, so that a clear demarcation between the real and the fraudulent cannot be glibly made.

By the mid 1840s, nonetheless, a clear decline in musical taste may be discerned. The enthusiasms of the 1820s had waned and there was a pitifully unresponsive audience for Berlioz's *La Damnation de Faust* in 1846, one of the supreme achievements of French Romanticism. A relentless diet of *opéra-comique* and the pretty evocative pictures of *Le Désert* had undoubtedly seduced the public from greater things, and a trend towards sentimentality, the bane of the mid Victorian age, is clearly evident. The disorders of 1848 were for Berlioz a manifest signal of art's decline, even its death. His *Mémoires*, begun in that year, have a distinctly valedictory tone. Mendelssohn, Donizetti and Chopin were soon dead and the new stars of French music were Thomas and Gounod, both masters of a lyrical style of great craft that lacked the commitment of an earlier generation and did not eschew the sentimental. For Berlioz a serious setback was Liszt's espousal of Wagner's cause, for he was convinced that Wagner represented a dangerous tendency that could only undermine the most sacred traditions of music, as indeed it did. When Wagner played the *Tristan* prelude in Paris in 1860, Berlioz was among the vast majority who were unable to accept this radically new music; Baudelaire was among the very few who perceived its worth and guessed at its enormous later influence in France.

Perhaps it was the open-door attitude of the French that inhibited the flowering of native talent in the Romantic period, as it had in English music in the eighteenth century. After the Siege and the Commune, when French composers under Saint-Saëns's leadership began to think of the need to rebuild their national traditions, fewer foreigners came to Paris and more French composers rose to prominence. Their work

inherited a Romantic language forged by Beethoven, Berlioz, Meyerbeer, Schumann and others and was a worthy match for the new schools
in Russia and Bohemia if not perhaps for the mighty voices of Wagner
and Brahms. They remained true to long-established French virtues in
their attachment to the *spectacle* and ballet and to critical values derived
largely, as had always been the case, by literary men from literary
practice. Music was still not accorded the supremacy among the arts the
true Romantic in Germany or Italy might have given it, but it continued
to contribute to a predominantly literary culture with some weakening
of the centrality of Paris but with the same enthusiasm and diversity in
taste and achievement that had marked French music throughout the
century.

NOTES

1. René Dumesnil, *La Musique romantique française* (Aubier, 1944).
2. Louis Véron, *Mémoires d'un bourgeois de Paris* (3 vols., G. de Gonet, 1853–5), vol. III,
   p. 122.
3. Despite Puccini's use of it in *Madama Butterfly*.

BIBLIOGRAPHY

Two broad studies of the place of music in the French Romantic movement stand out:
Léon Guichard's *La Musique et les lettres au temps du romantisme* (PUF, 1955), and J.-M.
Bailbé's *Le Roman et la musique sous la monarchie de juillet* (Minard, 1969). General histories
of French music in this period have been written by Paul Landormy, *La musique française
de la Marseillaise à la mort de Berlioz* (Gallimard, 1944) and René Dumesnil, *La musique
romantique française* (Aubier, 1944). More general studies are Julien Tiersot's *La Musique
aux temps romantiques* (Félix Alcan, 1930) and Claude Laforêt's *La Vie musicale au temps
romantique* (Peyronnet 1929, reprinted Da Capo, New York, 1977). The fullest treatment
of French music after 1870 is Martin Cooper's *French Music from the Death of Berlioz to the
Death of Fauré* (Oxford University Press, London, 1951).

The music of French grand opera is a neglected field, although the social background
is covered in William L. Crosten's *French Grand Opera: an Art and a Business* (King's
Crown Press, New York, 1948), and the libretti are closely studied in Patrick J. Smith's
The Tenth Muse (Gollancz, London, 1971) and Karin Pendle's *Eugène Scribe and French
Grand Opera of the Nineteenth Century* (UMI Research Press, Ann Arbor, 1979).
Meyerbeer's journals and letters are available in the series of *Briefwechsel und Tagebücher*
edited by Heinz Becker (Walter de Gruyter, Berlin, 1960–), and a general essay by
Martin Cooper is found in *Fanfare for Ernest Newman*, ed. van Thal, (Arthur Barker,
London, 1955).

The *romance* and *mélodie* are the subject of Frits Noske's admirable *La Mélodie française
de Berlioz à Duparc* (PUF, 1954) with its second edition in English, *French Song from Berlioz
to Duparc* (Dover, New York, 1970). On Liszt and Chopin one may consult the
comprehensive symposia edited by Alan Walker published (Barrie and Jenkins,
London) in 1970 and 1966 respectively. Paganini's impact on France is the subject of a
special number of the *Revue internationale de musique française*, 9 (November 1982) and is

fully treated in G. de Courcy's *Paganini the Genoese* (University of Oklahoma Press, Norman, 1957).

Berlioz's writings are published by Flammarion (*Mémoires*, 2 vols., Livre de Poche, 1969) and Gründ (*Les Soirées de l'orchestre*, 1968; *Les Grotesques de la musique*, 1969; *A travers chants*, 1971). The *Correspondance générale*, edited by Pierre Citron, so far consists of four of a projected seven volumes (Flammarion, 1972–   ). English readers are referred to David Cairns's excellent translation and edition of the *Memoirs* (Gollancz, London, 1969, revised edn 1975). The illustrated catalogue of the Victoria and Albert Museum Exhibition, *Berlioz and the Romantic Imagination* (1969) is highly evocative and informative. Jacques Barzun's *Berlioz and the Romantic Century* (Little Brown, Boston, 1950) gives a broad cultural perspective. Hugh Macdonald's *Berlioz* (Dent, London, 1982) provides a general study of Berlioz's life and works. For other individual composers, consult *The New Grove* (20 vols., Macmillan, London, 1980). An essential adjunct to the aesthetics of the period is Peter le Huray and James Day, *Music and Aesthetics in the Eighteenth and Early-Nineteenth Centuries* (Cambridge University Press, 1981).

Recordings of Berlioz, Liszt and Chopin are plentiful, but they are very scarce in the field of opera. Of the operas under study only *Guillaume Tell*, *Les Huguenots*, *Benvenuto Cellini*, *Le Prophète*, and *Les Troyens* have been recorded complete. Of the others one may occasionally find extracts or taped broadcasts, but the music of Spontini, Auber and Halévy remains largely inaccessible to those unversed in score-reading.

XI · *Romantics on the fringe (Les Romantiques marginaux)*

MAX MILNER
(translated by Janet Lloyd)

We have grown more or less accustomed to calling them 'the minor Romantics', although it is recognised that the description is somewhat unjust. One of their most recent historians has admitted: 'Je ne m'en suis servi que faute de mieux, et avec toutes les restrictions qu'on imagine.'[1] The fact is that, initially, the description implied a value judgment which an evolution in taste has partially belied or rendered absurd. Nowadays there can be no question of such a description extending to Gérard de Nerval whose *Les Chimères*, *Aurélia*, *Sylvie* and *Pandora* must be counted among the sublime achievements of the art of literature. And Théophile Gautier, who belonged during his youth to the group of artists subsequently dubbed 'the minor Romantics', wrote some of his most original and powerful works during that period. His membership of that group in no way accounts for our reluctance to count him among the 'major Romantics'.

The very distinction made between 'major' and 'minor' is brought into question by the existence of the writers to whom this chapter is devoted: not only because of the relative nature of all aesthetic judgments but also because the destinies of misfortune and failure to which most of these writers seemed called in such an exemplary fashion, even in respect of the posthumous fate of their works, was intrinsically bound up with the 'glad tidings' that Romanticism was to announce. One of the essential qualities of Romanticism would be lacking if there had not existed human beings sufficiently courageous, poverty stricken or mad to stake their whole lives upon an artistic activity destined to produce only abortive, unrecognised or profoundly atypical works. In the literature of the classical age the writers who fully realised the aesthetic ideal of the age are relatively easy to distinguish from all the 'minor masters' who, with varying degrees of success, strove in that direction. But it is scarcely paradoxical to suggest that the essence of Romanticism is present in those whose excesses, exaggeration and 'bad luck' denied them careers crowned with success and recognition just as much, if not more so, as in those who, through the power of their genius but in many cases also through making judicious compromises, managed to win the favour of the public.

If the criterion of stature or quality implied by the description 'minor Romantics' thus seems particularly misleading in the case of the writers with whom this chapter is concerned, it would seem in contrast that the idea of a literary 'fringe' expresses an essential quality that they all share, notwithstanding their extreme diversity. To be 'on the fringe' means, in effect, to belong to a social body or class (in this case almost invariably the lower or middle bourgeoisie) with which one has not broken all links, but to reject its values not only on an ideological level (as often happened even in the cases of the most well-established Romantics) but also on an existential one. The writers that we are concerned with are thus, in a sense, 'on the fringe' on two counts: in respect, first, of the bourgeois society whose values they oppose with a particular bitterness and in some cases dramatic personal commitment and, secondly, of the various groups that make up the Romantic movement – groups with which they cannot or will not completely identify themselves.

This is a new phenomenon the origins of which are to be found in the divorce that progressively took place, during the first quarter of the nineteenth century, between, on the one hand, a society increasingly dominated by the bourgeoisie and, on the other, a concept of the artist that tended to make him a being apart, invested with a mission that transcended that of all other social groups, and endowed with a dignity that forbade him to devote himself to anything other than the cult of Art: this last conceived as a veritable priestly calling. Whereas still, in the mid eighteenth century, the word 'artist' had denoted no more than a craftsman with a particular technical skill,[2] it gradually became restricted to those who practised the Fine Arts and acquired new prestige that stemmed from the notion of the artist's affinity with the creative power of the divine and his communication with a source of beauty that transcends all human values.[3]

It is not hard to see that, endowed with such prestige, the condition of artist could become an idealised refuge for those who found themselves, through the evolution of history, plunged into disarray and condemned to an existence without future prospects. Such was no doubt the case for those *méditateurs* whom Nodier frequented in Paris between 1800 and 1803 and who prefigured, in a number of respects, the groups with which we are concerned. Among them painters and writers were brought together in the celebration of a 'primitive art' which afforded them a means of escape from an increasingly regimented society which offered their desires no hope of fulfilment and from which they marked their dissociation through their eccentric dress. 'Le sentiment général qui leur tenait lieu d'abord de religion . . . c'était au commencement l'amour, le fanatisme de l'art', Nodier wrote in 1832, describing this period of his youth.[4]

The new prestige attached to the condition of artist certainly continued to fuel the dreams of those who, during the Empire and the Restoration, could find no place that matched their ambitions in the society that was establishing itself without them.[5] But it was not until 1830 that the incompatibility between these dreams and reality was shatteringly revealed by the movement of history. The beginnings of Romanticism had engendered huge hopes. The Romantic doctrine as it developed in France from 1820 onwards not only conferred a sacred role upon the poet but also encouraged him to expect benefits to accrue from this priesthood, making him either an auxiliary or a councillor for religious power, with the mission of revealing the paths of providence to his fellow men, or the depository of some autonomous spiritual power charged with guiding the social body along the perilous paths of liberty. It is for this reason that there were no truly 'fringe' artists during this period. Some, who were soon to become such, were still more or less assiduously frequenting Victor Hugo's coterie. These were young people his juniors by about ten years (Gérard de Nerval and the sculptor Jean Duseigneur, both born in 1808, being the eldest among them), over whom Victor Hugo exerted a veritable fascination that was to take full effect in the battle over *Hernani*. Their enthusiasm it was that ensured success for the play which symbolised in their eyes all the promises held out by the new art. Although infected by a certain demagogy, Victor Hugo's influence and open-mindedness was extensive. The solitary Alphonse Rabbe, Hugo's senior by six years, did not share his aesthetic ideas but found in him a sympathetic ear for his passion for liberty and his despairing stoicism. The provincial, Aloysius Bertrand, ventured out of the isolation to which his poverty condemned him to read his first prose-poems in Hugo's salon.

1830 was marked by the relative but highly significant success of *Hernani*, believed by the more advanced or anti-conformist groups in the artistic world to herald the total liberation of art. It was also the year of the July revolution, which appeared to signal the definitive demise of a social order incapable of revering beauty and offering her promoters their rightful place in the enterprise of building the future. Before the year was out, however, the surge of hope that had carried forward those advanced groups began to recede. The causes for this were both internal and, above all, external.

Despite the renewal of fervour that accompanied the battle of *Hernani*, the atmosphere within Victor Hugo's circle was not what it had been in the early days. Serious cracks were beginning to appear in the friendship between Hugo and Sainte-Beuve, upon which the cohesion of the group and its wider influence to some extent depended. Nodier, Musset and Dumas disengaged themselves from the group. And, with his publishers at his heels, Hugo himself retreated to complete his *Notre-Dame de Paris*.

Above all, however, it was the social order established in the aftermath of the July revolution that engendered such bitterness, disillusion or despair among those who had taken part in the struggle, or followed it with sympathy in the belief that political change would be accompanied by social reform of a kind to match their aspirations. This society, which was supposed to allow each individual to develop his own talents and take part in the transformation of the world, turned out to be a thwarted society in which the tyranny of money was even more pitiless than had been that of rank and birth, and the economic, prudent, conformist behaviour of the French bourgeoisie of the period was encouraged and rewarded to the detriment of the generous dreams, absolute ideals and open-handed attitudes that seemed part and parcel of the condition of artist. Far from managing to impose its own values upon the intellectual world, the class that possessed the reality of power became the object of systematic denigration to the point where the epithet 'bourgeois', given a positive connotation by the *philosophe* movement in the eighteenth century, now became a kind of mark of infamy, as the humorists and caricaturists demonstrated in a thousand and one ways.[6]

The 'disenchantment'[7] that followed almost immediately upon the euphoria of July 1830 extended far beyond the artistic avant-garde. Among the leaders of the Romantic movement, it provoked efforts to adapt to the new reality or attempts to elaborate a mode of thought that would be capable of impinging upon it and sooner or later changing it. However, those who had placed in the revolution the greatest hopes that it would give Art every chance withdrew in contrast into attitudes of isolation, rejection or defiance which did, well and truly, make them artists on the fringe. Of course, their marginality took many diverse forms. In some cases it was lived out collectively, expressed in the formation of groups whose members lent each other encouragement to resist by professing the ideas they all held in common. In others it was lived out in solitude and it was certainly in this form that the image of the *poète maudit* acquired its most pathetic features. However, there were different degrees even to this solitude: Nerval and Lassailly were sinking into insanity even while maintaining an appearance of continuing to participate in the literary life of the period; Forneret constructed a fantastical universe within the cloistered refuge of the provinces; Aloysius Bertrand died in hospital, having won interest in his work from no more than two or three friends. We shall return to each of them to consider the personal destiny they either chose or were engulfed by. But let us meanwhile turn to the groups in which the Romantic fringe took the form of a collective response to the situation of the artist in the society of the July monarchy.

The oldest of these, known historically as the *Petit Cénacle*, was partly composed of members of Victor Hugo's *cénacle*, or circle, who, by the end of 1830, were feeling the need to find a venue where they could express the radicalism of their political and aesthetic opinions without constraint. The place they found was the studio of the sculptor Jean Duseigneur who, at the age of twenty-two, seemed destined to revolutionise French sculpture. Grouped around him were the engravers Célestin Nanteuil and Joseph Bouchardy (who later became an actor), the poets Jules Vabre, Théophile Gautier, Gérard de Nerval, Philothée O'Neddy, the novelists and playwrights Alphonse Brot and Auguste Maquet. Petrus Borel, a student of architecture simultaneously trying his hand at poetry, emerged briefly as their leader by reason of his magnetic personality, his tragic aura and the intransigence with which he professed his anti-social ideas. The fact that this brotherhood brought together artists using a number of different means of expression was in itself a phenomenon of some significance. Their contemporaries saw, in general, only its most superficial aspects: the provocative costumes, the black jokes, the affectations of exoticism, primitivism and cannibalism, the declamations round the punch bowl and the nocturnal rowdiness. In a series of articles between August and October 1831, the *Figaro* made a meal of those whom it had elected to call the *Jeune-France* group, explicitly attributing the excesses of the group to the union that it had occasioned between painters and men of letters: 'La Jeune-France est née du jour où la peinture a fait alliance avec la littérature romantique. Le poète a dit au peintre: vous peignez, mais vous ne savez pas parler: prenez mon jargon . . . Le peintre a répondu au poète: vous écrivez, mais vous ne savez pas peindre: prenez ma barbe . . . Et de ce jour les peintres ont su écrire, les hommes de lettres ont eu la barbe.'[8]

But even if Jean Duseigneur's studio – installed over a simple fruiterer's shop in the rue de Vaugirard – often rang with exalted paradoxes and declamations,[9] and the nocturnal calm of the streets of Paris was sometimes disturbed by the noisy jollities of the *Jeune-France*, the meetings of these young men all practising their different arts with an equal enthusiasm, brought to the fore one of Romanticism's newest and most productive ideas: that there is a profound affinity between the various arts, an affinity that consists not only in realising an ideal of beauty through a number of heterogeneous forms of expression but also in making use of the sensibilities and techniques developed from the practice of the various arts to the end of perfecting the production of such beauty and submitting it to criticism.

It was a confrontation, never before realised in such an assiduous and intimate fashion, that presupposed a concept of Art that transcended the frontiers established by history and for that very reason it acquired a power and prestige noted at the time by a contemporary with undoubted perspicacity but not without a measure of anxiety: 'Au lieu des beaux-arts que nous connaissons tous par leurs noms de famille ou leurs noms de baptême, nous avons l'Art, roi nouveau que le siècle a porté sur ses pavois, et qui le gouverne en despote ombrageux.'[10] The members of the *Petit Cénacle* were particularly sensitive to that despotism. For them, art was not only a privileged activity but an essential choice, a veritable rule of life that could demand the most costly of sacrifices and supersede all moral and religious rules. In a letter to Sainte-Beuve, written in 1832, Gérard de Nerval expressed with much delicacy what it was that these young artists derived from one another's company. Although his description of the situation may be somewhat idealised, it does give some idea of all the impassioned activity and devotion to the artist's calling that lay hidden behind the apparent dissipation. Referring to Jean Duseigneur, he wrote as follows:

C'est à propos de Jean Duseigneur, un grand travailleur, et qui, sauf quelques portraits d'amis, ne se prend qu'à des travaux longs et sévères; disposition bien louable, dans ce temps-ci où tous les jeunes gens de grand talent et de grande espérance s'épuisent en petits ouvrages tandis que les œuvres solides sont plus rares que jamais. J'ai bien compris tout cela depuis deux ans que je le connais et que je suis entré dans le Petit Cénacle dont il fait partie et où je m'attache de plus en plus. Certes, il n'a pas été formé dans l'intention de parodier l'autre, ce glorieux *cénacle* que vous avez célébré, mais seulement pour être une *association* utile et un public de choix où l'on puisse essayer ses ouvrages d'avance et satisfaire jusqu'à un certain point ce besoin de publication qui fait qu'on éparpille un avenir de gloire en petits triomphes successifs. C'est aussi un aiguillon bien puissant que de s'entendre demander tous les jours: qu'as-tu fait? et que de voir autour de soi des gens qui travaillent.[11]

For all those involved it was an unforgettable experience and the mediocrity of the years that followed were to lend their memories of this period an enhanced prestige. Twenty-five years later Théophile Gautier was to write: 'Être jeune, intelligent, s'aimer, comprendre et communier sous les espèces de l'art, on ne pouvait concevoir une plus belle manière de vivre, et tous ceux qui l'ont pratiqué en ont gardé un éblouissement qui ne se dissipe pas.'[12]

Long lasting the dazzling impression may have been, but the reality that produced it barely lasted into the first months of 1833. The members of the *Petit Cénacle* had not all reacted to the consolidation of Louis-Philippe's power in similar fashion. Some, Théophile Gautier for instance, were anxious to retain contact with Hugo and his followers who were openly criticising the excesses they deemed likely to compromise the cause of Romanticism. Others gave their approval to the increasingly provocative behaviour of Petrus Borel. During the summer of 1832, Borel installed himself, with a few other members of the group, in an isolated house at the top of the rue Rochechouart. There, they camped out on animal skins, without clothes, to the horror of their neighbours who threatened to get the police to evict what they called 'le camp des Tartares'. Borel then moved to a house in the rue d'Enfer. The house-warming was the occasion of a memorable orgy in the course of which Alexandre Dumas, who was a guest, was reputed to have consumed custard from a skull. It was now, at the end of 1832, that, together with a few friends, Borel founded a weekly journal, *La Liberté, journal des arts*, the manifesto of which sounded the battle charge:

C'est une vraie guerre que nous engageons et une guerre à mort . . . L'armée est prête, les cadres remplis, les soldats exercés, et le mot d'ordre qui n'avait été encore que bégayé . . . nous le crions aujourd'hui à voix haute: Mort à l'Institut! Mort au Professorat! Ainsi nous ne jetterons les armes que lorsque nous aurons fait à l'Académie Royale des Beaux-Arts une large tombe avec les pierres démolies du Palais des Quatre Nations.[13]

Alas! the army in question was already in rout. The members of the *Petit Cénacle* continued to maintain their friendly relations for a while, but they were no longer prepared to march against the cannons. In 1833 the total flop of Borel's *Champavert* and O'Neddy's *Feu et Flamme*, two works that ostentatiously sported the colours of the *Jeune-France*, no doubt hastened the dispersion of the *Petit Cénacle* and drove those who had founded their greatest hopes upon it back into bitterness and solitude.

The group that, in November 1834, began to gather in the apartment occupied by Gérard de Nerval and the painter Camille Rogier in the impasse du Doyenné, in an area under demolition between the arc du Carrousel and the place du Théâtre-Français, numbered a few figures from the *Petit Cénacle*: Gautier, Maquet, Nanteuil and, from time to time, Borel himself but it was quite different in character. In the first place, it was much more open. The artists met in the main room of the apartment, in a vast somewhat dilapidated salon that still retained a few traces of the splendour and elegance of the eighteenth century. They included poets and novelists such as Roger de Beauvoir, Alphonse Brot, Esquiros, Alphonse Karr, Alexandre Dumas, Arsène Houssaye, painters and engravers such as Préault, Gavarni, Boulanger, Devéria and Delacroix and even members of the administration and the army such as Falconnet, Couvent des Bois and Édouard Lhôte whose only credentials were that they were sincere lovers of the arts. The fact was that the spirit of the age was no longer in tune with abrasive exclusivity and passionate declarations of war against society. Following the rioting of April 1834 the power of Louis-Philippe had been consolidated and it was further strengthened after the Fieschi assassination attempt (28 July 1835). Prosperity was returning and with it social peace. Youth was turning away from action or dreams of action and becoming more concerned to enjoy itself. Nerval and Rogier's apartment, alongside which Théophile Gautier took up residence, was a place of gaiety with a décor to which a number of painters with a fine future ahead of them had contributed, (among them Chassériau and Corot). This was the scene of masked balls, dramatic performances and pantomimes; here many parties were held and many practical jokes to mystify the bourgeois concocted. The presence of Rogier's mistress, known as Cydalise, even introduced an affecting note of sentimentality as her Eastern grace grew ever more delicately refined with the advance of the tubercular consumption that was to carry her off.

One hesitates to apply the term 'fringe' to this hospitable milieu where life seems to have been so pleasant. Nevertheless, those who belonged most intimately to it did feel that they were enjoying a kind of 'extra-territoriality' with respect to bourgeois society, even society in general. In later years Arsène Houssaye wrote:

Ce qu'il y a eu de plus caractéristique dans notre Bohème, ce fut notre révolte ouverte contre tous les préjugés, je dirai presque contre toutes les lois. Réfugiés là comme dans une citadelle d'où nous faisions des sorties belliqueuses, nous nous moquions de tout. En dehors de l'esprit et du cœur, il n'y avait plus rien . . . Nous nous étions mis hors la loi.[14]

And Théophile Gautier put it as follows: 'On était là, en plein Carrousel, aussi libres, aussi solitaires que dans une île déserte d'Océanie.'[15] The members of the Bohemian community of Le Doyenné adopted a stance outside a society whose preoccupations they despised or disregarded (even political ideas, so heatedly discussed in the *Petit Cénacle*, found no favour here). At the same time, however, from an aesthetic point of view they manifested a growing independence. It stemmed from the great diversity of their interests and chosen mediums. Meanwhile, what united them consisted essentially in the lofty conception of art that they shared and the desire of each one to attain the highest pinnacle of perfection in his own particular way:

Nous avions l'air de dilettantes, plus préoccupés des aventures de la vie que des aventures de l'idée [writes Houssaye again], mais au fond nous étions studieux, obstinés, résolus; nous avions tous une vertu inappréciable dans les lettres, c'était de ne vouloir écrire que selon notre fantaisie. Nous étions pauvres, mais aucun de nous n'aurait consenti à s'attarder ou à se défaire la main dans le travail mercenaire.[16]

It will therefore be appreciated how difficult it is to give even a rough idea of the contribution to French literature made by these Romantics on the fringe, especially if we include those isolated writers who had no contact with the circles described above. At most, all we can hope to do is distinguish a few main trends, mindful from the start of how unequally they are reflected in the work of the various writers with whom we are concerned.

The most general characteristic they shared was their material poverty – poverty in some cases amounting to the most appalling destitution. The leaders of the Romantic movement all enjoyed fairly easy circumstances, many of them having started off with a personal fortune later supplemented by substantial royalties, and they commanded at least sufficient credit to allow them to lead relatively luxurious lives, even if at the cost of running up considerable debts. In contrast, not one of those known as the 'minor Romantics' managed to earn a decent living from his pen – without, that is, consecrating himself to literary chores quite alien to his ambitions, witness the cases of Rabbe, Lassailly, Esquiros, Nerval, and even Gautier who, throughout his life, was shackled to reviewing drama and to journalism to earn his daily bread. In *Stello* and *Chatterton*, Vigny denounced this state of affairs, which he regarded as the sign of a fundamental opposition between the poet and power; he took his examples from the eighteenth century in both its monarchical and its Revolutionary phases. But his theme of the curse afflicting the poet might well have been more accurately illustrated by the examples right there before him, of which – admittedly – he was planning to write in a sequel to his *Stello*. In 1832 the poet Escousse killed himself together with his friend Le Braz, leaving behind the following communication intended for the newspapers: 'Escousse s'est tué parce qu'il ne se sentait pas à sa place ici-bas, parce que la force lui manquait à chaque pas qu'il faisait en avant ou en arrière; parce que l'amour de la gloire ne dominait pas assez son âme, si âme il y a . . .' Jacques-Imbert Galloix, Hégésippe

Moreau and Aloysius Bertrand died in poverty in Paris where they had sought a literary renown that never came. To be sure, the failure of these provincials who came to Paris and foundered there was in many cases due to a lack of talent and a determination to persevere in a career to which they were not particularly suited but whose prestige was, in their eyes, such that they would have believed themselves dishonoured in adopting any other. Nevertheless, it is impossible not to admire the intransigence of, for example, Bertrand who staked his entire existence on a work which truly did contain elements of genius.

The difficulties they encountered in their quest for renown no doubt did count for much in the attitude of revolt adopted by these writers on the fringe, an attitude which was the second characteristic which they practically all shared in common. But that revolt took very different forms depending on the times and individuals concerned.

The *Petit Cénacle* was particularly associated with political revolt, the group having been formed in the aftermath of a revolution desired by each and every one of its members. The strong personality of Borel, who declared in the Preface to his *Rhapsodies* (1831) that he was a republican 'd'enfance' and a little further on justified what he called 'la haute mission de Saint-Just', was no doubt a strong influence upon the group. But his attitude, not so much of revolution as of revolt, did not imply any precise political commitment and in that same Preface comes over more as a response to essentially individual – or even individualistic – motivations. Borel proclaims:

Je suis républicain comme l'entendrait un loup-cervier: mon républicanisme c'est de la lycanthropie! – Si je parle de république, c'est parce que ce mot me représente la plus large indépendance que puissent laisser l'association et la civilisation. Je suis républicain, parce que je ne puis pas être caraïbe; j'ai besoin d'une somme énorme de liberté.

Philothée O'Neddy, with rather less oratory and more sense of solidarity, also aligns himself with those who hold the social order in contempt but does so by ascribing to the workers, with whom he wishes to identify, aesthetic preoccupations which come quite naturally to himself:

Ouvriers musculeux et forts, gardez-vous de repousser ma faible coopération; jamais vous n'aurez assez de bras pour l'érection d'une si grande œuvre! Et peut-être ne suis-je pas tout à fait indigne d'être nommé votre frère. Comme vous, je méprise l'ordre social et surtout l'ordre politique qui en est l'excrément . . . comme vous, je n'ai de pieux élancements que vers la Poésie, cette sœur jumelle de Dieu.[17]

The fact remains that the association between the *Petit Cénacle* and the political ideas of the extreme left was sufficiently close in the mind of the public for the name *bousingot* to be fairly generally applied to the members of the *Jeune-France* group. Originally, the word had denoted the hat of soft leather worn in July 1830 by volunteers from Le Havre, its application being subsequently extended to the most extremist of the young revolutionaries. The *Jeune-France* group adopted it in a show of bravado, giving it a certain esoteric significance with their own particular spelling of the word.[18]

The attraction of subversive political attitudes made itself particularly felt among the members of the *Petit Cénacle*. But it also, in some cases more lastingly, influenced such frequenters of the impasse du Doyenné as Esquiros who, in 1848, became a deputy and after 1870 a senator of the extreme left. It even influenced isolated individuals such as Aloysius Bertrand who, having returned to Dijon after his first spell in Paris, in the aftermath of 1830 threw himself into political journalism for a time, soon to find himself in trouble over the republican position he adopted. Similarly, the Lyonnais writer Louis Berthaud founded a satirical newspaper, *La Glaneuse*, in 1832 and later, in association with an exile from Savoy, Jean-Pierre Veyrat, set up *L'Homme rouge* which expressed violently anti-monarchical opinions first in Lyons and then in Paris. There, these two journalists soon found themselves stricken by extreme poverty.

Among these writers the passion for politics may, with a few exceptions, have been short-lived and of vague orientation, but it would be mistaken to believe it insincere. The trouble was, as in the case of the young who revolted in 1968 to whom they bear certain resemblances, that it was almost inevitable that their aspirations towards radical change in society should be without political consequence – and thus doomed to an ineffectiveness that soon became discouraging. Philothée O'Neddy declared that the literature of youth had managed to 'perfect its revolution' (a somewhat optimistic view in itself!), and furthermore displayed enough inventiveness and power to be 'the glorious herald of a metaphysical crusade against *society*, bracing all its energy to bring about the defeat of what it calls the *social lie*'; he then urged all young people with 'patriotic beliefs' (that is to say engaged in political action in the strict sense) to set aside 'republican fanaticism' and 'enlist in the armies of our Babel'.[19]

The weapons used in this struggle against the 'mensonge social' were, admittedly, not entirely new. The originality of these writers stemmed above all from the use they made of them and the way in which, in using them, they pushed literature to its limits. It is perhaps this that explains how it is that, paradoxically, they may seem to us somewhat archaic despite the fact that they were heralding the most modern literary tendencies. Their weapons – at least those that many of them favoured – were frenzy and Byronism.

In an article written in 1819, Nodier had suggested the name 'école frénétique' to denote a number of works the common feature of which was a recourse to the most brutal methods to provoke what a specialist of the genre, Cuisin, was to call 'les fortes émotions de la terreur'. The popularity that these works (for the most part translations or imitations of English or German horror stories) enjoyed in France dated from the Revolutionary period and Nodier, like the marquis de Sade in his *Idée sur les romans*, saw a connection between the violence they portrayed and the shocks sustained by the sensibilities of the public during the Terror, shocks which had, so to speak, raised the threshold of its excitability. Victor Hugo in *Han d'Islande, Bug-Jargal* and *Le Dernier Jour d'un condamné*, Balzac in *Le Centenaire* and Nodier himself in his *Smarra* had not despised the use of this somewhat basic but nonetheless powerful source of emotions. After 1826 the *genre frénétique* had been relegated to popular literature and a little later was replaced, in higher literature, by the *genre fantastique* which had certain affinities with it but acted upon the reader's sensibilities by rather more subtle means. But the *genre frénétique* now enjoyed a renewal of favour among the writers of the fringe to whom this chapter is devoted. What is distinctive about the way they used it is their declared intention to provoke the reader, to wrest him from his sense of comfort by thrusting before him frightful images and thus to break the implicit pact according to which literature is supposed to present him with a representation of the world with which he can spontaneously identify or to enable him to rise above himself painlessly, with sentiments of the sublime. Far from seeking to win over *l'ami lecteur,* Petrus Borel, who adopted the nickname of 'lycanthrope', deliberately set out to assault and offend him. *Champavert*, which is beyond question the masterpiece from this body of literature, thus presents, for instance (with deliberate changes of time and place), a public prosecutor complacently attending the execution of a girl who has killed her child and whom he had himself made pregnant and had subsequently condemned (*M. de l'Argentière*); two blacks from Havana tearing each other literally to pieces in a duel to the death over an imagined adultery (*Jacques Barraou*); an old doctor bent on promoting his reputation as a scholar who dissects the lovers of his young wife and then, when she dies of shock upon discovering their remains, dissects her too (*Andréa Vesalius*); and a student who drowns his unfaithful mistress in a well and reveals his crime to his rival just as the latter is on the point of killing him in a duel (*Champavert*). The celebration of violence and horror is not gratuitous as it very often was in the productions of the *école frénétique*. As in the followers of the marquis de Sade, whose influence here is omnipresent, it expresses a desire to attack the very sources of life and enter into alliance with the destructive forces that lurk in man's unconscious and are at work in nature itself. But whereas in Sade this alliance had represented a kind of paroxysm of a certain philosophy of nature, here it expressed an attempt to reflect in literature the power of negation, death and derision which these writers thought they could perceive at work in the history of their age, and whose victims they believed themselves, above all others, to be. There can be no doubt that in this respect their work runs counter to the main current of French Romanticism, one of the major preoccupations of which was to salvage that negativity by elaborating progressive mythologies featuring, among other elements, the redemption of Satan, the symbol of absolute negation.

In this respect there could be nothing more characteristic than the anti-providence which rules Petrus Borel's *Madame Putiphar* in which the schemes of the wicked are systematically favoured while the lot of the pure in heart is invariably suffering, misfortune and useless sacrifice, or again, the constant imprecations of Lassailly's *Roueries de Trialph* in which the hero sums up his course through life as follows:

Moi, je suis né avec le besoin de passions fortes et aventureuses. Le sang que j'ai ne coule pas sans bouillonner. Je deviens malade à me conduire sagement. J'ai trop rêvé de vertu d'ailleurs pour être vertueux; car mes rêves, mes inspirations d'enthousiasme dépasseront toujours mes plus grands efforts; et pour qui serais-je vertueux? Je n'ai de Dieu qu'à force de raisonner; je n'ai de patrie que si j'y crois; je n'ai de famille que dans les conditions d'arriver au bonheur; je n'ai d'amis que pour être dupe; je n'ai de nom que comme étiquette d'un sac vide. J'ai tout désaimé![20]

It could perhaps be objected that the sincerity of this nihilism – for that is really what it is – is rendered somewhat suspect by the note of detachment and humour that often accompanies this vitriolic literature. *Les Roueries de Trialph*, for instance, opens with the following epigraph which would appear to be a warning to the reader not to take all that follows too seriously:

Ah!

Eh! he!

Hi! Hi! Hi! Hi!

Oh!

Hu! hu! hu! hu! hu!

Profession de foi par l'auteur

The *Champavert* stories often oscillate between horror and burlesque, the best example of this explosive mixture being *Passereau*, in which – as just one of a number of incongruities – the hero, maddened with despair at his betrayal by his loved one, seeks out the public executioner to whom, apparently in all seriousness, he declares: 'Je désirerais ardemment que vous me guillotinassiez!' Uncertainty reaches a climax in Forneret's work where, alongside aphorisms either of a ponderousness worthy of Prudhomme or of an infantile naïvety, one comes across brilliant 'nonsense' such as: 'J'ai vu une boîte aux lettres sur une cimetière.'[21] Under the title *Un pauvre honteux*, Forneret published one of the strangest poems in French literature. In apparently colourless language, it expresses fantasies of sadism and orality which seldom find their way to the level of consciousness. Here are the last lines:

> Il l'a pliée,
> Il l'a cassée,
> Il l'a placée,
> Il l'a coupée,
> Il l'a lavée,
> Il l'a portée,
> Il l'a grillée,
> Il l'a mangée.
> Quand il n'était pas grand, on lui avait dit:
> Si tu as faim, mange une de tes mains.

No doubt this kind of humour played its part in dissuading contemporary readers from taking 'seriously' the texts in which it was manifested, the more so given that some of the works that faced them were pure parodies the purpose of whose 'frenzy' appeared to be simply to vaccinate Romanticism against its most glaring excesses. Such was the case with Jules Janin's *L'Âne mort et la femme guillotinée*, published in 1829, which blithely combined the filthiest eroticism with descriptions of the morgue, the guillotine and impalement. The inspiration behind *Les Jeunes-France* (Renduel, 1833) seems more ambiguous. In it Théophile Gautier gently castigates some of the obsessions of his friends from the *Petit Cénacle*, clearly indicating his own desire to distance himself from the shock-aesthetics which he had himself helped to provoke but which were not really in tune with his own temperament.[22]

This very special manner of playing with the unbearable would have to wait for rehabilitation until the advent of surrealism, at which point it was dubbed 'black humour'. In its destabilisation of conventional attitudes to life and death, and its aggressive exploitation of the surprises afforded by language, André Breton correctly perceived the prefiguration of the essential element of surrealism: namely, a general subversion of the relations between literature and reality. He was also quite correct when, taking a lesson from Freud, he detected here 'le triomphe paradoxal du principe de plaisir sur les conditions réelles au moment où elles sont le plus défavorables', with humour acting as a kind of lightning conductor that made it possible to discharge without danger the threatening impulses that 'frenzy' laid bare. But perhaps we should look further than these explanations which might appear to reclaim the more subversive side of Romanticism to the profit of a literary wholesomeness which Breton, all in all, never really renounced. In the humour that our fringe Romantics practised along with their frenzy, there is a desire to profane which strikes not only at the morality and intellectual complacency from which the bourgeois public derives satisfaction, but also at literature itself: with its own self-derision, it forces back into their initial destitution those who seemed to depend upon it most in order to escape from the misery of living.

The treatment of Byronic themes in this kind of literature also demonstrates a tendency to force literature to its limit, although in this case with fewer consequences for the future. An exaltation of passion, curses against a life too confined to allow that passion to develop freely, blasphemy against a God guilty of having given man a sense of the infinite while condemning him to live in a finite world (and, to cap it all, punishing him for seeking that infinity here on earth), apologia for Satan and invitations to imitate his own revolt: all this was part and parcel of something which all the French Romantics drew upon to a greater or lesser extent and with more or less of a sense of guilt. Most of them, however, borrowed from Byron only that which could reinforce their tenacious humanism: to reject God – a God increasingly absent from their work, at least in his Christian form – was to exalt man. In the most virulent of the fringe Romantics two tendencies are detectable: on the one hand a reactivation of the polar concepts of belief/blasphemy, for the purpose not of giving new life to belief (as was to happen in the case of Barbey d'Aurevilly), but of lending greater force to blasphemy; on the other, a radical rejection of all the values that man might claim in order to take the place of a dethroned God.

In a composition in *Feu et Flamme* entitled *Rodomontade*, Philothée O'Neddy wishes God to exist so that he can defy him:

Si dans le firmament des signes, des symboles,
Amenaient ma superbe à croire aux paraboles
Du Charpentier de Nazareth . . .

Ne croyez pas qu'alors, pénitent débonnaire,
Dans une église, aux pieds d'un prêtre octogénaire
     J'advolerais tout éperdu! . . .

Non, non. Je creuserais les sciences occultes:
Je m'en irais, la nuit, par des sites incultes;
     Et là, me raillant du Seigneur,
Je tourbillonnerais dans la magie infâme,
J'évoquerais le Diable . . .[23]

In a similar fashion, Borel's Champavert, brought to the depths of despair, defies a God in whom he does not believe but whom he challenges to manifest himself if he does exist: 'S'il était un Dieu qui lançât la foudre, je le défierais! Qu'il me lance donc sa foudre, ce Dieu puissant qui entend tout, je le défie! . . . Tiens, je crache contre le ciel! tiens, regarde là-bas, vois-tu ce pauvre tonnerre qui se perd à l'horizon? on dirait qu'il a peur de moi.'[24] However, these *rodomontades* should not lead to the conclusion that man is better than God and deserves to take his place. Taken to its extreme limits, the Byronic cursing of existence, (which in the case of the English poet was easily enough accommodated with a fine lust for life) becomes, for Alphonse Rabbe, an apologia for suicide, for Jean Polonius's Empedocle a dizzying invitation to self-destruction, for Lassailly's Trialph a rage unleashed against the whole of humanity, and for the painter Spinello, the hero of Lefèvre-Deumier's *Les Martyrs d'Arezzo*, an intoxicating identification with Satan: 'On eût dit que son esprit, traversant malgré lui tous les degrés de la révolte, arrivait avec son archange au bord de la chute qu'il voulait peindre. Il sentait s'imprimer sur sa face cette pâleur surhumaine qu'il voulait graver au front de Lucifer.'[25] Although a number of these writers manifest elements of the over-facile rhetoric of the abyss, made fashionable by Byron, their sufferings, their poverty, their failure itself must convince us that their way of expressing themselves, by all the means available, was aiming for a literary Beyond which, so long as they had the strength to continue to struggle, was for them both the supreme goal of existence and at the same time a way of expressing and confirming the inevitably cliff-hanging aspect of any existence. Armand Hoog has quite correctly written:

Le romantisme français, par eux, propose un *mode de vivre* et une expérience originale de l'âme. Au fond de leur sensibilité il y a autre chose qu'un goût inédit pour l'image et la couleur. Dans l'œuvre des 'petits romantiques' éclate toute nue une révélation extra-littéraire. Plus qu'à un développement lyrique, nous avons affaire à un développement de l'âme engagée dans une tragédie vécue.[26]

It has certainly been worth attempting to distinguish, within the extreme diversity of the writers with whom this chapter is concerned, the principal similarities that resulted from the fringe position that they occupied. Nevertheless, it must be repeated that some of them almost totally elude any such attempt to find characteristics shared in common. So we cannot avoid presenting them one by one, in a series of portraits that it would be artificial to attempt to classify in terms of affinities, literary genres (for most of them, with varying success, practised them all), or indeed any other criteria. Even chronology is of very little help. If we make an exception of Nerval – and there are many reasons for doing so – the most important of their works were published between 1830 and 1840, their individual dates not being particularly significant, except for specialists concerned to establish the influences that some of them may have exerted upon others.[27]

Alphonse Rabbe should certainly be the first mentioned. Born in 1786, he was the oldest of all the Romantic group. But should he really be included among the Romantics? Despite his friendship with Hugo, he never declared himself as his supporter. By virtue of his precise, analytic style, admirably suited to the maxim, to argument and an eloquent exposition of moral ideas, he was closer, rather, to classicism. But he had a way of confronting adversity, seeing it as a sign of special election and deriving from it both a bitter delight and at the same time resolute determination to say 'no' to life, that make him the first of the rebels we have mentioned in this chapter. And for him, adversity was not merely a literary theme. As a young man he launched himself on the conquest of life with a fervour that was heightened by his awareness of his physical beauty and intellectual gifts. After serving in the Spanish campaigns of 1808 to 1810, he embarked upon a brilliant career in Aix as a lawyer and political polemicist. But he soon became disenchanted with the Restoration, which, initially, he had passionately supported. His defection to the liberal opposition provoked a campaign of persecution which obliged him to flee his native Provence. In Paris, he found himself no more than an obscure scribbler earning a meagre living from historical rehashes of little merit. Furthermore, his handsome face became ravaged by the marks of a syphilitic complaint which, at the end of his life, induced him to shun all social contacts. In one of his prose-poems he wrote: 'Quand je me regarde, je frémis. Est-ce bien moi! Quelle main a sillonné ma face de ces traces hideuses!'[28] As a result of the suffering his illness caused him, he became immoderately dependent upon opium. It was probably from an overdose that, on 1 January 1830, he died, but there is no way of knowing whether it was an accident or the deliberate implementation of a projected plan of suicide which he had often mentioned to his friends and for which he had already in advance written a passionate defence. This defence constitutes a major part of his *Album d'un pessimiste*, published by L'Héritier with the help of those same friends in 1835. It was to fascinate the surrealists with its arrogant logic and also on account of the similarities between the death of its author and that of Jacques Vaché, and they proclaimed Rabbe to have been 'surréaliste dans la mort'. The *Album d'un pessimiste* also contains prose-poems reminiscent still, in their rather oratorical and wordy form, of the attempts at non-versified poetry that appeared at the end of the eighteenth century and beginning of the nineteenth. From the point of view of the subject-matter and the gloomy human experience that they record, however, they can from time to time be seen as prefigurations of the Baudelairian prose-poems.

Petrus Borel (1809–59) has already been mentioned several times by reason of his role as the pivotal personality around whom the *Petit Cénacle* revolved. If one had to propose a typical example of a fringe Romantic, his would no doubt be the name that would spring to mind. Like most of these fringe artists, he had roots from which he never broke away entirely. His family belonged to the lesser Savoyard nobility and had been ruined by the Revolution. His real name was Pierre-Joseph Borel d'Hauterive and he was, all in all, quite proud of his family connections. His choice of profession, first as architect and subsequently as writer occasioned a rift between himself and his father but he always maintained excellent relations with one of his brothers, an archivist of note. The violent need he felt for independence made him a frequenter of various studios and *cénacles*, and in 1837 it led him to withdraw to a little village in the Brie region where he lived in a hut with his mistress, suffering from cold and hunger, to write *Madame Putiphar*. But *Madame Putiphar* (Ollivier, 1839), the novel upon which he was counting to reveal his true literary stature to the world, obtained no more success than his *Rhapsodies* (Levasseur, 1831) or his *Champavert* (Renduel, 1833). He now found himself forced into collaborating to produce occasional articles or sketches of day-to-day life, very popular in the newspapers of the day, in a multitude of periodicals as the opportunities arose. Some of the sketches he wrote for *Les Français peints par eux-mêmes* in 1840–1 (*Le Croquemort* and *Le Gniaffe*, for instance) are the work of a caricaturist who knows just how far to go in exaggeration and zany humour. But his humour is unfortunately not always of that calibre. All this was still not enough to keep body and soul together. He tried his luck in a new enterprise: a return to the land, at Asnières, where he set about cultivating a small plot, meanwhile endeavouring to retain contact with his friends and with the periodicals of the capital – but with no greater success. In 1844 he returned to Paris where he continued in his struggle against a poverty which editorship of a number of ephemeral little magazines (the *Satan*, the *Revue pittoresque*) did little to alleviate. When his resources ran out – and his inspiration too, unfortunately, to judge by the pieces he produced during this period – he decided in 1846, on the advice of Théophile Gautier and with the help of Delphine de Girardin, to apply for a post as colonial inspector in Algeria. In the face of the spectacle of the 'werewolf' turning shepherd to the French colonials, critics today are inclined to resort to the word 'renegade' or to lamenting the harsh necessities of life – when, that is, they are not drawing comparisons with the way that Rimbaud cut himself off from poetry to lead the life of a mercenary smuggler. But such reactions are quite unjust. If Petrus Borel took his new functions seriously and proved himself an administrator devoted to the well-being of his charges, he was never harsh towards them or servile towards his superiors; it was his quarrels with the latter, marked by a touch of persecution-mania on his part, that eventually, in 1855, cost him his post. He married, yet it was with the daughter of his mistress with whom he continued to live. She bore him a child, yet he named him Aldéran-André-Petrus-Bénoni. The last four years of his life may not have been those of a 'werewolf', but they were certainly still those of a fringe artist. They were spent in solitude in the Castel de Haute Pensée, a modest little house he had built near the portes de Mostaganem where he died of sunstroke in July 1859.

Petrus Borel is one of those unfortunate writers who have so much come to be regarded as symbols that there is a tendency to forget what they actually wrote, remembering only their fate and the figure they cut. It is true that, even at his best, his work is marred by many weaknesses and infelicities. Baudelaire regarded these mistakes as one form taken by the bad luck that dogged the 'lycanthrope' and saw them as 'symptômes d'une nature morbide, amoureuse de la contradiction pour la contradiction, et toujours prête à remonter tous les courants, sans en calculer la force, non plus que sa force propre'.[29] Would Borel have been as he was if he had produced a perfect work? His *Rhapsodies* contain samples of most of what was fashionable at the time, including verse of the most insipid kind and certainly do not do justice to their inflammatory Preface. But throughout *Champavert* a high tension is sustained and in its better moments this work is successful in conveying the power of a death-wish that is not eclipsed either by Lautréamont or by Bataille. Furthermore, quite apart from its admirably melancholic and lucidly despairing prologue, *Madame Putiphar* conveys an obsessive theme of imprisonment, persecuted sexuality and impotent revolt which runs counter to all the happy endings and positive identifications traditionally offered by the novel genre and has the ring of a swan-song for this whole generation of sacrificed youth. That is what Baudelaire, with his customary penetration, perceived:

Cet esprit à la fois littéraire et républicain, à l'inverse de la passion démocratique et bourgeoise qui nous a plus tard si cruellement opprimés, était agité à la fois par une haine aristocratique sans limites, sans restrictions, sans pitié, contre les rois et contre la bourgeoisie, et d'une sympathie générale pour tout ce qui en art représentait l'excès dans la couleur et dans la forme, pour tout ce qui était à la fois intense, pessimiste et byronien; dilettantisme d'une nature singulière, et que peuvent seules expliquer les haïssables circonstances où était enfermée une jeunesse ennuyée et turbulente.[30]

A comparison between the destinies of *Philothée O'Neddy* and Petrus Borel illustrates the contrasting forms that fringe Romanticism some-times took. Born in Paris in 1811, O'Neddy spent his entire life there. When his father, a civil servant at the Ministry of Finance, died of cholera in 1832 he was obliged, as the sole support of his mother and sister, to take a job as a clerk in the same ministry. There he remained for the rest of his life, ever hoping for unlikely promotion. His short membership of the *Petit Cénacle*, where he changed his too bourgeois name of Théophile Dondey for the more exotic Philothée O'Neddy and where his swarthy but blonde 'moorish' looks attracted much admir-ation, was the only glorious period of his existence. It came to an end – with, alas, no glory at all – with the publication, at the author's own expense, of his *Feu et Flamme* (Dondey-Dupré, 1833). Thereafter, during his lifetime, Philothée O'Neddy's presence in the literary life of his age made itself felt only through the publication of fragments of novels and occasional dramatic pieces in *L'Estafette*, *Le Voleur*, and *La Patrie*, but he remained faithful to the republicanism of his youth and also to his glowing memory of the *Petit Cénacle* (letter to Asselineau dated 23 September 1862). By the time he died, 19 February 1875, he was almost totally forgotten.

Less fantastical and explosive by temperament than Borel – and, almost certainly, less of a genius – O'Neddy expressed in a rigorous and skilfully elaborated form a detestation of life which was neither any less profound nor – understandably enough – less well-founded. The confidence of his sense of rhythm, his art of giving life to abstractions and a kind of intimate solemnity and mystic resonance to the expression of *ennui*, pain and certain morbid or macabre meditations mark him out as a precursor to Baudelaire, who must surely have profited from reading his work. It was he who made words such as 'spleen', 'dandysme', 'électrique' and 'miasmes' poetically acceptable. In his *Feu et Flamme*, it is not so much the glittering colours, daring neologisms and resounding blasphemies that move us still, but the metaphysical anxiety stemming from his conviction that he lives in a world of evil and his hopeless aspirations towards a paradisiacal state attained through the medium of art alone. The poems that he persisted in writing even after the fiasco of his only publication continued to express the new *mal du siècle* with a certain originality:

> Névrose, maladie, hallucination,
> Velléité de spleen et de consomption,
> Travers byronien, fantaisie inquiète[31]

They also, in a somewhat over didactic fashion, transmit the credo of a radical pessimism which is summed up well enough in the following line:

> L'absolu, c'est la nuit, l'absolu c'est le mal.[32]

However, although much appreciated by Valéry Larbaud,[33] Dondey's posthumous poems suffer from his prolonged lack of contact with the public. He continued to write verse in the manner that Hugo had already abandoned. All things considered, there was a better chance for the disorderly genius of Borel to survive across the years than for the intellectual harmonies of this impassioned introvert.

Théophile Gautier was the only one of all the members of the *Petit Cénacle* to achieve such a survival across the centuries (or perhaps, *the* century) and he seems to have managed it without too much trouble. His success was, however, directly connected with the fact that, as early as 1833–4, he began to distance himself rapidly from the fringe *Jeune-France* group. His *Albertus, ou L'Âme et le Péché, légende théologique* (Paulin, 1833) already contains a strong measure of parody in a barely concealed autobiographical manner: the work treats the theme of a young man who delivers himself up to the devil in the mistaken belief that he is embracing a young woman of perfect beauty. In *Les Jeunes-France, romans goguenards* (Renduel, 1833) the split appears complete, although it did not affect his friendship and personal loyalty towards individual members of the group. His theory of art for art's sake, sketched out in the Preface to *Mademoiselle de Maupin* (Renduel, 1835), which was to orientate his future work, placed him in the position to be hailed as a master both by Baudelaire (who remained sensitive to the element of Romantic inspiration in his work) and by the pundits of Parnassus. And, as a quite gratuitous stroke of good luck, just at the point when

Parnassus appeared to be of interest only to literary archaeologists, the critics of our time discovered in Gautier's fantastic side (which owed much to his *Jeune-France* period) a thematic thread of remarkable coherence. It gave forceful expression to, first, the narcissistic tendencies of the author, second, his refusal to abandon the dream of a love of totally fulfilling fusion (one that set a prohibition upon all accessible women), and third, the threat of castration that is cast over this dream by a number of father-figures who may be seen as the inadequate incarnations of the Law and Reality. *La Cafetière* (1831), *Omphale* (1834) and *La Morte amoureuse* (1836) introduce the first in a series of women of this kind, untouchable or to be touched only at one's peril by reason of the death or fascination that emanates from their hieratic beauty – qualities more or less inseparable from their association with an omnipresent maternal image. Gautier's construction of imaginary exotic paradises miraculously preserved from the flatness of contemporary existence (*Fortunio*, Desessart, 1838), his refuge within an antiquity where desire could flourish free from Christian constraints and bourgeois platitudes (*Arria Marcella*, 1852, *Le Roman de la Momie*, 1858), and his dream of a hermaphrodite being through whom the wound of the difference between the sexes might be healed (*Mademoiselle de Maupin*) are all indications of the unconscious forces that preserved his sense of dereliction and exile despite the fact that, as a writer, he appeared well enough integrated into the literary and social life of his age.

Alphonse Esquiros (1812–76) did not himself belong to the *Petit Cénacle* but he probably knew all its members, including those who had frequented Victor Hugo's salon in rue Notre-Dame des Champs. It was indeed there that he made his first contacts with the world of letters while completing the advanced studies he had started at the Petit Séminaire Saint-Nicolas du Chardonnet. A contemporary in that establishment had been Alphonse-Louis Constant, the future magus Éliphas Lévi; and the influence of abbé Frère-Colonna, a mathematician preoccupied with the problems of animal magnetism, probably helped to awaken in both young men an interest in the occult sciences to which Esquiros devoted a number of pieces which appeared in various reviews. He was, in fact, interested in and stimulated to write by anything at all out of the ordinary: prostitutes (*Les Vierges folles*, Le Gallois, 1840), madmen, heraldry, alchemy.

Of all the fringe Romantics, it was he who demonstrated the most positive and enduring political commitment. The republican ideas that he professed in *L'Évangile du peuple* (Le Gallois, 1841) earned him an eight-month prison sentence, the fruit of which was a collection of verse entitled *Chants d'un prisonnier*, containing a number of fine poems not without influence upon Baudelaire. He was a deputy for Paris under the Second Republic, then spent the years of the Empire in exile in Holland and England, sending a number of excellent articles to the *Revue des deux mondes*. He finally returned to France and there ended his days as a senator.

Of Alphonse Esquiros's diverse literary production – worthy of interest from a number of points of view – we should single out his novel, *Le Magicien* (Desessart, 1838), a masterpiece that deserves to be better known. In a series of short chapters composed with a cinematic jump-cutting technique, it combines a number of intrigues in which Esquiros's personal preoccupations give a profoundly original form to a number of themes traditional to Romanticism. Thus, the political intrigue (the work is a historical novel set at the time when Catherine de Medici was seeking to muster the forces of the populace in order to thwart the ambitions of her son) gives the author an opportunity to expound his own ideas about black magic, witchcraft and the witches' sabbath which, he suggests, may during the Middle Ages have represented 'the voice of the people'. They were themes which, as is well known, Michelet was to manipulate with considerable brilliance in his *La Sorcière*.

The central character in the novel is, as the title indicates, a magician, Auréole Hab Hakek. He may be seen as a Faustian type of sage in league with the devil, with whom public rumour identifies him. But for Esquiros he also represents the scientist of the future, confident that his own intellectual powers will suffice to fathom the enigmas of the universe and support his plans of world domination. Thus, the prodigious feats that he accomplishes all have, in principle, a rational explanation and it is this that inclines the fantastical side of the novel in the direction of what was later to be known as science-fiction. The presence at the magician's side of a robot who acts as his factotum accentuates this modernistic element. But, although this recourse to a supernatural with a rational explanation is, it must be admitted, somewhat clumsy, it does not deprive *Le Magicien* of all mystery and poetry. These qualities stem principally from the confrontation of the young hero, the sculptor Stell, with the powers of evil embodied on the one hand by Hab Hakek and his ill-starred wisdom and, on the other, by the black Amalthée who inspires the hero with a love that conflicts in his heart with the mystical adoration that he feels for the blonde and seraphic figure of Marie. Torn between these two 'simultaneous and contradictory demands', Stell little by little gives way to a fascination for the abyss that is connected 'aux ténèbres, aux gouffres, aux profondeurs qu'il avait dans son cœur'.[34]

However, to describe the successive stages through which his Satanic temptation passes, Esquiros abandons the laborious and over familiar psychology through which most fantastical authors seek to render plausible the mechanisms of possession. Instead, he gives free rein to the creative powers of the unconscious, allowing himself to be guided by that logic of imagery in which the secret of all poetry lies. His images are dominated by three haunting themes: water which, like the heart of the hero, is sometimes deceptively calm, sometimes wild and tempestuous; the forest, where Amalthée's green eyes lie in wait for him; and metamorphosis. But Stell is not alone in giving way to delirium. All the characters in the novel, including a dwarf who is in love with a giantess, succumb to a passion for the impossible which *Le Magicien*, despite the superficial clumsiness which thwarted its success, expresses with a power seldom matched in Romantic literature.

Jules Lefèvre-Deumier is the next writer to consider, even though he did not belong to the same generation or even share the same manner as Esquiros. Born in 1797, he belonged to the very first Romantic group, *La Muse française*, and in 1823 published a poem entitled *Le Parricide*, the Byronic elements of which were tempered by the author's sentimentality and moral scruples. However, it was not until 1839, one year after the publication of *Le Magicien*, that his most interesting work appeared. This was *Les Martyrs d'Arezzo*, and it has a number of features in common with Esquiros's novel. It too is a historical novel, set in the fifteenth century in Italy. The theme is again that of the artist drawn to Satan but Lefèvre's hero, the painter Spinello, becomes the helpless victim of diabolical temptation through the very practice of his art. He agrees to paint a picture representing the fall of the rebel angels and decides to invest the visage of Satan with a superhuman beauty that will, better than conventional representations, convey a sense of the fascination that he exerts. Spinello is thus, quite involuntarily, affected by the influence of the doctrines of the *fraticelli* which his painting was intended to oppose. In the eyes of the *fraticelli* Satan was not an angel of evil but a courageous rebel who had tried to rescue mankind from divine tyranny, 'ce sublime Porte-Lumière qui fait les penseurs, les héros, les poètes, les artistes'.[35] Upon completing his masterpiece, Spinello realises that he has given his rebel angel the features of Béatrix, the woman whom he loves. He becomes obsessed with this image, identifying himself ever more completely with it and, whatever his subject, makes it the centre of all his compositions. After many adventures he perceives it in the waters of the ocean itself where (like Esquiros's hero) he contemplates it with horrified fascination and eventually casts himself into the waves. In this work, marred unfortunately by *longueurs*, Jules Lefèvre thus expresses not only the curse that rests upon the creator of genius condemned to rebellion by his rivalry with God, but also what is probably an obsession of a more personal nature: the strange impotence that afflicts the artist who is possessed by a single idea and is incapable of doing anything but endlessly repeat it: what Lefèvre, strikingly enough, calls 'le martyre de la mémoire'.

The dissatisfaction and anguish evident in *Les Martyrs d'Arezzo* were not the result solely of his intellectual speculations. The life he had led also played its part. Jules Lefèvre started his career as an employee of the Ministry of Finance and ended up as a librarian of the Tuileries. In between times however, because of an unhappy love-affair, he had followed in Byron's footsteps and set sail for Greece to fight against the Turks. He stopped off in Italy and then, still suffering from his despairing love, set off once more to assist the insurgents in Poland. There he was several times wounded fighting in the rebels' ranks, suffered extreme poverty, then in 1842 inherited a fortune from a wealthy aunt. Within a few years he had dissipated the entire sum thanks to prodigal living and the subsidies he gave to *L'Artiste*. He can surely be included without too many misgivings among our Romantics on the fringe.

The career of *Charles Lassailly* was full of paradoxes. One was, that of all the writers with whom we are concerned not one – with the possible exception of Nerval – was more involved in the literary life of his period nor yet at the same time more solitary. Lassailly's solitariness stemmed from personal idiosyncracies which eventually led to insanity. He was twenty years old when he settled in Paris after leaving the town of Orléans where he had been born in 1806. He soon became a member of Victor Hugo's intimate circle and played a prominent role in the 'great days' of Romanticism, the days of *Marion de Lorme* and *Hernani*. The few sentimental, satirical or political poems of his that were published by a number of reviews sympathetic to the movement are in no way exceptional of their kind. In 1832 his *Poésie sur la mort du fils de Bonaparte* bore witness to a budding humanitarian messianism, but the Saint-Simonian ideas of *Le Globe* were still too advanced for him. Yet this apparently rather conformist young man of letters, remarkable only for his extraordinary emaciation (no doubt in part a consequence of his hunger-stricken life), his proverbially large nose and the style of dress of an impoverished dandy that he adopted, published the most frenetic and impudent novel to come from the pen of any Romantic: *Les Roueries de Trialph, notre contemporain avant son suicide* (1833). It is a statement of absolute despair with an underside of black humour of the kind mentioned above, incorporating, in the midst of a continuous stream of imprecations against society and life in general, a bewildering series of ambushes, long-pondered acts of revenge and wild scenes of love that are a blithe mixture of burlesque and sadism, the final and most remarkable one being where Trialph, before departing to cast himself into the sea, cold-bloodedly assassinates his mistress by dint of tickling the soles of her feet.

Did Lassailly really take himself seriously? The *Roueries de Trialph* contains plenty of passages that expound his literary, political and philosophical ideas and would incline one to think so. But we should beware of overestimating his naïvety. The infiltration of the most artificially literary episodes into the hero's life is quite deliberate. Confronted by Satan who, in a dream, asks him how he plans to get out of the inextricable labyrinth he has entered, Trialph replies: 'par des extravagances méditées, par des combinaisons de drame ridicules, par des effets pitoyables qui intéresseront probablement'.[36] That is just one way, among others, of making good his declaration: 'je suis mon siècle, moi, Trialph', and of doing justice to the fantastical etymology of his name, apparently derived from a Danish word meaning 'a mess' or 'hash'. In an article that appeared in 1835,[37] Lassailly was to claim that his intention had been to write a kind of *Don Quixote* for his own times. The comparison is not as absurd as it might appear. It helps to make more understandable how it was that, after the incredible extravaganza of his only novel, Lassailly settled down as a worldly journalist. He wrote for a large number of fashionable periodicals, founding and editing the short-lived *Ariel, journal du monde élégant* (March–May 1836) and became a severe critic of the excesses of the Romantics (with the exception of Vigny). He languished unhappily for the love of a string of inaccessible high-society ladies (this, it should be said, has been much exaggerated by legend). Meanwhile he was slipping gently into an insanity aggravated by his poverty which neither a brief collaboration with Balzac (on *L'École des ménages*, in 1839) nor the financial assistance that Vigny collected for him during his confinements first in the care of Dr Blanche, then in that of Dr Brierre de Boismont (1840–3), were able to redress.

The marginal or 'fringe' quality of the life of *Aloysius Bertrand* (1807–41) is compounded by a number of factors certain of which were common to some of the writers discussed above, but in his case the combination of them all is quite unique. First, his poverty: he was the son of a captain in the *gendarmerie* and an Italian mother who settled in Dijon in 1814. Following his father's retirement and subsequent early death, he entered a state of destitution from which he was never to escape. It was aggravated by his touchy pride, the obligation he felt never openly to accept any work he considered demeaning to his vocation as an artist, and the shame he felt at being seen poorly dressed in public. This penury forced him to leave Paris in 1830, only two years after his arrival there, even though during that period he had managed to attract the attention of Victor Hugo and, above all, Sainte-Beuve, to the prose-poems that he had been composing. He returned to Dijon but, after a stormy passage in political journalism there, in 1832 he made his way back to the capital where he subsisted by performing obscure tasks of one kind or another (they have remained shrouded in mystery for his biographers). Having contracted tuberculosis, he was moved from one hospital to another, eventually to die in the Necker hospital in 1841. It was only in the following year that his friends Sainte-Beuve and David d'Angers has his *Gaspard de la nuit* published (by Victor Pavie, in Angers). Apart from one drama and a number of mostly mediocre poems, this was his only work. Louis Bertrand (Aloysius was, of course, a pseudonym) was, furthermore, a provincial, one who was not only born and brought up in the provinces like so many other Parisians but who also derived his essential inspiration from his provincial background. One quite individual aspect of him as a fringe writer is that in his dreamer's eyes Dijon became a sort of enclave of the past within the present. André Breton was to call him a 'surréaliste dans le passé', and it is true that he was not satisfied with the superficial kind of picturesqueness that provided a facile means of escaping from the present world for many of his contemporaries. He animated the end of the Middle Ages, the sixteenth and the seventeenth centuries with a life that was anything but a reflection of the hypothetical life of the past. Rather, it was a means of creating a vision in which the interplay of light and shadow, the mannered figures borrowed from Italian comedy or the theatre of the fantastic, and the combination of unexpected details and dreamlike sequences produced in the reader that sense of wonder which is born of novelty and which Baudelaire considered as the very principle of creative imagination. Bertrand's vision was fuelled by his contemplation of pictorial works, as is suggested by the subtitle of *Gaspard de la nuit*: '*fantaisies à la manière de Rembrandt et de Callot*'. But his work is a far cry from a simple description of real or imaginary paintings; it draws, rather, upon the resources of language alone to create rhythms, discontinuities and silences which put the reader more in mind of music.

'*Blanchir*' (that is to say 'arrange the spacing') 'as if the text was verse', Bertrand instructed his publisher. But the point (which, of course involved a marginal type of aesthetics that understandably baffled his contemporaries) was that this was not verse but a type of prose which turned resolutely away from the lyrical *legato* to which earlier compositions of prose-poems had attempted to correspond. It is striking to note how every time Bertrand makes a correction to his text, it is to make it less limpid, more elliptical, more stark. Bertrand pierced windows in reality, windows to look upon some spectacle of enchantment, as in the 'magic peep-shows' of the period, creating a spark of beauty in between images that were, so to speak, surrounded by space. Despite his inclination to direct his gaze towards the past rather than the present, this technique of his establishes him as the precursor of a form of art that is resolutely modern. And Baudelaire, Mallarmé and the surrealists were all to recognise Aloysius Bertrand as its initiator. Because, despite his modesty, he was conscious of the importance of his work, he sacrificed everything to it, just like the alchemist to whom he compares himself in the prologue of *Gaspard de la Nuit*: 'Trente ans! et l'arcane que j'ai sollicité de tant de veilles opiniâtres, à qui j'ai immolé jeunesse, amour, plaisir, fortune, l'arcane gît, inerte et insensible comme le vil caillou dans la cendre de mes illusions!'[38] Having been one of the first to make art 'la pierre philosophale du XIXe siècle',[39] he was denied the consolation of seeing the transmutatory powers of his 'alchimie du verbe' bloom in other hands.

The last of these miniature portraits must be that of *Xavier Forneret*: first, because, of all the writers we have mentioned, he was the last to die – in 1884 at the age of seventy-five; secondly, because his manner of being a marginal writer was so exaggerated that it almost places him outside that category. Far from suffering from poverty, Forneret inherited from his father, a rich landowner from Beaune, a sufficiently handsome fortune to enable him to produce luxurious publications of his work at his own cost. However, he used his fortune to finance eccentricities which brought him discredit in the eyes of his compatriots, to initiate a whole string of infamous law-suits, to seduce an honest girl whom he subsequently dragged through the mud (and yet had the nerve to dedicate one of his pamphlets 'to my natural son'), and to surround his works with vulgar publicity campaigns which automatically rebounded against him: the one and only performance of his drama *L'Homme noir*, at the Dijon theatre on 10 March 1837, was a fiasco as lamentable as the play itself, curtailed in the third act in the midst of jeering and hilarity, and none of his publications elicited anything but jibes from the newspapers when, that is, they were mentioned at all. Was this a case of a bourgeois in revolt against his class, like a number of others who had preceded him? Not at all. While the frenetic nature of his early works is reminiscent of the *bousingot* literature, his political ideas in 1848 did not venture beyond a very moderate republicanism. Both Cavaignac and Louis Bonaparte were hailed by him as men of providence and he spent the rest of his life singing the praises of order, property and the necessary social inequality. Furthermore, he remained totally cut off from the literary circles of the capital, except for the time when his drama *Mère et Fille* was put on at the Théâtre Montmartre in January 1855 and won him a few not too unfavourable notices (for which, however, he had in all likelihood had to foot the bill). Only one far-seeing article, by Charles Monselet, in *Le Figaro* of 26 July 1859, rescued his name from total oblivion. He was, to some extent, on the fringe of the fringe. However, his desire to escape from the norm, or his inability to conform to it, is transmitted by everything about his novels. The titles: *Rien – Quelque chose*, '*au profit des pauvres*' (1836); *Sans titre, par un homme noir, blanc de visage* (1838); *Vapeurs, ni vers ni prose* (1838); *Pièces de pièces, Temps perdu* (1840); *Lettre à Dieu* (1846); the presentation and typography: a title in white lettering against a cover in colour, pages blank except for one or two lines, only the *recto* side of the sheet used, and so on. But what is most disconcerting about them is, as André Breton writes: 'l'extrême inégalité de sa production, où la trouvaille la plus authentique voisine avec le pire redite, où le sublime le dispute au niais, l'originalité constante de l'expression ne laissant pas de découvrir fréquemment l'indigence de la pensée'.[40] Let us mention only the 'pearls'. Some are in the frenetic style, where Forneret sometimes surpasses even Borel in the vigour and forthrightness with which he expresses his fantasies of sadism, orality and necrophilia. But the most remarkable are to be found in the domain of the maxim, a form of expression not at all in favour among most of the fringe Romantics. The irony encouraged by this lapidary form to which German Romanticism in its early stages had been so attracted here turns into black humour ('Le sapin dont on fait des cercueils est un arbre toujours vert') or meditations on language ('J'imagine que personne n'a remarqué (et tout le monde a eu raison), que brise désignait le vent le plus doux')[41] . . . when, that is, the 'prudhommesque' platitudinous type of crassness in which Forneret appears to delight does not gain the upper hand. This disconcerting man who derived such unique effects from the dry terseness of the maxim was equally capable of writing accounts of dreams in which the control of reason appears to present only the most minimal of barriers to the invasion of images.[42] He also produced poetic prose of an extreme fluidity in which the enchantment of nocturnal nature, paroxysms of love and the imminence of death are sensations that melt into an ecstatic contemplation that was to evoke the enthusiasm of the surrealists: 'Et la lune donnait et la rosée tombait' (1838) and 'Diamant de l'herbe' (in *Pièces de pièces, Temps perdu*).

If the literary career of *Gérard de Nerval* had been halted in February 1841, the date when he was first admitted to a mental hospital (and when Jules Janin had the bad taste to write an obituary to his mind), there would have been no grounds for considering him separately from the fringe writers whose portraits we have so far sketched in. It would even have been difficult to cite a single particularly original work from his pen to set alongside those with which his contemporaries had by this time indicated that they had already set out along the difficult path that was to lead to a certain influence and renown. And yet he was by no means either the youngest or the least precocious of the group. He was born in 1808 and by the age of twenty had already won fame with a translation of the first *Faust* that had eclipsed the two earlier ones to have appeared in French; and his name often appeared in poetry collections during this period.

Like many others, he had chosen a literary career, the only one that interested him, in defiance of his family's wishes. His father, a former medical officer in Napoleon's army, who had been retired in 1814, never reconciled himself to the choice. And the need his son felt to rehabilitate himself in his eyes by proving himself capable of earning his living by his pen accounts for much of the sense of guilt and failure that dogged him in his last years. It also explains the choice of the life of a literary hack, aggravated by ill health, that he inflicted upon himself from 1836 onwards, having rapidly dissipated his inheritance from a maternal grandfather in the launching of a critical periodical, *Le Monde dramatique*. In the meantime he had been a member of Victor Hugo's coterie, the *Petit Cénacle*, the Bohemian group of le Doyenné, and had established friendly relations with most of the writers of the age. However, apart from a number of poems in which the sound of his real voice is sometimes detectable and a historico-fantastical novella, *La Main de gloire* (Le Cabinet de lecture, 1832), Gérard de Nerval's name was generally known only by virtue of a number of theatrical works composed in collaboration with Dumas which appeared now under the one, now the other, signature. These included the libretto for a comic-opera, *Piquillo* (Marchant, 1837) and two plays, *L'Alchimiste* and *Léo*

Burckart (Barba, 1839), which did not enjoy the success that was really their due.

But in the course of these years, Nerval accumulated experiences, reading and plans, and envisaged themes for future works which were to make him not only a writer extremely representative of the fringe group of Romanticism to whom this chapter is mainly devoted, but also something much more: the most perfect and moving French incarnation of the qualities of Romanticism, capable of reaching out to the reader across the centuries.

Without claiming to solve the secret of what really constitutes genius, one might say that this paradoxical achievement (paradoxical in the sense that it took more than a century for it to be recognised as such) was a result of the transmutation of personal experience into a series of mythical configurations. These reflected an ever-disappointed but ever-renewed effort to use literature as a medium to give some form to destiny. To this end, the writer drew upon a cultural heritage that was constantly subject to reinterpretation in terms now of the particular historical moment, now of hallucinatory fantasies deeply rooted within himself.

Seen as whole, Nerval's work seems altogether designed to fill a void, compensate for a loss, balance a deficiency, that stems both from the author's own early life and from the origins of life in general. It would be simplistic to fall back upon a biographical explanation that identified that loss with the loss of the author's mother who died when he was only two years old, far away in Eastern Prussia where she had followed the path of her husband's career. But there can be no doubt that her death did, in more senses than one, represent an empty square on the chequerboard of his duel with existence. In the first place, it made him, quite unconsciously, invest with the role of a persecutor the father-figure who was guilty of having torn mother from child, thereby shattering a fundamental primitive unity. And, by extension, the same persecutory role was allotted to those deities whose paternal, virile and dominatory characteristics have been stressed by the religious traditions of mankind: the god Knelph in *Les Chimères*,[43] above all the biblical Jehovah[44] with his stupid, intolerant servants, and also the Soliman of 'L'Histoire de la reine du matin' in *Voyage en Orient*. Anything that could be identified with the maternal image, in contrast, was regarded as providing protection against the anguish caused by dereliction and the rupture of the continuities that allow life to be lived. Thus, the Valois, where he spent the first six years of his life, in the bosom of his maternal uncle's family, gradually – and increasingly – once his mental illness began to make him all the more conscious of his isolation – became, in his memory, the blessed land of all continuity where traces of druidic ceremony were harmoniously interwoven with those of the ancient kings of France, the friends of Jean-Jacques Rousseau and his own childhood. The choice of his pseudonym could not be more significant in this respect: for posterity, Gérard Labrunie was to be Gérard de Nerval, after the name of a property belonging to his mother's family in the region of Mortefontaine. Germany and German culture also benefited from this favourable transference, but with a greater ambivalence. Germany was both the consecrated land where his mother rested and also the sombre kingdom that had wrested her from him and it thus became associated with the destructive forces that were threatening his sanity: 'On ne me trouve pas fou en Allemagne', he wrote in a notebook during his last journey, six months before his death; and that perception was, to be sure, comforting and at the same time alarming. It was, without doubt, also his lost mother that he was seeking in the series of women with whom he fell in love. But in this quest a new ambiguity comes to light. For the loved ones to play to perfection the role of substitute mother, it was necessary that nothing in their several personalities should frustrate the amalgamation of their countenances upon one another and the projection on to them of the ideal maternal image. Hence, his fascination with actresses, first and foremost Jenny Colon whom he literally worshipped, whatever the place she held in his real life. But it could be said that the facility with which they could assume a series of personalities was also the price that had to be paid for their incapacity for being, that is to say for living. The dizzying fascination of resemblance, one of the major themes of *Sylvie* (1853) is both a promise and a snare. It was only during the last period of his life, when he was putting the finishing touches to *Aurélia*, that he managed, in a progress still mined with snares, to produce a harmonious fusion of all the female figures who had polarised his emotions: Isis and Marie, goddess and woman, mother and lover, Saint and Fairy.

But Nerval's personal drama cannot be isolated from the history of his age. When reflecting upon his complaint, he lucidly connects its causes with the disarray of an entire generation that suffered from a sense of frustration and deprivation. This amplified the personal distress that the absence of a mother occasioned him. It is altogether in keeping with his intellectual style that he should consider this collective drama to be essentially played out on the level of philosophic and religious convictions, and it is also on that level that he sets out, although in ways peculiarly his own, to seek a solution. 'Dieu est mort'[45] is the conclusion that he restates repeatedly, in different forms, in all his attempts to diagnose the *mal du siècle*. But in his case, unlike in that of many of his contemporaries, this *mal du siècle* does not give rise to a vain nostalgia that is simply the complement to a feeling of resignation. On the one hand Nerval is much too honest and too imbued with the spirit of his century to believe in the possibility of a return purely and simply to traditional Christianity: 'L'arbre de la science n'est pas l'arbre de la vie. Cependant, pouvons-nous rejeter de notre esprit ce que tant de générations intelligentes y ont versé de bon ou de funeste? L'ignorance ne s'apprend pas.'[46] On the other hand, he perceives in this very century a confused anxiety which may contain a promise of regeneration:

Nous vivions alors dans une époque étrange, comme celles qui d'ordinaire succèdent aux révolutions ou aux abaissements des grands règnes . . . . C'était un mélange d'activité, d'hésitation et de paresse, d'utopies brillantes, d'aspirations philosophiques ou religieuses, d'enthousiasmes vagues, mêlés de certains instincts de renaissance; d'ennui des discordes passées, d'espoirs incertains, quelque chose comme l'époque de Pérégrinus et d'Apulée.[47]

Nerval, again very much in tune with his period, sought to promote this renaissance by reactivating the most ancient beliefs of mankind and reconciling them with Christianity. For many of his contemporaries this kind of syncretism was no more than a symbolic presentation of a frame of mind ready to abandon all transcendental belief. But Nerval, for his part, truly revered the reality of the sacred, whatever the veils that shrouded it, to such an extent that he was scarcely joking when he told a questioner, 'Moi, pas de religion? J'en ai dix-sept . . . au moins', and it was in all sincerity that he wrote about his journey to the East as follows: 'Oui, je me suis senti païen en Grèce, musulman en Égypte, panthéiste au milieu des Druses, et dévot sur les mers aux astres-dieux de la Chaldée.'[48] The fact is that the religious distress common to his whole period takes a special form in Nerval as a result of his own personal dread of a kind of haemorrhage of the vital forces, a dousing of the creative fire which would condemn the world to darkness and death: 'Hélas, et si je meurs, c'est que tout va mourir!', cries his Christ aux Oliviers. This, really, is the source of his distrust and rancour for the God of the Christians: 'Celui qui donna l'âme aux enfants du limon' was either unwilling to or incapable of keeping alive that creative spark that the ancient deities had passed on from one to another. And this is also the reason for the affinity that, mixed with an intense sense of guilt, he felt for the rebellious deities of the underworld, for magicians and alchemists, for the 'saintes de l'abîme' who had dared to defy divine prohibitions and take over the responsibility for the creation of life. We find clear testimony to the fact that Nerval considered himself at least in part to be the descendant of such a line in the passage in 'L'Histoire de la reine du matin' where the architect Adoniram, who has descended into the depths of the earth, recognises in his ancestor Tubal-Kaîn the protector who will enable him to succeed in whatever he undertakes.

It was thus with the means that he commanded as an artist that Nerval proceeded to attempt to reascend the slope, fill the void, repair the rent that caused his own life and those of his contemporaries to suffer the malignancy of a linear historical development dominated by chance and ruination. Many Romantics attempted to escape from a similar sense of disarray by resurrecting, renovating or creating myths that made it possible to dream of a return to origins and a reactivation of the forces present in the first ages of mankind; and Nerval's erudition, although disordered and sometimes superficial, covered a huge field ranging from legends of the Pre-Adamites to the powerful symbolic structures of the Second Faust and encompassing every form of esotericism, alchemy and illuminism. It thus placed at his disposal a vast body of mythical material. From 1841 onward, each of his works drew heavily upon this, but the peculiar feature of Nerval's writing is that, far from giving rise to one of those vast syntheses which authors such as Ballanche, Quinet and, later, Victor Hugo strove to produce, the confidence that Nerval derived from those myths was constantly undermined by doubts. He repeatedly reinvested the same images with new and contradictory meanings with the result that in his case what that mythical material inspired was not so much a confirmation of faith, but rather a groping quest or even an appalled doubt. The modern quality of his writing, particularly in the hermetic sonnets of *Les Chimères*, but also in apparently transparent works such as *Sylvie* or *Promenades et Souvenirs*, seems to stem from the fact that the meaning is subject to pressures not easy to define and to insidious shifts of meaning that render all dictionaries useless and elude all the keys one might be tempted to employ to crack the code.

Hence the difficulty of conveying, in such a short space, any picture of these works that can claim to be any more than a caricature. It is a difficulty that is compounded by the fact that, as they appeared in their definitive state, most of the works were the result of a juxtaposition or re-utilisation of fragments composed and published at different times, under the duress of journalistic or editorial necessities; and this has inevitably detracted from the unity of inspiration behind the definitive text. Thus, *Voyage en Orient* first appeared in 1847 in the form of articles in *L'Artiste* and the *Revue des deux mondes*. Then, in 1848, the first part,

Les Femmes du Caire appeared as a single volume, published by Sartorius, and in 1850 *Le National* published the *Nuits de Ramazan*. The work did not appear in its entirety until 1851, published by Charpentier and having undergone considerable changes. *Les Filles du feu*, published in January 1854, comprises two novellas written shortly before, in 1853, *Sylvie* and *Octavie* (reworking the themes of earlier compositions); quite a large fragment of a serialised novel, *Les Faux Saulniers* (1850), here entitled *Angélique*; a dramatic piece from 1839, *Corilla*; a novella, *Isis* (1845) most of which is adapted from a German article; a novel written in 1839 in collaboration with Maquet, a quasi-translation, *Jemmy* (1843); a study devoted to the songs of the Valois region which had appeared elsewhere six times already; and the twelve sonnets that make up *Les Chimères*. In *Les Illuminés*, published in 1852, the text of the first, very brief chapter was the only one that had not, once or several times, already appeared elsewhere.

One remarkable aspect of the Nerval miracle is that, despite all these deconstructions and reconstructions which affect not only the details of the myths involved but also the very structure of the works, there remains always detectable if not an intact message, at least a recognisable method and an insistent questing which mark them out unmistakably as coming from the hand of Nerval and none other. Underlying all these works is a quest for identity (one that, given the circumstances of Nerval's life was to cost him his sanity). It is this quest that determines their 'géographie magique', to borrow an expression from *Voyage en Orient* which Jean-Pierre Richard has felicitously applied to Nerval's work as a whole.[49] The explanation for the family resemblance between the mythical figures that inhabit this world is that, notwithstanding the diversity of their origins, they all, either simultaneously or in succession, both mirror his own destiny and also intercede to incorporate it within a drama of revolt, expiation and regeneration bounded only by the history of the cosmos. It is in *Aurélia*, which was at the press at the time of his death (26 January 1855), that this progress, regularly illuminated by the revelations of dreams and the hallucinations of madness, is presented in its most perfected form. But most of his earlier works can also be read as progressions towards a point that is ever-elusive, in the course of which it nevertheless becomes possible to draw aside one or two of the veils that shroud the enigma of destiny. Hence the importance of the theme of the voyage in Nerval's work and indeed in his life, which was, even more than Rimbaud's, that of 'un homme aux semelles de vent'. Nerval's *Voyage en Orient* is something quite other than a piece of journalistic reporting, a collection of travel sketches or a grandiose enterprise in the manner of Chateaubriand. Rather, it is a pilgrimage towards the cradle of religions, the light of origins; and, in the context of the pilgrim's own destiny, the two great stages along the way, 'L'Histoire du calife Hakem' and 'L'Histoire de la reine du matin', assume the significance of founding myths while, at the same time, they stand as premonitory warnings of the painful martyrdom to come. *Lorely* (Giraud, 1852), a combination of the memories of a number of travels in Germany and the Netherlands, is placed under the sign of *la nixe*, whose name means both enchantment and falsehood ('[le] nom même signifie en même temps charme et mensonge'), and whom Nerval explicitly identifies with madness, in his prefatory letter to Jules Janin. In *Promenades et Souvenirs* (1854), he turns back to his own past which is intimately linked with that of a region that epitomises the past of France, a past in which he seizes upon a number of threads interwoven into his own existence. The technique is reminiscent of that used in *Sylvie* in which the imaginary voyage is plotted in accordance with the rigorous rules of a symbolic itinerary. *Les Nuits d'octobre* (1852) takes the form of an account of fantastical wanderings in the manner of Sterne, a veritable descent into hell, the circles of which are represented by scenes of everyday existence and the 'combinaisons bizarres de la vie'.[50]

Are these ritual voyages of initiation? Assuredly not, to the extent that the attempt to integrate himself into a living tradition, to transform his being by entering into possession of a wisdom transcending the centuries constantly clashes with the evidence of the death of the gods and the interchangeable nature of mythical images in which Nerval finds it impossible to seize upon anything other than his own countenance. That is the ambivalent significance of the theme of the double, which pervades his work from *Le Roi de Bicêtre* (1839), through *Les Illuminés* and right on into *Aurélia*. Léon Cellier writes:

[Nerval] s'est identifié tour à tour à Faust, Werther, W. Meister, Fr. Colonna, au héros de *Élixirs du Diable*, à Charles VI, au calife Hakem, à Adoniram, à R. Spifame, à Cazotte, à Restif, au Biron de Shakespeare et au Christ de Jean-Paul, à Lucius et à Saint-Germain, à Mausole, à Astolphe, à Thésée, à Orphée, à Dante, à Virgile. Et l'on pourrait allonger cette liste presque à l'infini.[51]

Far from enabling him to escape from himself, however, these projected identifications constantly bring him face to face with his own drama. Instead of confirming his identity, they simply intensify his sense of being torn asunder and his self-doubt: 'Suis-je Amour ou Phébus? Lusignan ou Biron?'[52]

The price that Nerval had to pay for this impassioned quest was, as we have remarked, madness. In falling back upon literature to fill the

mysterious void that might have made Nerval's life simply that of yet
another mentally sick person, he may not have found a cure. Indeed his
suicide sadly confirms that he did not. But at least he discovered the way
to penetrate, beneath the brilliant, varied, iridescent, sensory albeit
sometimes superficial surface of the language and modes of thought of
his period, through to more subterranean ways that convey a superabun-
dance of senses to ravish the modern reader and immeasurably extend
the field of human experience. At the beginning of *Aurélia*, Nerval
proclaims: 'Le Rêve est une seconde vie.' In doing so he does more than
just carry forward the lesson of German Romanticism and open up the
path to surrealism. As Mallarmé was to say of Poe but as might equally
well be said of all writers of genius, he found the way to 'donner un sens
plus pur aux mots de la tribu'.

NOTES

1. Jean-Luc Steinmetz, *La France frénétique de 1830* (Choix de textes, Phébus, 1978),
   p. 32.
2. *Dictionnaire de l'Académie*, 'artiste' (4th edn, 1762).
3. On this subject, see Paul Bénichou, *Le Sacre de l'écrivain* (Corti, 1973), in particular
   pp. 420–7.
4. Article in *Le Temps*, 5 October 1832, cited by Bénichou, *Le Sacre de l'écrivain*, p. 211.
5. Cf. these lines by Lamartine to his friend Virieu, dated 1810: 'Des artistes surtout,
   mon cher ami, des artistes, voilà ce que j'aime, de ces gens qui ne sont pas sûrs de
   dîner demain, mais qui ne troqueraient pas leur taudis philosophique, leur pinceau
   ou leur plume pour des monceaux d'or!'
6. This discrepancy between the values of the dominant social class and the intellectual
   world is one upon which Paul Bénichou lays considerable emphasis (*Le Sacre de
   l'écrivain*, in particular pp. 425–6). It nevertheless masks certain areas of agreement
   which might be revealed by a deeper analysis of the social mechanisms at work. To
   the extent that the power of the bourgeoisie rests upon the development of the
   capitalist mode of production, critics who take issue with the bourgeoisie's external
   behaviour, its ideas or its morality without bringing into question the organisation
   of property and labour which is the basis of that power, can impinge hardly at all
   upon it, and may even play a distractionary role in the social struggles that are
   developing. This may account for the ease with which certain of our artists 'on the
   fringe' became reassimilated within the bourgeois order although, even then, it
   would remain to be seen how total that reassimilation proved to be.
7. 'École du désenchantement' was the expression that Balzac, in one of his *Lettres sur
   Paris*, published in *Le Voleur* (9 January 1831), used to refer to a number of works
   that appeared in the immediate aftermath of the July revolution.
8. *Le Figaro*, 30 August 1831.
9. The piece entitled 'Pandaemonium' in *Feu et Flamme* by Philothée O'Neddy gives
   some idea of this, although it is no doubt considerably embellished in the interests of
   the picturesque.
10. Charles Deglény, 'Le langage à la mode', in *Nouveau Tableau de Paris au dix-neuvième
    siècle*, vol. VI, 1835. Cited by Bénichou, *Le Sacre de l'écrivain*, p. 423.

11. Gérard de Nerval, *Œuvres* (2 vols., Pléiade, 1974), II, 785.
12. *Histoire du romantisme* (1874), p. 86.
13. The seat of the Institut de France and the Académie Française.
14. Arsène Houssaye, *La Confession* (Dentu, 1885), I, 310.
15. T. Gautier, *Ménagérie intime* (Lemerre, 1869), p. 58.
16. *La Confession*, p. 305.
17. *Feu et Flamme*, published with an introduction and notes by Marcel Hervier, (Éd. des Presses françaises, 1926), Foreword, p. 2.
18. On this complicated question, see the excellently researched article by Paul Bénichou: 'Jeune-France et Bousingots', *Revue d'histoire littéraire de la France* (May–June 1971), pp. 439–57. The spelling 'bousingo' is used in the publicity for a collective anthology, *Contes du Bousingo*, that appeared repeatedly during 1832–3. According to a letter addressed by Philothée O'Neddy to Asselineau in 1862, the word had been invented with that particular spelling during a fairly inebriated evening at the end of which the members of the *Jeune-France* group spilled out into the streets singing 'nous ferons du bousin (noise)-go'. However, they were evidently familiar with its usual spelling and meaning and there can be no doubt that the title *Contes du Bousingo* represents an oblique reference to this, although with a wink and a nudge aimed at the initiated.
19. *Feu et Flamme*, Foreword, p. 3.
20. Charles Lassailly, *Les Roueries de Trialph, notre contemporain avant son suicide* (Silvestre, 1833), pp. 10–11.
21. In *Encore un an de sans Titre, par un homme noir blanc de visage* (Duverger, 1840).
22. However, the problem of parody throughout this period remains a very complicated one: there seems no way of distinguishing the element of irony and mystification in Victor Hugo's *Han d'Islande*, Musset's *Contes d'Espagne et d'Italie* or Mérimée's *Le Théâtre de Clara Gazul*. On the problem of parody, see G. Genette, *Palampsestes* (Seuil, 1982).
23. *Feu et Flamme*, p. 20.
24. *Champavert, contes immoraux* (Renduel, 1833), p. 66.
25. Jules Lefèvre-Deumier, *Les Martyrs d'Arezzo* (Ambroise Dupont, 1839), I, 182.
26. 'La révolte métaphysique et religieuse des petits romantiques', in *Les petits romantiques français* (Les Cahiers du Sud, 1949), p. 14.
27. These works of significance (usually one or two in the case of each writer) are the only ones we shall be considering. For reasons that are obvious, these fringe Romantics were seldom published or else, in order to earn their livings, they dissipated their energies in works that do not reflect their true talents. Alternatively – and this was no doubt both a consequence and a cause of their marginal position – they lacked the discernment necessary to see where their talents really lay. Except in those cases where the entire production amounted to a single work, there therefore exists a mass of rubbish which it would be quite pointless to mention.
28. 'Horreur', *Album d'un pessimiste*.
29. Baudelaire, *Œuvres complètes* (Pléiade, 1976), II, 154.
30. *Ibid.*, p. 155.
31. 'Une fièvre de l'époque' (1837), in *Poésies posthumes de Philothée O'Neddy* (Charpentier, 1877), p. 147.
32. 'Velléités philosophiques', *ibid.*, p. 477.
33. See *Ce vice impuni, la lecture* (Gallimard, 1941).
34. *Le Magicien*, preface and notes by Max Milner (Lausanne, L'Âge d'Homme, 1978), p. 72.

35. *Les Martyrs d'Arezzo* (Ambroise Dupont, 1839), I, 169.
36. *Les Roueries de Trialph, notre contemporain avant son suicide* (Silvestre, 1833), p. 260.
37. *L'Indépendant, furet de Paris*, 24 December 1835.
38. *Gaspard de la Nuit: fantaisies à la manière de Rembrandt et de Callot* (Angers, V. Pavie, 1842), p. 22.
39. *Ibid.*
40. *Minotaure*, no. 10 (1937).
41. *Encore un an de sans Titre* (1840).
42. 'Un rêve, c'est', in *Pièces de pièces, Temps perdu* (Duverger, 1840) and *Rêves* (Beaune, Romand, 1846).
43. See the sonnet 'Horus'.
44. See the sonnet 'Antéros'.
45. Epigraph, borrowed from J.-P. Richter, from the *Jardin des Oliviers*.
46. *Aurélia, Œuvres*, I, 386,
47. *Sylvie, ibid.*, I, 242.
48. *Voyage en Orient, ibid.*, II, 624.
49. See *Poésie et profondeur* (Seuil, 1955).
50. *Les Nuits d'octobre, Œuvres*, I, 80.
51. *Gérard de Nerval, l'homme et l'œuvre* (Hatier-Boivin, 1956), p. 185.
52. 'El Desdichado', *Les Chimères*.

BIBLIOGRAPHY

Up until the 1920s the writers known as the 'minor Romantics' were studied mainly by collectors of literary curiosities more intent on emphasising their eccentricities or lamenting their sufferings than on evaluating their works: J. Claretie, *Élisa Mercœur, Hippolyte de la Morvannais, Georges Farcy, Charles Dovalle, Alphonse Rabbe* (Bachelin-Deflorenne, 1864); Charles Asselineau, *Mélanges tirés d'une petite bibliothèque romantique* (Pincebourde, 1866), (on Jean Polonius, Gustave Drouineau, Philothée O'Neddy); L. Derome, *Causeries d'un ami des livres* (E. Rouveyre, 1886); E. Asse, *Les Petits Romantiques* (Techener, 1896), (on Jean Polonius and Charles Lassailly); H. Lardanchet, *Les Enfants perdus du romantisme* (Perrin, 1905), (on Émile Roulland, J.-P. Veyrat, Charles Lassailly, Louis Berthaud, Laurent Ausone de Chancel, Napoléon Peyrat).
During the 1920s, the controversies – partly of a political nature – that developed around Romanticism caused some critics to draw attention to works that were particularly characteristic of the movement as a whole, in some cases with a view to caricature (e.g. Jules Marsan, *Bohème romantique*, Les Cahiers libres, 1929), in others in a manner moving and deeply poetic even where their studies are partially flawed and abortive. Notable among the latter are Aristide Marie, who published the first serious biographies of Gérard de Nerval (Hachette, 1914) and Petrus Borel (Éd. de la Force française, 1922), and undertook to edit the complete works of both these authors; and Henri Girard who in 1924 launched the 'Bibliothèque romantique' (Presses françaises), which included publications of the works of Alphonse Rabbe, Jules Lefèvre-Deumier and O'Neddy. During this same period the surrealists were discovering in the 'minor Romantics' their own precursors and were devoting many pages of eulogy to them in the *Nouvelle Revue française* (an article on Bertrand by Breton in 1920, reprinted in *les Pas perdus*, Gallimard 1944), in *Littérature* (in particular nos. 2 and 13, on Rabbe), in *La Révolution surréaliste* (nos. 9–10, 1927), and in *Minotaure* (no. 10, 1937) on Forneret. Breton's *Anthologie de l'humour noir* (Éd. du Sagittaire, 1950) devoted considerable space to Borel and to Forneret. The first thesis devoted to the 'minor Romantics' was on the subject of the influence of surrealism. It was defended by Jules Kreiser in 1942 with the

title, 'Ascendances romantiques du surnaturalisme contemporain', and was published later that year by Calmann-Lévy under the pseudonym of Francis Dumont and with the title *Naissance du romantisme contemporain*. The same author, still using the name Francis Dumont, in 1949 brought out a special number of the *Cahiers du Sud* entitled *Les Petits Romantiques français*. Together with *La France frénétique de 1830* by Jean-Luc Steinmetz (Phébus, 1978) this, despite a number of inaccuracies in certain articles, is still the best introduction to the subject.

So far as the individual authors are concerned, listed here are only the most interesting modern editions of their works together with the principal critical studies that are relevant.

Alphonse Rabbe. *Album d'un pessimiste, Le Centaure, Le Naufrage, L'Adolescence*, published by J. Marsan (Presses françaises, 1924). Criticism: Lucienne de Wieclawick, *Alphonse Rabbe dans la mêlée politique et littéraire de la Restauration* (Nizet, 1963).

Petrus Borel. Texts: *Rhapsodies* (Éd. de la Force française, 1922); *Champavert, Contes immoraux* (same publisher, 1922); *Madame Putiphar*, with a preface by Jules Claretie and introduced by '*Madame Putiphar*, roman sadien?' by Béatrice Didier and followed by 'Les malheurs du récit' by J.-L. Steinmetz (Ed. Régine Desforges, 1972); *Champavert* (Éditions des Autres, 1979) (the Slatkine reprints yielded a reproduction of the original edition of this work). Works of criticism: Jules Claretie, *Petrus Borel, le lycanthrope* (Éd. de la Force française, 1922); Enid Starkie, *Petrus Borel, his life and his time* (London, Faber and Faber, 1954).

Théophile Gautier. (We will mention only the works connected with his 'Romantic on the fringe' side). Texts: *Les Jeunes-France*, introduced by R. Jasinski (Flammarion, 1973); *Mademoiselle de Maupin*, introduced by G. van den Bogaert (Garnier–Flammarion, 1966); *Contes fantastiques*, introduced by H. Juin (Éd. 10/18, 1973); *Contes fantastiques*, introduced by M. Eigeldinger (Garnier-Flammarion, 1982). Works of criticism: R. Jasinski, *Théophile Gautier, les années romantiques* (Vuibert, 1929); H. van der Tuin, *L'Évolution psychologique de T. Gautier* (Nizet et Bastard, 1933); P.G. Castex, *Le Conte fantastique en France de Nodier à Maupassant* (Corti, 1951); B. Delvaille, *T. Gautier* (Seghers, 1970).

Philothée O'Neddy. *Feu et Flamme*, with introduction and notes by Marcel Hervier (Les Presses françaises, 1926). Criticism: Valéry-Larbaud, *Ce vice impuni, la lecture* (Gallimard, 1941).

Alphonse Esquiros. *Le Magicien*, introduced by Max Milner (Lausanne, L'Âge d'homme, 1978). Criticism: Jacques P. van der Linden, *Alphonse Esquiros, de la bohème romantique à la république sociale* (Nizet, 1948).

Jules Lefèvre-Deumier. Criticism: Georges Brunet's preface to *Vespres de l'abbaye du Val* (Les presses françaises, 1924).

Charles Lassailly. *Les Roueries de Trialph* (Silvestre, 1833) has not been republished. Criticism: Eldon Kaye, *Charles Lassailly* (Droz, 1962).

Aloysius Bertrand. Texts: *Gaspard de la Nuit*, introduced by Jean Richer (Flammarion, 1972); *Gaspard de la Nuit*, introduced by Max Milner (Gallimard, 1980). Works of criticism: Cargill Sprietsma, *Louis Bertrand, dit Aloysius Bertrand* (Champion 1926); Fernand Rude, *Aloysius Bertrand* (Seghers, 1971); Henri Corbat, *Hantise et imagination chez A. Bertrand* (Corti 1975).

Xavier Forneret. Many of Forneret's texts have been reprinted in reviews and anthologies which it is not possible to list here, but there is no modern edition of his works in existence, even in the form of selected excerpts. Criticism: Eldon Kaye, *Xavier Forneret, dit 'l'homme noir'* (Droz, 1971).

Gérard de Nerval. Some idea of the considerable bibliography for Nerval can be formed by consulting J. Senelier's *G. de Nerval, Essai de bibliographie* (Nizet, 1959, and

Bibliographie nervalienne (Minard, 1969–). Texts: the Champion edition of his complete works remains unfinished. The volume devoted to *Filles du feu*, with an introduction by N. Popa will still be found useful. Most of Nerval's work is to be found in the Garnier edition, introduced by Henri Lemaître and in the Pléiade edition compiled by A. Béguin and J. Richer (2 vols., most recent revision, 1974). This most recent edition contains most of the writer's correspondence. It may be complemented by the *Œuvres complémentaires* published by Minard. The edition of *Voyage en Orient* compiled by G. Rouger (4 vols, Ed. Richelieu, 1950) remains unrivalled to date. A much improved Pléiade edition under the supervision of Claude Pichois and J. Guillaume is under preparation. It is to contain all Nerval's known texts. J. Guillaume has produced critical editions of *Les Chimères* (Brussels, Palais des Académies, 1966) and of *Pandora* (Presses Universitaires de Namur, 1976).

Works of criticism: An excellent introductory study is Léon Cellier's *Gérard de Nerval, l'homme et l'œuvre* (Hatier-Boivin, 1956), also R. Jean's *Nerval par lui-même* (Éd. du Seuil, 1969). The thesis by Jean Richer, *Nerval, expérience et création* (Hachette, 2nd edn, revised and completed, 1970), is the fullest study of Nerval's sources, in particular the esoteric ones, and of some of the aspects of his creative methods. Other works of importance are: A. Béguin, *Gérard de Nerval* (Corti, 1945); J. Richer, *Gérard de Nerval et les doctrines ésotériques* (Le Griffon d'Or, 1947); M.-J. Durry, *Gérard de Nerval et le mythe* (Flammarion, 1956); J. Gaulmier, *Nerval et 'Les Filles du feu'* (Nizet, 1956); K. Schaerer, *Thématique de Nerval, ou 'Le Monde recomposé'* (Minard, 1968); R. Chambers, *Gérard de Nerval et la poétique du voyage* (Corti, 1969); P. Bénichou, *Nerval et la chanson folklorique* (Corti, 1970); J. Geninasca, *Analyse structurale des 'Chimères'* (Neuchâtel, La Baconnière, 1971); G. Schaeffer, *Une double lecture de Gérard de Nerval, 'Les Illuminés' et 'Les Filles du feu'* (Neuchâtel, La Baconnière, 1977); M. Jeanneret, *La Lettre perdue, Écriture et folie dans l'œuvre de Nerval* (Flammarion, 1978).

We should also mention a number of chapters or review articles which have made important contributions to Nervalian criticism: G. Poulet, '*Sylvie* ou la pensée de Nerval', in *Trois essais de mythologie romantique* (Corti, 1966); J.-P. Richard, 'Géographie magique de Nerval', in *Poésie et profondeur* (Seuil, 1955); G. Gaillard, 'Nerval, ou les contradictions du romantisme', *Romantisme*, nos. 1–2 (1971); H. Meschonnic, 'La poétique de Nerval', *Europe* (September 1972); S. Felman, *La Folie et la chose littéraire* (Seuil, 1973). Finally, a number of literary periodicals have devoted important special numbers to Nerval: the *Mercure de France* (June 1951, November 1952, May 1955); the *Cahiers du Sud*, no. 292 (1948); *Europe* (September 1972).

Index